D0866747

A Poisoned
Chalice

Jeffrey Freedman

A Poisoned
Chalice

Published by Princeton University Press,
41 William Street, Princeton, New Jersey 08540
In the United Kingdom:
Princeton University Press, 3 Market Place,
Woodstock, Oxfordshire OX20 1SY

Library of Congress Cataloging-in-Publication Data
Freedman, Jeffrey, 1957–
A poisoned chalice / Jeffrey Freedman.
p. cm.
Includes bibliographical references and index.
ISBN 0-691-00233-9 (alk. paper)
1. Enlightenment. 2. Good and evil—History—18th century. 3. Trials (Poisoning)—Switzerland—Zurich—History—18th century. 4. Lord's Supper—Wine—History—18th century. 5. Europe, German-speaking—Intellectual life—18th century.
I. Title.
B2621 .F74 2002
364.15'23'0949457—dc21 2001051040

British Library Cataloging-in-Publication Data is available

This book has been composed in Galliard

Printed on acid-free paper. ∞

www.pup.princeton.edu

Printed in the United States of America

10 9 8 7 6 5 4 3 2

What establishes the worth of any man is not the truth he possesses—or supposes himself to possess—but rather the sincere effort he has applied to pursuing the truth. For it is through the search for truth, not the possession of it, that he expands those powers which are the sole constituents of his ever-increasing perfection

Nicht die Wahrheit, in deren Besitz irgend ein Mensch ist, oder zu seyn vermeynet, sondern die aufrichtige Mühe, die er angewandt hat, hinter die Wahrheit zu kommen, macht den Werth des Menschen. Denn nicht durch den Besitz, sondern durch die Nachforschung der Wahrheit erweitern sich seine Kräfte, worinn allein seine immer wachsende Vollkommenheit besteht

—G. E. Lessing, "Eine Duplik" (1778), vol. 13 of *Sämtliche Schriften*, ed. K. Lachmann (Stuttgart, 1893), p. 23

Contents

Illustrations

Preface

THE WRITING OF THIS BOOK IS A TALE of many cities. It began a number of years ago in the western Swiss city of Neuchâtel, where I was conducting research for my dissertation about an eighteenth-century publishing firm, the Société Typographique de Neuchâtel. There, among the papers of the publisher, I stumbled upon a mysterious and arresting letter from a Frankfurt bookseller who had just published a pirated edition of two sermons by the Zurich pastor Johann Caspar Lavater. The bookseller urged his correspondent in Neuchâtel to undertake a French translation of the sermons, explaining that Lavater had delivered them in the aftermath of a dreadful crime: the poisoning of the communion wine in the main cathedral in Zurich. German editions of the sermons were being published left and right, and the bookseller's own edition had sold out in four weeks. Whoever published a French translation, he reasoned, would be able to capitalize on the extraordinary appeal of a sensational event. As it happened, the Neuchâtelois did not follow the advice of their Frankfurt correspondent (there never was a French translation of Lavater's sermons on the poisoning of the communion wine), but I resolved to pursue the matter further if only to satisfy my own curiosity. Not immediately, of course—I still had a dissertation to write. At the time, I simply made a note to myself and filed it away, and for years afterward the note gathered dust—layers upon layers of dust—until circumstances allowed me to return to it. It was not until the winter of 1999, dissertation behind me and PhD in hand, that I finally set out for Zurich, hoping to uncover some evidence about the mysterious poisoning that the Frankfurt bookseller had mentioned to the Neuchâtel publisher. Fortunately, the crime had led to a trial—fortunately for me, if not for the accused man—because criminal trials leave a paper trail. I pursued that trail through the archives in Zurich, and from there I followed it northward into the wider world of German-speaking Europe—to Bremen, Berlin, and Leipzig—before returning home, laden with note cards, to New York, where I settled down to write this book, a book that tells the story of a strange and long-forgotten criminal case from the age of Enlightenment.

Tracking across Europe in search of my quarry, I would undoubtedly have lost my way if not for the help of colleagues who took the trouble to steer me in the right direction. In Zurich, I had the good fortune to have numerous guides. Martin Hirzel in particular has been unstinting in his support of this project. He taught me a great deal about the life and work of Johann Caspar Lavater; he carefully read and criticized an earlier draft of the book; and he was tireless in responding to my numerous email inquiries from this side of the Atlantic, providing me with a constant stream of precious information that saved me from many errors, both big and small. The collaboration with Dr. Hirzel has been one of the most rewarding aspects of my work on this book. Rolf Graber and Franz Mauelshagen were enormously helpful in a variety of ways. Dr. Graber helped me to locate sources in the Zurich archives, and Dr. Mauelshagen graciously read an earlier draft of the book and provided support through his challenging and probing questions.

Thanks to Katja Hürlimann and her generous hospitality, my research trips to Zurich were not only productive but enjoyable. Bruno Weber was of great assistance to me in locating illustrations. And Chantal Lafontant, Thomas Hildbrand, Simone Zurbuchen, Andreas Suter, and Jakob Tanner all took the time to meet with me and discuss my project, providing encouragement at a moment when the project was still in its infancy. Hans Stickelberger, pastor of the main cathedral in Zurich, took me on a walking tour of the cathedral so that I was able to inspect the scene of the crime. I also offer my special thanks to the staffs of the Zurich State Archives and the Manuscript Collection of the Zurich Central Library, and in particular to Ruth Häusler, who patiently deciphered numerous passages from documents written in what seemed (to me, in any event) to be an illegible eighteenth-century scrawl.

In Bremen, I had the pleasure of meeting Holger Böning, whose lively and engaging conversation frequently beckoned me away from the reading of eighteenth-century German newspapers. But as if to compensate for the distraction, Dr. Böning gave me an invaluable crash course on the history of German newspapers and then read and criticized the section of my book devoted to the newspaper coverage of the crime.

In Berlin and Leipzig, I incurred large debts of gratitude to three colleagues in particular: Pamela Selwyn, Ursula Goldenbaum, and Mark Lehmstedt. Dr. Selwyn guided me through the labyrinth of the Friedrich Nicolai papers in the State Archives in Berlin and helped me to decipher passages from Nicolai's correspondence; Dr. Goldenbaum taught me a great deal about Leibniz and the problem of evil in eighteenth-century German philosophy; and Dr. Lehmstedt brought to my attention some very important letters to and from the Leipzig publisher Philipp Erasmus Reich, and provided critical responses to various aspects of my book. Even now I recall with fondness a warm spring evening in Leipzig when Dr. Lehmstedt and I sat at the table of an outdoor café in the shadow of the Thomaskirche talking about the poisoning of the communion wine and its broader implications.

On a more recent trip to Germany, I had the good fortune to be able to present a paper on the affair of the poisoned communion wine to the Medieval and Early Modern History Colloquium at the University of Bielefeld. Many thanks to the members of the colloquium for an evening of lively and stimulating discussion.

Finally, to close the geographic circle, I would like to acknowledge my debts to institutions and colleagues in the New York City area. I am grateful to Yeshiva University, which supported this project by granting me a sabbatical during the autumn and spring semesters of 2000–1. Among colleagues, I owe a particular debt of gratitude to Gary Hentzi, who read his way through this book more times than I care to mention, and to James Schmidt, who generously shared with me his wide knowledge of the German Enlightenment and helped me to clarify my thinking on a number of important points. Gabrielle Starr, Isser Woloch, Anthony Grafton, Manfred Laubichler, Natalie Davis, Robert Darnton, William Jordan, Lawrence Vogel, and Herman Lebovics deserve my thanks for their helpful comments on all or parts of the book, as do the members of the Columbia University Faculty Seminar on Eighteenth-Century Culture, to whom I presented a version of my book in the spring of 2000; their many thoughtful responses proved helpful to me as I prepared the final version of my manuscript. Tim Sullivan, my production and copy editor, gave this manuscript a careful and thorough reading and saved me from several embarrassing solecisms and infelicities of style. Annie Chamberlin provided invaluable assistance in preparing the index. Thanks of a slightly different variety are due also to my former roommate Fazia Aitel, who had to contend with me from day-to-day as this book was taking shape, and who had to endure constant talk of poisoned wine at the very same time that we were both, as it were, drinking from the same chalice.

To write a book about a crime can be a somewhat gloomy experience. Occasionally, therefore, I would escape the gloom by retreating to the Copper Kettle, the always convivial and high-spirited watering hole of my neighborhood in Queens. Few of the regulars had any idea that I was writing a book, much less a book about so macabre a subject. By offering me a retreat from the solitary labor of writing, however, they have rendered to me a great service, and for that they deserve a toast. So here's to the lads at the Copper Kettle. On many an evening as this book was being written, we raised our glasses high, and not one of them ever contained poison. Cheers!

New York City
March 2001

A Poisoned Chalice

Introduction

HIS IS A BOOK ABOUT A CRIME. NOT just any crime, to be sure, but one of the worst, most heinous, most abominable crimes imaginable to Christians. On Thursday, 12 September 1776, according to the magistrate in the Swiss city of Zurich, somebody placed deadly poison in the communion wine of the main cathedral in the heart of the city. And to crown the infamy, this particular Thursday coincided with one of the most important dates of the liturgical calendar: the General Day of Prayer and Repentance. To poison the communion wine in a cathedral on such an occasion was nothing less than the consummate act of desecration, a sacrilege so monstrous that one contemporary pastor compared the poisoner to Judas and the poisoning to the Crucifixion.[1]

Besides being a horrific act of desecration, such a crime was a serious threat to the cohesion of a tightknit community. Scarcely 10,000 inhabitants dwelled within the heavily fortified walls of eighteenth-century Zurich, and all of the citizens of the city belonged to the reformed Protestant church, the only one tolerated since the Reformation, which had abolished the mass and transformed the sacrament of communion. In the reformed Protestant church, taking communion in both kinds was not a privilege reserved for the clergy (both clergy and laity drank the wine), nor was the sacrament handed down from on high, distributed from the altar by a priest who mediated between God and the faithful. The communion service was organized, as it were, along a horizontal rather than a vertical axis. The communion cup circulated throughout the congregation, passing from hand to hand and from mouth to mouth. As a result, the communion service took on a double role: it was not only a sacrament but also a civic rite—or rather a sacrament of citizenship. When Zurichers came together to celebrate communion, they were affirming not only their individual ties to their God but also their collective ties to one another, cementing their bonds of fellowship through the sharing of a common meal: literally, a "supper" [*Abendmahl*]. The poisoning of the communion wine threatened to dissolve those bonds, sowing seeds of suspicion and mistrust, turning citizen against citizen.[2]

And finally, of course, such a crime was an act of attempted murder. But against whom? The cathedral was not just any church. It was one of the four main parish churches within the walls of the city and the one where some of the most prominent citizens, such as the mayor, came to worship:[3] a few drops of a lethal substance placed in the communion wine of the cathedral and virtually the entire ruling class of an Old Regime state could be dispatched in the twinkling of an eye. No wonder that the government took the affair so seriously, and that for months afterward it gave as much attention to this as to any other matter of state.[4] But members of the ruling councils were not alone in treating the affair with such gravity. Pastors in Zurich devoted their sermons to it, thundering from their pulpits against this monstrous crime. Newspapers and journals throughout the German-speaking world discussed it. And so too did countless individuals in Germany and Switzerland, giving voice to all manner of rumors, the echoes of which can be detected in letters of the period.

For all of its importance to contemporaries, however, the affair of the poisoned communion wine has attracted virtually no attention from historians. The general histories devoted to Zurich in the eighteenth century pass it over in silence, and so too, for the most part, do more specialized studies, which mention it, if at all, in a footnote or a brief sentence.[5] How to explain this silence?

The answer, presumably, is that Zurich historians have viewed the affair of the poisoned communion wine as an ephemeral event unconnected to the larger themes of eighteenth-century history. Such a view is wrong, as we shall see. But it is quite possible that some readers of this book may be harboring a similar prejudice. Before proceeding, therefore, we need to understand why the affair of the poisoned communion wine deserves to be rescued from oblivion and what is at stake in a book of this sort.

IN ZURICH, THE POISONING OF THE COMMUNION wine quickly escalated into a political affair. It led to a trial that opponents of the government denounced as a farce, and it culminated the following year in a major constitutional crisis, the most serious crisis faced by the government in the last decades of the Old Regime. Almost from the very beginning, however, the affair was also unfolding in an arena much broader than that of Zurich. Within weeks of the General Day of Prayer and Repentance, news of the crime had spread all across the German-speaking world, transmitted by scores of newspapers, which blanketed the territories of the old Reich. Even Germans who cared little about Swiss politics now found their attention riveted upon the spectacle unfolding in Switzerland, as if Zurich had suddenly become the stage for a drama of universal significance. And in a sense, the poisoning of the communion wine *was* a drama of universal significance, a drama that enacted one of the most fundamental problems confronted by intellectuals in the age of Enlightenment: the problem of evil. If the various currents of Enlightenment thought converged at any one point, it was their common rejection of the Christian doctrine of original sin, the quasi-biological notion of hereditary fault, which traced the origin of evil to the disobedience of Adam and Eve in the Garden of Eden. To Enlightenment thinkers, this doctrine defied rational comprehension and offended the dignity of man. But the poisoning of the communion wine was no less a challenge to rational comprehension and no less offensive to the moral dignity of humanity than the notion of a corrupt and enslaved will passed on like an ancestral curse from generation to generation. Not even a political motive (assuming there was one) could adequately account for the deliberate, premeditated attempt to massacre hundreds upon hundreds of worshipers, most of whom were simple artisans with little or no connection to the small circle of governing magistrates. Such a crime seemed to expose the very limits of rational understanding and to point beyond reason toward a moral depravity so terrifying that it could only be described as diabolic. "How does [this affair] concern us?" a Hamburg newspaper asked rhetorically in 1779, long after the criminal investigation and the ensuing trial had come to an end in Zurich. "In fact, it concerns us a great deal, for besides the Swiss, did not the entire public of the civilized world [*das ganze gesittete Publikum*] shudder at the wickedness of such a deed?"[6]

Because the crime posed a problem of such fundamental importance, it captured the interest of some of the leading figures in the German republic of letters: Friedrich Nicolai, Johann Caspar Lavater, Johann Gottfried Herder, Christoph Martin Wieland, Isaac Iselin, Johann Zimmermann, Johann Eberhard, and Johann Joachim Spalding. In sermons, journal articles, pamphlets and personal letters, German and Swiss intellectuals debated the implications of the crime, advancing interpretations and counter-interpretations in a sequence of passionate exchanges. Not all of the contributors to the debate identified themselves with the Enlightenment. Indeed, one of its two main participants, the Protestant pastor Johann Caspar Lavater, was an outspoken critic of the Enlightenment, and he used the poisoning of the communion wine to illustrate his criticisms, claiming that attacks on traditional Christian faith had undermined the foundations of morality and were thus responsible for the commission of the crime. In its form, however, if not its content, the debate was very much in the spirit of the Enlightenment. Even Lavater advanced grounds for his claims; he appealed to evidence; and, most importantly, he took his stand in public, in printed texts, which were themselves subject to further critique. Conducted in this fashion, the critique of Enlightenment was part of the Enlightenment; it belonged to a process of self-clarification by which the Enlightenment came to examine its own prejudices and assumptions. By following that process as it unfolded in response to the crime in Zurich, this book brings to life an important episode in the intellectual history of the late eighteenth century, an episode in which the Enlightenment was forced to interrogate the very limits of reason itself.[7]

NOW, THE SELF-CLARIFICATION OF ENLIGHTENment may sound like a rather abstract intellectual enterprise, and in some cases it was (most notably in the philosophy of Kant, whose *Critique of Pure Reason*, published five years after the poisoning, sought to expose the limits of the understanding from the lofty perspective of a transcendental critique). But the debate about the poisoning of the communion wine was nothing if not concrete. Grounded in a single, empirical event, it never strayed so far from the event as to lose itself in airy speculation. The problem was that the ground itself was unstable, more like the shifting sands of a desert than the hard rock of an Alpine mountain. Nobody had actually witnessed the poisoning, which was presumed to have taken place under cover of darkness, so the reconstruction of the crime rested on secondary evidence—physical traces left by the criminal, the results of scientific investigations, and circumstantial evidence culled from the testimony of witnesses. To draw inferences from such evidence was anything other than straightforward. What had actually happened in the cathedral, no less than what it might mean, was open to interpretation, and the two questions were inextricably connected (bound together, so to speak, in the same hermeneutic circle) because every attempt to establish the meaning of the event rested on a particular reconstruction of the facts and every attempt to reconstruct the facts rested on a particular view of their meaning. Lavater, for example, who regarded the crime as a sign of diabolic evil, interpreted the evidence in such a way that the facts of the crime appeared correspondingly sinister. Others, who rejected as irrational the very existence of the devil, did precisely the opposite, and their reconstruction of the facts made the event seem relatively benign. The two versions of the facts differed so profoundly as to be irreconcilable. Both of them could not be right, and yet it was difficult, if not impossible, to find a neutral and objective standpoint from which to adjudicate between them. On the face of it, every attempt to pin down what had happened in the cathedral seemed doomed to validate its own interpretative prejudice.

At the center of this book, therefore, lies not an event so much as a problem. What counts as valid evidence? How can one interpret it? To what extent can one obtain objective knowledge about events in the past? The problem of evidence is, of course, an eminently historical one inasmuch as standards of evidence have changed over time.[8] But it is equally a problem of historical method, confronted, at least implicitly, by all historians, who struggle in the manner of Leopold von Ranke to reconstruct the past "as it actually was" [*wie es eigentlich gewesen*]. I say "implicitly" because most historians confront the problem without "problematizing" it. They go about their business without bothering to spell out their methodological presuppositions, and if they do spell them out, they consign them to a separate publication or a separate chapter within a larger book, distinguishing clearly between the writing of history on the one hand and reflections on the writing of history on the other. What sets this book apart is that it collapses the historical and methodological levels: it is bound to confront the problem of evidence explicitly because that problem lies at the center of the story it seeks to reconstruct.

SO THE AFFAIR OF THE POISONED COMMUNION wine opens onto some very large topics indeed—from the political crisis of an Old Regime state, to the self-critique of Enlightenment and the problem of evil, to the interpretation of evidence and the nature of historical knowledge.

But enough of such large and weighty matters! As it is, this introduction may already have gone on too long and frightened off some potential readers with all of its highfalutin talk about the limits of reason and the hermeneutic circle. Rather than crushing the affair under the weight of philosophy and theory, therefore, I would like to end by emphasizing another of its aspects: it is a good story. It contains a kind of formal symmetry, framed as it is by two dramatic acts of bloodletting: the spilling of the blood of Christ in the cathedral and the spilling of the blood of a condemned man on the scaffold. It features a colorful cast of characters, including an anticlerical, oath-swearing gravedigger, a desperate, hard-drinking drifter, and a defrocked minister. It offers plenty of suspense. And it may even point to a moral, although on that score, to be sure, readers will have to make up their own minds. Such a story calls to mind various literary genres, but none fits it so well as that of detective fiction, which always begins with a mystery—a crime shrouded in darkness—and which derives its dramatic power from the efforts of the detective to solve the crime. As I sat down to write this book, therefore, nothing seemed so natural to me as to cast myself in the role of the detective and to give the story of the poisoned communion wine a narrative treatment—modeled loosely on the genre of detective fiction—rather than chopping it up according to the analytic mode of the social sciences. The larger issues raised in this introduction are not set apart and treated in isolation but woven into the fabric of the narrative.[9]

It has often been remarked that the historian works in the manner of a detective, building inferences based on clues—"fingerprints," as it were—left by those whose lives he seeks to reconstruct.[10] How much more does he resemble the detective when the object of his investigation is itself a criminal case—and not just any criminal case, but one so full of twists and turns that it reads as if it came from the pen of Arthur Conan Doyle. "The Case of the Poisoned Communion Wine" would be a worthy match for the deductive powers of Sherlock Holmes. If only one were allowed to smoke a pipe in the archives. . . .

Chapter One

Murder in the Cathedral

PERCHED ATOP A STEEP RISE ON THE right bank of the Limmat River, the cathedral with its high bell towers dominated the urban landscape of eighteenth-century Zurich just as it had done two and a half centuries earlier when Zwingli had inaugurated the Reformation in German-speaking Switzerland. The interior of the cathedral, too, looked much the same as in the Reformation, reflecting transformations effected by Zwingli and his fellow reformers in the early sixteenth century. Its walls remained cleansed of images, and its aisles free of statues. The nave, emptied of its pews, was a vast uncluttered space, dominated at the far end by a high pulpit from which the pastor, enthroned beneath the vaulted ceiling, preached the Word of God to the congregation below. On the site of what had once been the altar, where medieval priests had performed the miracle of transubstantiation, stood a "baptismal stone," which served as a communion table for the purpose of celebrating the Lord's Supper. The overall atmosphere of the cathedral remained as austere as ever—its somber hues unbrightened by stained glass, its air unsweetened by incense, the voices of its psalm-singing congregants unaccompanied by the chords of an organ (which the reformers had removed lest the dulcet tones of the instrument divert attention from the preaching of the Word). To all appearances, nothing much had changed in the great citadel of Swiss Protestantism in 250 years.[1]

But appearances were somewhat misleading. For one thing, the battle against Catholicism was a thing of the past (the last religious war in which Zurich participated dated from the early eighteenth century).[2] Gone, therefore, was the passion of an epochal struggle, and gone, too—or at least on the wane—was the oratory that such passion had inspired. From the pulpit, the fiery rhetoric of the early reformers had given way to cooler, more sober-minded sermons, and preachers now placed less stress on fine points of dogma than on the practical, moral needs of their congregants—a shift in emphasis that bore witness to the influence of the Enlightenment within the Church itself.[3] As the oratorical temperature began to drop, moreover, the churches were emptying. From the mid-eighteenth century onward, compulsory attendance at church services was no longer enforced, and many Zurich citizens simply chose not to attend the full regimen of weekly sermons—twelve in all in the cathedral alone—which kept employed a veritable army of unbeneficed clergymen.[4] Add to this the discontent expressed by some of the laity in response to recent liturgical reforms and revisions of the song book, and one can well understand why a few clergymen were beginning to fear that the Church was growing alienated from its flock.[5]

Perhaps, then, all was not well in the cathedral where Zwingli had launched the Swiss Reformation. Yet we would do well not to attach too much significance to the jeremiads of clergymen, in whom such alarmism has always been something of a *déformation professionelle.* The truth is that Zurich was still a city of pious church-goers, especially when it came to communion, which was celebrated only four times during the liturgical calendar: at Christmas, Easter, Pentecost, and the General Day of Prayer and Repentance. It was one thing to skip the early morning sermon on

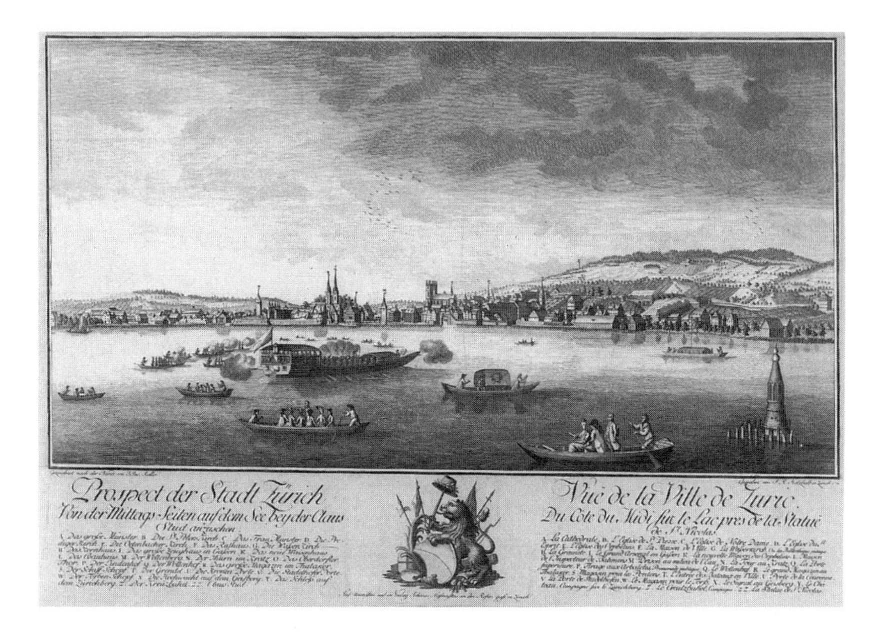

FIGURE 1. Zurich from four different angles.
a. From the south. Etching and copper engraving by Johann Jakob Heidegger, 1778. After Johann Jakob Koller.
b. From the north-east, 1778. Same as illustration a.

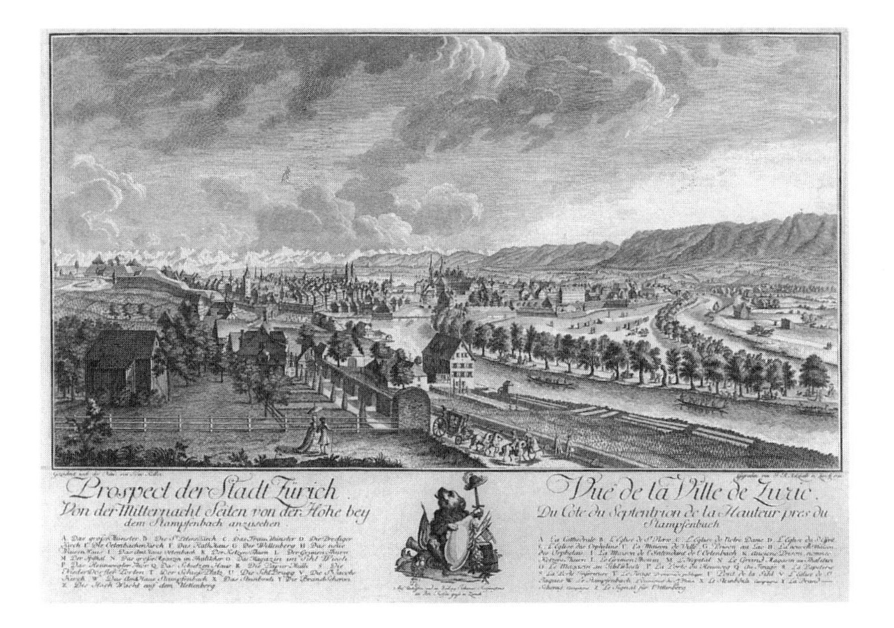

c. From the north. Etching and copper engraving by Johann Rudolf Holzhalb, 1781. After Johann Jakob Koller.
d. From south-west, 1783. Same as illustration c. Courtesy of the Zentralbibliothek Zürich, Graphische Sammlung.

FIGURE 2. The right bank of the Limmat between the cathedral and the town hall. Etching by Johann Balthasar Bullinger the elder, 1772. Courtesy of the Zentralbibliothek Zürich, Graphische Sammlung.

Monday (held, it should be noted, at six o'clock in the winter, and at five in the summer!) and quite another to miss communion, which was one of only two sacraments—the other was baptism—retained by the reformed Protestant Church. When communion was celebrated, the nave and the galleries of the cathedral were likely to be full of worshipers performing both a religious and a civic duty. To accommodate the many communicants, moreover, communion was celebrated twice at the time of the General Day of Prayer and Repentance: on the Sunday before the holiday and on the holiday itself. It was not the least bit unusual, therefore, when twelve hundred worshipers packed into the cathedral on the morning of Thursday, 12 September 1776.[6] Nor was there anything so unusual about that morning which might have given those in the cathedral cause for alarm. Whatever the signs of spiritual alienation between the Church and its flock, no one could have foretold a deed so blasphemous that it would shake the Zurich Church to its foundations and send shock waves across German-speaking Europe.

I

Somehow (no one knew exactly why) the custom had been established in the Zurich cathedral that all the preparations for the

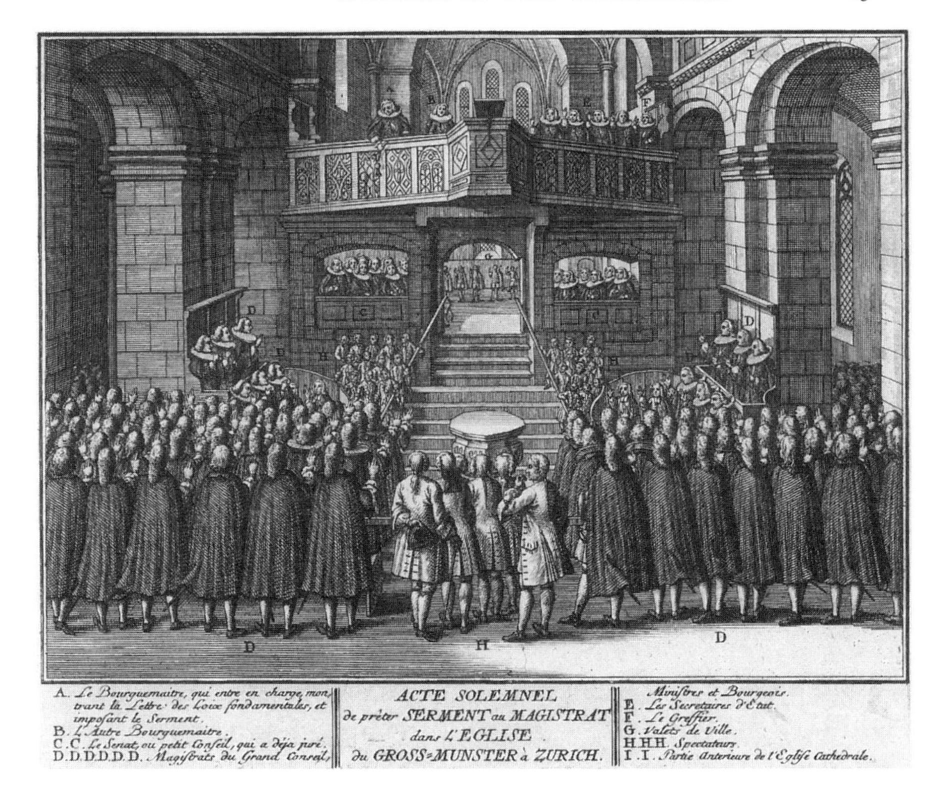

FIGURE 3. The interior of the main cathedral in Zurich on the occasion of the semi-annual oath-taking ceremony that accompanied the investiture of the Small Council. The "baptismal stone" appears in the middle foreground. Etching by David Herrliberger. From Herrliberger, *Heilige Ceremonien [. . .] der heutigen Reformirten Kirchen der Stadt und Landschaft Zürich* (Zurich, 1750). Plate 8, no. 2.
Courtesy of the Zentralbibliothek Zürich, Graphische Sammlung.

communion service were made on the preceding evening.[7] Accordingly, just as soon as the evening prayers had come to an end on Wednesday the eleventh, the cellar master and his two assistants went to fetch the communion wine, which came from a single large keg located in the wine cellar of a former convent, the *Chorherrenstift*, adjacent to the cathedral. All of the wine used in the cathedral came from this keg, and so, too, did the wine used in the *Prediger-*

kirche, the other of the two main parish churches on the right bank of the Limmat, to which a supply of wine had already been transported on the previous Saturday. Inside the wine cellar, the cellar master [*Küfer*] and his two assistants tapped the keg and poured the wine into carrying vessels. Then his assistants took turns transporting the vessels into the nave of the cathedral, making several trips until all the wine for the communion service had been deposited in the cathedral. Several doors connected the front of the cathedral to the *Kreuzgang*, a cloister that ringed the interior courtyard of the convent. In all likelihood, the cellar master's assistants transported the wine through one of these doors, proceeding from the wine cellar to the cloister and thence into the front of the cathedral.[8]

Meanwhile, in the nave of the cathedral, the sexton [*Sigrist*], Hans Conrad Keller, along with his wife, daughter, and female servant had been preparing the communion table. To create the table, they had placed a wooden plank across the baptismal stone and covered it with a tablecloth. On top of this makeshift table, they had set thirty-two plain wooden cups (the plainness of the cups symbolized the humility that Zwinglians strove to cultivate), and beneath it they had arranged five wooden barrels and a dozen tin cans, all of which they now filled with the wine brought from the cellar. Once all the others had departed, the sexton assured himself that everything was in order; he locked the doors to the cloister, the only doors on the ground floor of the cathedral equipped with locks (all of the other doors were simply bolted from the inside); and then he too went home, not returning until the following morning shortly before the worshipers began to arrive. During the night, the cans and the barrels of wine lay unprotected and unwatched underneath the communion table in the nave.

The first to arrive on the morning of 12 September was the sexton's female servant, who went to the cathedral at four o'clock to ring prayer bells. Using the sexton's keys, she entered through one of the doors in the cloister, which she found securely locked. After she had finished ringing the bells, she went home, locking the door behind her and returning the keys to their usual spot in the sexton's house.[9] Soon afterward, the sexton awoke. He removed

FIGURE 4. Wooden communion cups and communion plate. Photograph of nineteenth-century copies modeled on seventeenth-century originals. Courtesy of the Züricher Amt für kantonale Denkmalpflege.

FIGURE 5. Tin cans used for pouring the communion wine. Photograph of eighteenth-century originals. Courtesy of the Züricher Amt für kantonale Denkmalpflege.

the keys from where his servant had left them and set out in the company of his daughter to open the cathedral. He, too, found the door securely locked. When he advanced into the nave of the cathedral, however, he made a surprising discovery. There, on the floor in front of the communion table, he noticed "red spots" that looked like spilled wine, and on the table he found one cup that had been smeared around the rim with a gluelike substance.[10] Everything else was just as he had left it the previous evening, so he did not bother to bring his discovery to the attention of his clerical superiors. Instead, he ordered his daughter to wipe the moisture from the floor and to wash the smeared cup while he tidied up as best he could, finishing just as the first worshipers began entering through the main portals in the middle of the cathedral.

The congregation assembled at about a quarter after six, several hours before the communion service, which was held between nine and ten o'clock.[11] For so important an occasion as the General Day of Prayer and Repentance, it is likely that chairs and benches, reserved mainly for citizens of high social standing, had been set up along the aisles of the nave, as well as in the gallery, or the "upper church" as it was sometimes called. The majority of the worshipers, however, would have stood, either milling about along the central axis of the nave or leaning against columns; and there they would have remained while the Antistes, the head pastor of the cathedral, delivered his sermon, which ended with the recital of the Our Father.[12] The communion service itself began when the Antistes descended from the pulpit and headed to the communion table. There, with the other clergymen gathered around him in a tight semicircle, he read from the liturgy while the sexton began pouring wine from the first of the five barrels into the cups.

The wine was of dreadfully poor quality. As it came out of the barrel, the sexton recalled, it was covered with a "white foam" that looked like milk. Nevertheless, he continued to pour the wine until he had filled twelve of the cups; then he filled the remainder of the cups from the second barrel, in which the wine was somewhat less "murky." As was customary, the first to drink the wine were the clergy, who were standing near the communion table. Those who drank from the first twelve cups were immediately taken aback at the color of the wine. Later, they too would describe the color as "murky," declaring that the wine looked "as if it had been sitting in dirty vessels." Discreetly, so as not to create a commotion, one of the clergymen then approached the sexton and signaled him to replace the murky wine. This the sexton did, emptying the cups of murky wine into the first barrel and refilling them with wine from the tin cans and from the fifth of the five barrels. The wine contained in the tin cans and in the fifth barrel turned out to be fine; from this point forward, it was the only wine used to refill empty cups. In the meantime, however, some of the clergy had already begun, "from overhastiness," to fan out into the congregation bearing cups filled with the murky wine. So some of the bad wine did circulate among the communicants, although it is not clear from which of the barrels it came or how much of it the communicants, in fact, drank. According to one published source, little of the wine is likely to have been drunk since the worshipers found its color (here described as "bluish") and its "sweet and insipid" taste so repulsive that either they drank only a drop of it, or they spat it out after drinking it, or they passed on the cup without drinking from it at all. "This time the wine was truly awful," one of the communicants is reported to have muttered under his breath.[13]

Nobody collapsed on the spot, but there was a good deal of grumbling about the poor quality of the wine. And so, if nothing else, the affair was embarrassing—especially for Caspar Hess, the cathedral canon who served as administrator [*Stiftverwalter*] of all the properties belonging to the cathedral chapter. Along with his other functions, Hess was responsible for overseeing the wine cellar. To determine where the fault lay (and perhaps also to deflect criticism from himself), he decided to launch an investigation.

Immediately after the conclusion of the service, Hess went into the wine cellar to examine the wine in the keg. It looked fine, not at all like the wine in the wooden barrels in the cathedral, which Hess described as "yeasty" and "fermented." Upon inspection, a bit of wine left in the carrying vessels also turned out to be flawless, and so, too, did a sample of wine that Hess gathered from the

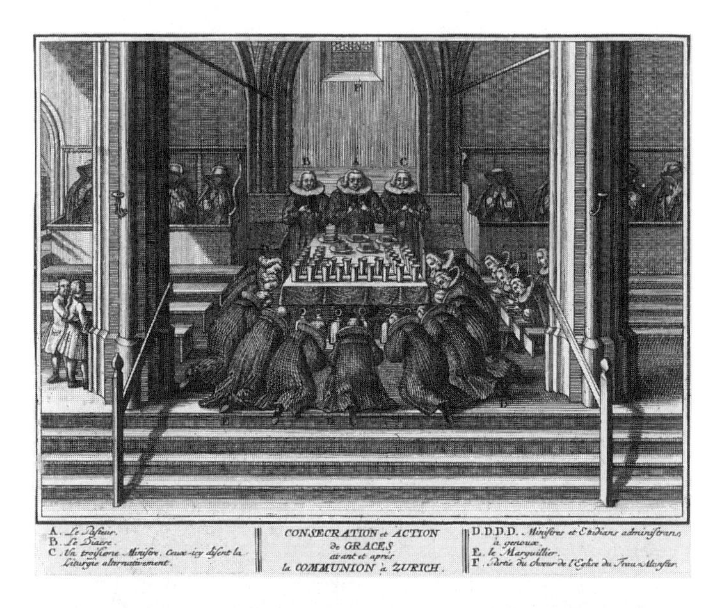

FIGURE 6. The communion service as celebrated in the Fraumünster in Zurich, a church opposite the main cathedral on the left bank of the Limmat. Etching by David Herrliberger. From: Herrliberger, *Heilige Ceremonien [. . .] der heutigen Reformirten Kirchen der Stadt und Landschaft Zürich* (Zurich, 1750). Plate 7, nos. 1-2. Courtesy of the Zentralbibliothek Zürich, Graphische Sammlung.

Predigerkirche. Because all the wine came from the same keg in the wine cellar, the problem could not have lain at the source. Instead, Hess reasoned, it must have come from the barrels themselves. And what, indeed, could have been more natural than for wine sitting in barrels to become discolored, given that the barrels were made of wood and that wood was apt to become moldy?

The main difficulty with this conclusion was that not all of the barrels contained murky wine. Four of them did, but one of them did not. When questioned, moreover, residents of the neighborhood around the cathedral testified that they had seen the barrels laid out to dry as late as five o'clock on Wednesday afternoon. As Hess saw it, this testimony was important. It militated against the explanation of moldy wood and raised the possibility of a more sinister explanation—a possibility that hardened into a virtual certainty when the sexton revealed to Hess the discoveries he had made upon arriving in the cathedral earlier that morning. According to Hess, the moisture on the floor and the smeared cup pointed to the presence of an intruder during the night. Add to this the fact, already established by the comparison of the various wine samples, that the wine contained in the barrels had undergone some kind of transformation during Wednesday night, and it was difficult to avoid the conclusion that someone had tampered with the wine in the barrels. For his part, however, the sexton did not see how anyone could have gained access to the cathedral, unless the intruder had his own key or had been in the cathedral since the previous evening, because there had been no signs of a break-in.

To clarify the mystery, Hess decided to enlist the help of scientists. It was now late on Thursday afternoon. But the matter seemed too important to allow for delay. Laden with samples of wine from the first three barrels, Hess went calling at the home of Johannes Gessner, an esteemed doctor of medicine who lived opposite the cathedral and who happened at that very moment to be receiving a visit from two other doctors of medicine—Dr. Schinz and Dr. Ziegler. Gessner agreed to perform a chemical analysis of the samples, and Schinz and Ziegler agreed to conduct their own experiments together. Setting to work immediately, the three of them performed experiments until late on Thursday evening, then resumed their labors on the following day. At first, their results seemed too shocking to be believed, so they repeated the experiments to confirm the results. In the end, however, there was no denying the horrible truth: the wine, affirmed Gessner and his colleagues, contained "a mixture of a gluelike substance and Spanish pepper dissolved in vinegar, jimson weed, Iris, fly poison, and true arsenic."[14]

Yes, "true arsenic"! The result seemed incredible, yet the leading scientist in Zurich and his team of eminent collaborators had certified its accuracy. No doubt shaken by this astonishing turn of events, Hess immediately conveyed word of what had transpired to the magistrates of the Secret Council, the most powerful of the three ruling councils in Zurich, who convened in an emergency session on Sunday. It is not hard to imagine the atmosphere of that session. The resolution adopted by the Council was full of such expressions as "heartfelt sorrow," the "greatest dismay," and the "sad discovery."[15] Here, the magistrates instinctively realized, was a criminal case of the most shocking sort, and one so serious in its implications that it demanded all the resources at the disposal of the state. To meet this momentous challenge, the Council ordered a follow-up chemical analysis and a thorough review of the records of apothecaries in Zurich who might have provided the arsenic; it appointed two of its own members as investigators, directing them to undertake a thorough examination of the cathedral and to interrogate everyone who had been in the cathedral at any time from Wednesday evening to Thursday morning; and, finally, it ordered the results of the investigations to be submitted to the Small Council, the council usually responsible for criminal investigations, so that the latter could take up the matter during its regularly scheduled session on Wednesday, the eighteenth.

Proceedings of the Secret Council [*Geheimer Rat*] were meant to be secret [*geheim*], but secrecy was out of the question with investigators snooping around the cathedral and interrogating witnesses. In a matter of days, therefore, Zurich was buzzing with talk of the crime. Dozens of those who had taken communion in the cathedral the previous Thursday now declared (why only now?) that they had been taken ill either during or after the communion service, stricken by attacks of colic and fits of vomiting. And as panic spread, the most shocking revelation of all came to light: sometime after having taken communion, a certain Captain Burckhard had died! Immediately, word spread that Burckhard had been a victim of poisoning. But Burckhard's own physician, Dr. Diethelm Lavater, doubted that this was so. Lavater approached members of the Secret Council to explain that his patient had been ill before the communion service. It was likely, Lavater argued, that the deceased had died from his illness rather than from poisoning, and it was all the more likely because Burckhard's daughter had now contracted the same illness and was near death herself. After giving his opinion on the matter, Lavater received the order to perform an autopsy, and he was prepared to do so when family members of the deceased declared their opposition, thus blocking the operation. In the end, no autopsy was ever performed; the death remained a mystery.[16]

With Burckhard's death, rumors began to circulate that several—even hundreds—of worshipers had perished after taking communion on the General Day of Prayer and Repentance. But even if the rumors were wrong, blood had been spilt in the cathedral nonetheless: the blood of Christ.[17]

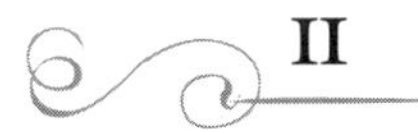

II

Before long, word of the crime in Zurich had spread all across the German-speaking world, conveyed by the scores of newspapers that covered the far-flung territory of the old Reich.[18] Thus, for example, one finds the following report published in a Stuttgart newspaper on 8 October 1776, less than a month after the General Day of Prayer and Repentance in Zurich:

> *Letter from Zurich, 19 September*
>
> Will you believe me if I recount to you a deed so abominable that everyone must regard it as fiction? But it is not fiction, it is the

> truth. If word of it had not already begun to spread . . . then I would not have mentioned it, preferring that such a monstrous deed might pass into oblivion. Never would I have suspected any trace of such a foul crime in our quiet and virtuous Zurich. Oh, my friend! Imagine, a monster, a devil, dared, on the Day of Prayer, to break into the church in the cathedral or to creep inside—or God knows how he got in—and to poison the wine that was lying in the church for use in the morning communion service. Four wooden barrels were opened by his accursed hand; into these he poured, in unequal quantities, a mixture of coloquint, Spanish pepper, jimson weed, fly poison, mouse poison, and sublimate of quicksilver; and adding glue to this mixture, he smeared it on one of the thirty-two cups that stood on the communion table.[19]

Where did such a report come from? And how did it find its way into the hands of a newspaper editor in Stuttgart? Clearly, each of the many newspapers in Germany did not have its own correspondent in a sleepy provincial town like Zurich. But it was not necessary for all of them to receive their reports directly from Zurich. The political fragmentation in Germany made it impossible to enforce a uniform system of copyright (the very concept of which was only beginning, in any event, to take shape). So newspaper editors were able to pilfer from one another with complete impunity, simply lifting reports printed in other newspapers, and the result, in practice, was not so different from the journalistic world of late-twentieth-century America, where the same dispatches from UPI, AP, and Reuters appear in suburban newspapers from Maryland to Montana. A report published by the *Hamburgischer unpartheyische Correspondent* (the *HC*), the most widely disseminated daily in Germany and the leading newspaper of record, would reach not only the readers of the *HC* (roughly 30,000, according to a conservative estimate) but also untold numbers of other readers who encountered the same report reprinted in other provincial newspapers.[20] If the *HC* published a misleading report (and that was bound to happen), then the errors contained in the report could prove stubbornly resistant to correction, acquiring a dynamic of their own as they moved through the journalistic chain.

And so it happened that the initial reports on the crime in Zurich conformed to two principal versions, copied and recopied, often verbatim, at intervals of several days. According to one of these versions, close to three thousand communicants had been in the cathedral on that Thursday morning, nearly thirty of them had been taken ill, and "several" of them had died.[21] According to the other account, no one had died as a result of poisoning and the reports of illness were exaggerated.[22] Spinning off from this second version, however, were still other reports whose main contention was that a full-blown massacre could easily have occurred, although no one had in fact died, and that only a lucky combination of factors had prevented the massacre. One such report claimed that the poison was mixed in such a way as to grow more lethal over time, and that if it had sat in the barrels only two hours longer, all those who drank the wine would have either died or gone stark raving mad.[23] Similar reports declared that the poison had not had time enough fully to dissolve. If it had dissolved, so the reports continued, the wine would not have been so murky, its color would not have appeared so disgusting as to deter people from drinking it, and a great many people would have died.[24]

With all of this press attention focused on Zurich, the authorities found themselves in an unaccustomed position. Usually, nobody cared very much what actually happened in Switzerland. To its many enthusiastic admirers in the late eighteenth century, Switzerland scarcely belonged to real historical time. It was a myth—a land of Alpine pastures, virtuous peasants, and freedom-loving burghers, enshrined in majestic and sublime mountain peaks—not the site of contemporary events, and certainly not the site of events worthy of notice, such as occurred in Paris, London, Vienna, Berlin, Rome, or, for that matter, Boston and Philadelphia.[25] Now, to be sure, the story of the poisoned communion wine had its mythic and timeless elements (we'll come back to this point in the next chapter), but it was also a contemporary event and it generated press reports that presented a rather unflattering image of sleepy old Zurich. In this unusual situation, the government tried to improvise a strategy of press management.

The subject of foreign news reports came up at a meeting of the Small Council in the first week of October. The councilors voiced their displeasure at the distorted and misleading account of events presented in a recent issue of a Frankfurt newspaper, comparing it unfavorably to what they regarded as a truthful and accurate account published in Schubart's *Teutsche Chronik*, which seems to have been the model for the second version described above. To set the record straight, they decided to write to the editor of the Frankfurt newspaper, instructing him to publish a new report modeled on the account in the *Teutsche Chronik*.[26] Then, less than a week later, another highly misleading news story came to the attention of the councilors, this one from a Stuttgart newspaper, which reported, under the dateline "Zurich, 25 September 1776," that the poisoner had been found and convicted. Immediately, the councilors fired off a letter to the government in Stuttgart demanding to know how the publisher of the newspaper had come by such a report.[27] It turned out, however, that the report had not originated in Zurich at all. It was a cut-and-paste job, which the publisher had assembled from two discrete sources: the article in Schubart's *Teutsche Chronik* and the statements of a "few unknown people" who had wandered into the editorial offices of the newspaper. Under questioning from the magistrate in Stuttgart, the publisher admitted, somewhat sheepishly, that the dateline was simply intended "to create the impression of a written report" submitted from Zurich.[28]

Against journalistic practices of this sort, the efforts of the Zurich government could avail little. Eventually, however, the most wildly exaggerated reports seemed to vanish of themselves, as if driven out of circulation through a kind of journalistic process of natural selection. Not that the newspapers were inclined to publish retractions: of all the newspapers that carried reports of deaths, not one openly admitted that it had been mistaken. But neither did any of them repeat their initial reports—they simply allowed the matter to drop.[29] From the many confusing press reports of late September and early October, therefore, something like a standard version of events began gradually to emerge. It evolved out of the article in the *Teutsche Chronik*, took on added detail in an issue of the *Erlanger Real-Zeitung* from late December, and achieved its final form in a lengthy account written by the famous Zurich pastor Johann Caspar Lavater, which appeared in early 1777 in the *Teutscher Merkur* of Christoph Martin Wieland.[30] Lavater's account affirmed that someone had managed to gain entry to the cathedral during the night before the communion service, and that the intruder had placed poison in the wooden barrels; but it vigorously denied that anyone had died as a result of poisoning, explaining this apparent contradiction by noting that the communicants had drunk only a few drops of the tainted wine and that the poison in the barrels was not sufficiently concentrated to cause death when drunk in such small quantities. Because Lavater was such a prominent figure in Zurich and because he maintained very close relations to the ruling councils, his account had almost the character of an official pronouncement: its goal was to lay to rest, once and for all, the many rumors elicited by the crime.

But how did the rumors of multiple deaths arise in the first place? And what of the rather fanciful story about the narrowly averted massacre? The truth is that the government had only itself to blame for fostering such rumors. Once word of the crime had leaked out, it was pointless to deny it. So the Small Council officially took up the matter in its session on Wednesday, the eighteenth, instructing pastors in Zurich's four main parish churches to preach sermons devoted to the crime on Sunday, the twenty-ninth, and ordering an official government decree read from the pulpits on the same day.[31] Otherwise, however, the government attempted to draw a veil of secrecy over the whole affair. It did not allow the publication of the chemists' reports submitted by Gessner and his colleagues, nor did it make available the results of the investigation initiated by the Secret Council on Sunday, the fifteenth. And it did not relax its general policy of censorship, maintaining a near total news blackout even though the affair was almost certainly on everyone's lips. Throughout the autumn of 1776, the printed newspapers and journals published in Zurich carried the obituaries of Zurich citizens, lists of the names of those nominated or promoted to official positions, reports on the weather, natural disasters, and the wine harvest, and stories about official ceremonies in other Swiss cantons and foreign states—but not a single word about the one event that was the object of news reports all over the German-speaking world.[32] In the absence of an open and public debate in Zurich itself, nothing restrained wild flights of fancy, and rumors were bound to result, with some of them finding their way into German-language newspapers through Zurich correspondents, who may earnestly have believed that they were relating the truth.

By their very nature, rumors tend to be elusive, but we can hear an echo of a few of the rumors that circulated in and around Zurich during the autumn of 1776 by turning to the one Zurich publication exempted from the news blackout imposed by the authorities: a handwritten news sheet edited by a local schoolmaster and copied by his pupils. This was not a clandestine news sheet. It appeared with the connivance of the authorities, who tolerated it because its circulation was so limited, and also no doubt because it was useful to them, as in such cases when they wished to orchestrate leaks. So it was not at liberty to report information hostile to the government, but at least it was able to report on events in Zurich, which the printed newspapers and journals were forbidden to touch, and it recorded what people were writing in their letters and saying in their conversations, sometimes with critical comment and sometimes with no comment at all.[33] In it, one finds the story about the narrowly averted massacre that found its way into several of the German newspapers, a good deal of speculation on the search for the criminal, and, in the issue of 4 October, a report about a letter written by a correspondent in Strasbourg to a friend in Aarau, a Swiss city not far from Zurich. According to this report, the correspondent in Strasbourg had inquired whether it was true, as he had heard, that 120 victims had died as a result of the poisoning in the cathedral. The news sheet hastened to point out that it was not true at all, that "God be praised, no one had died."[34] But even with such disclaimers, the letter as reported gave eloquent testimony to the macabre fantasies that the crime inspired.

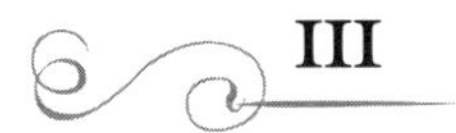

III

With rumors flying fast and furious, the pressure on the authorities to catch the villain must have been enormous. But who could have done such a dreadful deed? And how to find him? Nobody had been in a better position to commit the crime than the sexton, who had keys to the cloister, and who, by his own testimony, had been the last one to leave the cathedral on the evening before the communion service. The investigators interrogated the sexton on the sixteenth, subjecting him to longer and more detailed questioning than they did any of the other witnesses.[35] Under questioning, he repeated what he had told Hess about the smeared cup and the spots of moisture on the ground, adding that despite the best efforts of his daughter, it had not been possible to remove the spots—a claim that the investigators were able to confirm for themselves when they examined the area around the communion table.[36] As for the wine, it had looked perfectly fine to him on Wednesday evening when he had poured it into the barrels and tin cans. After the communion service, however, he had taken home the barrels, still partially filled with wine, and two days later he observed that a "nasty looking sediment" had formed at the bottom of all of them—though especially in one—while the wine had grown somewhat clearer.

The sexton received a reprimand from the Small Council for having failed to report the smeared cup before the beginning of the communion service, but the investigators did not suspect him of having committed the crime, largely, it would seem, because he was known to be an honest man with regular habits. Nor, in the end, did they suspect any of the others who had come in contact with the wine, such as the sexton's wife, daughter, and female servant or the cellar master, Caspar Burckhard, and his assistants, all of whom were able to give convincing accounts of their comings and goings.[37] When questioned about the wine, moreover, the cellar master and his assistants all confirmed the sexton's testimony, claiming that the wine had appeared perfectly fine to them on Wednesday evening; and the cellar master added that he had, in fact, tasted a little bit of the wine in the cellar just before it was transported into the cathedral.[38] The Secret Council had hoped that the examination of apothecaries would turn up helpful evidence, and it did enable the investigators to compile a list of all those who had made purchases of arsenic in recent months. The list, however, led nowhere because all of those who had purchased arsenic had legitimate grounds for doing so—either they were using the poison to drive away rats, mice, and insects, or they were veterinarians, who needed it to put ailing animals out of their misery—and none of them had any connection to the cathedral or any motive for committing the crime.

Eventually, however, the investigators picked up a scent. After having barked up several wrong trees, they began to focus their attention on a suspect named Hartmann Wirz. Wirz's main occupation was that of gravedigger (and in the documents he is always described as "gravedigger Wirz"). But he was also a bell ringer and watchman in the cathedral tower; and on the night of the eleventh he had been in the tower, ringing the cathedral bells and keeping the watch. There was no evidence that he possessed a key to the cloister—or any other keys to the cathedral, for that matter. As a bell ringer, however, he had no special need of a key. In the eighteenth century, it was possible to pass directly from street level to the gallery by means of an exterior staircase mounted against the facade of the cathedral, and from the gallery a door opened onto a winding staircase that led up through the tower to the bell room. Both the door on the gallery level and the door to the bell room were equipped with locks, but the locks had fallen into such a state of disrepair that a virgorous kick or a strong shove was enough to force them open.[39]

From the tower, it was possible to descend into the nave of the cathedral. So Wirz could have committed the crime even without a key, and there were two good reasons for suspecting that he had done so: first, he was alleged to have a motive—a longstanding grudge against the Antistes, Johann Rudolph Ulrich—and, second, he was thought to be a man of somewhat intemperate and dissolute habits, in stark contrast to the sexton, whose respectability had shielded him from suspicions.

On the afternoon of Saturday the twenty-first, rumors of Wirz's guilt were circulating throughout the city, set in motion by an original rumor (which proved to be groundless) that Wirz had taken flight the previous evening to escape prosecution. This rumor put the investigators on his trail. On the very same Saturday, however, the investigators discovered that there was nothing at all to the rumor of Wirz's flight. Wirz was sitting at home, and from there the investigators had him brought for questioning. "Did he have any idea why he had been called for questioning?" the investigators asked him. "On account of [my] miserable debts," replied Wirz. When the investigators explained to him the true reason for the questioning, "he maintained his composure and answered in such an uncharacteristically soft tone" that the investigators let the matter drop and allowed Wirz to return home.[40] But this was only a brief reprieve. Three days later, the Secret Council reversed itself and ordered Wirz to be placed under arrest, either because new evidence had come to light, or (one cannot exclude the possibility) because the pressure to arrest someone—anyone—had grown so strong as to be irresistible.[41]

When the authorities came for him, Wirz was with a mason in Kraz preparing a burial stone.[42] From there he was removed to the town hall and placed in a cell. Imprisonment in the town hall was hardly the worst form of imprisonment meted out to criminals in Old Regime Zurich. (It was mild compared to the rigors of confinement in the Wellenberg, a dank and horrid dungeon located on an island in the Limmat, which will be the setting for the final chapter of our story.) Nor was imprisonment the same thing as a death sentence. While imprisoned in the town hall, Wirz was to be interrogated and confronted with other witnesses; and the Small Council was to deliberate on his fate, receiving regular reports on the progress of the investigation, which continued even as Wirz sat

FIGURE 7. The town hall in Zurich. Etching by David Herrliberger, 1740. After Johann Melchior Füssli.

behind bars. On the following Sunday, the twenty-ninth, an official government decree was read from the pulpits in Zurich, expressing the horror of the government at the crime, summoning the citizenry to help in gathering evidence, and offering a reward of 200 Thaler for information leading to the arrest and conviction of the poisoner and his accomplices.

Still, Wirz's situation looked bleak. From their pulpits, the Zurich pastors preached such "heart-rending sermons that most of their auditors nearly melted into tears."[43] In such an atmosphere, the desire for revenge was bound to be strong, and fantasies of revenge found vivid expression in the sort of rumors recorded by the handwritten news sheet mentioned earlier. An edition from mid-November recorded a letter written by a woman in Bern who inquired of her son, a hosier's apprentice in Zurich, whether it was true, as she had heard, that "red-hot pincers had been employed to tear off the poisoner's skin" and "horses to draw and quarter him."[44] The editor hastened to point out that the report was false, but was it far-fetched? In Old Regime Zurich, torture (or, in any case, the threat of torture, the mere presence of the executioner at an interrogation being sufficiently persuasive) was still used to extract a confession.[45] And though somewhat less frequent than in previous centuries, executions were still common, as Wirz himself knew quite well from bitter personal experience: several decades earlier, when Wirz was still a young man of twenty-one, his own brother had been condemned of theft and bigamy and had perished beneath the executioner's sword.[46] As the gravedigger Wirz contemplated his fate from his prison cell in the town hall during the autumn of 1776, he had good reason to be filled with dark foreboding.

Chapter Two

Proof and Persuasion

T THIS POINT, LET US PAUSE FOR A moment to review what has so far transpired. A great many people in Zurich—from the councilors in the government to members of the clergy to the many communicants who complained of having felt ill after the communion service—believed that someone had gained entrance to the cathedral in the wee hours of the morning on Thursday, 12 September, and had dropped poison in the communion wine in the wooden barrels beneath the communion table. Whether the gravedigger Wirz was that someone had not yet been proved, but the "fact" of the crime had been sufficiently well established for the Secret Council to treat it as *corpus delicti* and for the Small Council to order all the pastors in the city to preach sermons on the subject of the crime. Beyond the boundaries of Zurich, it was well enough established to find its way into dozens of German newspapers, which transmitted news of the crime to a widely scattered public throughout German-speaking Europe.

How exactly did this "fact" come to be established? And how persuasive and compelling was the evidence for it?

I

It is difficult to contemplate the affair of the poisoned communion wine without thinking of historical parallels. For example, there are the various accusations laid against Jews in the Middle Ages: that they sacrificed Christian children at Passover (the infamous blood libel), that they poisoned wells (as in the so-called "Leper's Plot" in 1320), or that they desecrated the host.[1] In mid-eighteenth-century Paris, it was widely believed that royal agents were kidnaping young boys from working-class neighborhoods and sacrificing them to provide a bath of pure child's blood for an ailing member of the royal family who suffered from leprosy and for whom such a bath was the only cure.[2] In our own day, there is the *affaire du sang contaminé* so much discussed in the French media and now occasionally described as the *affaire du sang empoisonné*. What unifies these various historical episodes is a number of overlapping elements: poisoning, purity, pollution, blood, human sacrifice, desecration. All of the elements are not present in each of the episodes, nor are they combined in quite the same ways. But their recurrence over a long stretch of history points to the existence of certain archetypal or mythic narratives that translate fears and fantasies lodged deep in human consciousness. Seen from this perspective, the affair of the poisoned communion wine belongs to a history of the *longue*—indeed, the very long—*durée*: what made it so powerful and so captivating was its congruence with a preexisting narrative.[3]

The thesis of a mythic narrative raises interesting possibilities. It invites speculation that Hess may already have had the story of the poisoned communion wine in his mind, consciously or not, when he launched his investigation, and that he interpreted the evidence accordingly until he confirmed what he had always suspected. Once it had begun to circulate, one might argue, the story then spread so rapidly because it dramatized deep-seated fears associated with purity, pollution, and the violation of taboos.[4] The main objection to the thesis of a mythic narrative is precisely that it is speculative and that it cannot, by its very nature, be proved. To what sort of evidence could one appeal to demonstrate the operation of a mythic narrative? Nor, it must be admitted, does such a thesis advance us very far in understanding the historical circumstances peculiar to the affair of the poisoned communion wine. There may well be something to the argument that the story preceded the event, but to be convincing, the argument has to be less abstract and more firmly grounded in the soil of the late eighteenth century. To accomplish this, we need to shift our attention to the actual medium through which the story of the poisoned communion wine was spread: the printed newspapers of late-eighteenth-century Germany.

II

In the eighteenth century, Germany was unquestionably the leading newspaper producer in all of Europe, its many daily, semiweekly, and weekly newspapers reflecting the political fragmentation of the old Reich: hardly any princely residence, commercial town, or independent imperial city was so small and insignificant as to be without its own newspaper.[5] Until the very end of the eighteenth century, moreover, when newspaper editors began experimenting with a form of popular journalism, German newspapers addressed themselves primarily to a hybrid public of educated (though not necessarily university-educated) readers: princes, courtiers, statesmen, members of the liberal professions, academics, merchants, and, in some cases, urban artisans.[6] As befitted such a public, most of the newspapers were sober-minded and earnest, not sensationalist rags or eighteenth-century ancestors of the modern tabloid, and they concentrated on serious political news: wars, diplomatic negotiations, domestic high politics in major states, constitutional crises.[7] In 1776, as the reader would have no difficulty guessing, the most serious political news came from the New World and concerned the revolt of the American colonies against their British sovereign, which dominated press reports and transfixed the German reading public.[8] The affair of the poisoned communion wine might seem to pale by comparison when set alongside a great world historical event like the American Revolution. For a brief moment in the autumn of 1776, however, the two events did appear side by side—or, rather, one on top of the other—in the pages of the same newspapers.[9] How to explain such a bizarre juxtaposition?

Ever since the printed newspaper had begun to develop in the seventeenth century, commentators recognized that one of the main sources of its appeal was the curiosity inherent in human nature.[10] To traditional Christian moralists, who considered curiosity a vice rather than a virtue, the nature of the newspaper's appeal made it seem dangerous. Defenders of the newspaper countered by emphasizing the utility of the newspaper to different orders of society—especially to princes and their ministers and to merchants, who needed to keep abreast of events in a world wider than that of their own town or principality. But the defense of the newspaper did not rest entirely on its supposed usefulness. Even apologists of the new genre admitted that the reading of newspapers afforded not only utility but pleasure—*Lust und Nutz*—and that the pleasure derived from human curiosity, which the newspaper both stimulated and satisfied by exposing its readers to unusual events in faraway places.[11] What this meant in practice is that newspapers combined reporting on political, military, and economic matters with curious tales drawn from a repertoire first developed by the illustrated pamphlet of the sixteenth century. To this repertoire belonged stories of prodigies, miracles, and criminal cases of the most spectacular and gruesome sort. Such stories never dominated the pages of eighteenth-century newspapers, but they occupied a well-established, if subordinate, position, and their continuing importance to journalistic practice raises important questions about the significance of newspapers to the broader cultural transformations of the eighteenth century.[12]

According to historians today, one of the most important cultural transformations of the eighteenth century was the "reading revolution."[13] Traditionally, so it is argued, most nonacademic readers confined themselves to a narrow corpus of texts, which they read over and over again. The main object of such reading was to allow readers to recapitulate truths known to them from their earliest years, not to broaden their intellectual horizons. Around mid-century, however, this traditional style of repetitive reading gave way to a new style of "extensive" reading. Instead of circling perpetually within the same narrow orbit, extensive readers set off in search of novelty, seeking not familiar texts but new ones, which they read once and then discarded. On the face of it, the great popularity of newspapers in the eighteenth century would seem to provide the perfect example of this reading revolution. Here, one could argue, was a genre whose very name expressed the importance of newness. It offered the reader a continuous chronicle of new events, with each issue of the newspaper superseded by the next in an endless sequence. And precisely because the sequence went on ad infinitum, it fostered an association of "time" with calendar time—with linear rather than cyclical movement—which corresponded to modern philosophies of historical progress first elaborated in the eighteenth century.

For all its apparent persuasiveness, such an argument runs aground on one basic problem: news was not necessarily new. In practice, newspaper editors could not publish stories on every single criminal case in Germany, much less in the whole of Europe. Whether a particular murder or abduction or rape found its way into print depended on its suitability to excite the curiosity of readers, the criterion for which was not its novelty but rather its conformity to one or another of the traditional horror tales featured in newspapers since their advent in the early seventeenth century. Paradoxically, therefore, the stories designed to stimulate curiosity were the ones most likely to be familiar. Newspaper readers who went looking for such stories were not practicing extensive reading at all, but the very epitome of repetitive reading.[14]

So we have come back to the idea that the affair of the poisoned communion wine fitted a preexisting narrative. Now, however, the fit is not with some vague mythic narrative but with one derived from journalistic practice. If newspaper editors were so quick to snap up the affair of the poisoned communion wine, this was almost certainly because they recognized in it all the elements of a sensational and horrific crime story. And when they published the story, they not only gave it wings, allowing it to take flight and to spread more rapidly than would otherwise have been possible, they also gave it added credibility. Once it had materialized in newspapers, the story of the poisoned communion wine enjoyed all the authority of the printed word.

YET EVEN THE AUTHORITY OF PRINT WAS NOT enough, in itself, to establish the "fact" that someone had poisoned the communion wine in the cathedral in Zurich on the General Day of Prayer and Repentance. At no time have newspaper readers been so uniformly gullible and simple-minded as to believe everything they read, least of all in the age of Enlightenment, which prided itself on subjecting all forms of received wisdom to rigorous critique. Even defenders of the newspaper recognized that sometimes editors got things wrong, not out of maliciousness—it was not their object to deceive their readers—but simply because they depended on reports submitted from distant locations, which they were not always in a position to verify. To compensate for this failing, apologists for the new genre sought to promote a kind of reading pedagogy, arguing that the reading of newspapers was an "art" [*die Kunst, Zeitungen zu lesen*], the object of which was to establish criteria of credibility and to distinguish reliable reports from erroneous ones.[15] Three criteria in particular stood out: how far reports devoted to the same event and published in different newspapers agreed with one another, whether the newspapers in question enjoyed a reputation for scrupulous and careful reporting, and whether the reports rested on eyewitness accounts or merely on hearsay.[16] When measured by this yardstick, how persuasive were the press reports devoted to the affair of the poisoned communion?

In the last third of the eighteenth century, it was not uncommon for newspaper readers to consult several newspapers simultaneously. Nor was it difficult for them to do so, thanks to the proliferation of reading societies and reading cabinets, which had become fixtures even in small provincial towns. Typically, such institutions subscribed to several different newspapers, making them available to members and thereby enabling readers to compare different accounts of the same event far more easily and at a far lower cost than would otherwise have been possible.[17] If applied to the story of the poisoned communion wine, such comparative reading would have uncovered some discrepancies, as we noted earlier. But it would also have revealed that the discrepancies gradually faded as new reports were printed, giving way to what I have called the official version, and that, in any event, the discrepancies concerned only the consequences of the poisoning—whether anyone had died—not the "fact" of the poisoning itself. That the wine had been poisoned none of the newspapers disputed directly, not even so circumspect and highly regarded a newspaper as the *HC*.

Initially, to be sure, the *HC* treated the reports of the poisoning somewhat hesitantly, cautioning against overhasty conclusions and registering a certain note of skepticism. The first mention of the affair was a brief item (only six lines) on 2 October that appeared at the end of the news section, just before the announcements and classifieds. The item referred to "letters from Switzerland" that conveyed word of the poisoning, and from those letters it drew a very sketchy account—some of it, as it happened, wrong—to which it appended the warning: "This news report requires further confirmation."[18] Then two days later, a second report on the affair appeared, this one somewhat longer and more detailed—it ran to fifteen lines—though still located at the very end of the news section and surrounded, as it were, by journalistic red flags. The editor set off the report typographically by placing it in quotation marks, which implied that he was merely reproducing a report sent to him from Zurich, not endorsing its contents. The report itself contained such expressions as "supposedly" and "reportedly." And it concluded by declaring: "May so dreadful an event remain unconfirmed."[19] Two months later, however, the *HC* published a report—this one placed in the middle of the news section—that concerned the search for suspects in Zurich. It declared simply that "the poisoners of the communion wine have not yet been discovered," as if to say that the poisoning itself was no longer in doubt, only the identity of those responsible for it.[20] Even this report, it is true, did not amount to a positive endorsement of the accounts advanced so hesitantly two months earlier; but for so prudent a newspaper as the *HC*, it came very close.

So the press reports on the poisoned communion wine satisfied at least two of the criteria for evaluating the credibility of a story: the endorsement of a highly reputable newpaper and broad agreement among different accounts of the event. But they did not fulfill the third and final criterion—namely, the appeal to eyewitness testimony—nor were they in a position to do so. Even a correspondent who had been present in the cathedral in Zurich on the day of the communion service could not have claimed to have seen the crime. The most he could have confirmed was the poor quality of the wine and the complaints about it made by the communicants. Had the crime produced victims, then it would have been possible to witness, at least, the effects of the crime. A victimless crime carried out by a solitary person shrouded in darkness could not, by its very nature, have been witnessed.

In the absence of eyewitness testimony, newspaper stories deployed various rhetorical techniques to persuade readers of their truthfulness. One such technique was to allege that some people had denied the reality of the poisoning, and then to discredit such denials by claiming that they sprang from self-interested motives:

> It is perfectly natural that patriots in Switzerland would wish to silence and suppress [reports] of the intended poisoning of the communion wine. . . . Who would wish to see his own state, whatever its innocence in the matter, saddled with the ignominy of having had among its citizens so infamous a human soul? As

> the denials speak with great confidence, however, we would like our readers to know how things stand and to whisper into their ears that despite what is said about it, the report of the poisoning is accurate.[21]

Another technique, this one deployed by Johann Caspar Lavater in his article in Wieland's *Teutscher Merkur*—"True History of the Communion Poisoning"—was to compensate for the lack of an eyewitness by drawing attention to the "heavy, murky, viscous sediment" at the bottom of the barrels. Though the crime itself may have been invisible, the sediment was not: it was a hard physical reality, containing perceptible traces of the crime, which witnesses had seen with their own eyes.[22] Finally, two newspapers adopted the strategy of reproducing what purported to be an original letter from a correspondent in Zurich. This, the reader may recall, was the technique the editor of the Stuttgart newspaper used in the report cited in chapter 1: "Will you believe me if I recount to you a deed so abominable that everyone must regard it as fiction? But it is not fiction, it is the truth."[23] With its first-person narrative, such a report conveyed a sense of directness and intimacy, and so replicated the form, though not the content, of an eyewitness account.

What stood in for the content of eyewitness testimony was the result of the chemical analysis performed by Gessner and his colleagues. All of the newspaper reports that affirmed the fact of the poisoning appealed to the results of the chemical analysis as evidence, and so too, of course, did Hess and the magistrates in the Secret Council, who were already convinced that the wine had been poisoned, several weeks before the first press reports on the poisoning appeared in German newspapers.[24] Strictly speaking, not even Gessner and his colleagues were eyewitnesses to the presence of poison in the wine: what they witnessed was not the poison itself but signs of the poison. Yet even so, they were the primary witnesses and the most important source of evidence for the "fact" of the poisoning. In the end, the persuasiveness of the story elaborated by Hess, the Secret Council, and the German newspaper editors rested on the authority of science.

III

I say the "authority of science" rather than the "authority of scientists." But the status of the scientists mattered, too. Johannes Gessner, who performed the chemical analysis along with his two colleagues, was by all accounts the leading scientist in Zurich. An esteemed doctor of medicine and specialist in the field of botany, he had studied with the renowned Herman Boerhaave at the University of Leiden in the Low Countries, taken his degree at the University of Basel, and founded the *Naturforschende Gesellschaft* (also known as the *Physikalische Gesellschaft*), which attracted more than seventy members, and which established itself as the center of scientific activity in Zurich during the second half of the eighteenth century.[25] With such impressive credentials, Gessner could be relied upon to observe the most rigorous standards of scientific method. This did not give him the same type of authority as had once attached to such a figure as Aristotle, who had defined the truth by the simple fact of his being Aristotle. In theory, the authority of a modern scientist derives from the method he employs rather than from who he is, and his personal qualities are important only to the extent that they stand surety for the promise contained in the method. But that's the theory. In practice, Gessner enjoyed a good deal of personal authority—so much so that his conclusions compelled assent, even among those of his contemporaries who had not the faintest idea what his method was.

It mattered little, therefore, that the report submitted by Gessner and his colleagues was never published, and that in all likelihood hardly anyone has ever read it. In this report, the esteemed scientists were careful to record each of their experiments and to explain, step by step, how they arrived at their conclusions. To confirm those conclusions, the Secret Council did order a follow-up analysis. In the meantime, however, it operated on the assumption that a crime had been committed, and so did everyone else. This was a leap of faith. What lay behind it?

FIGURE 8. Johannes Gessner, professor of mathematics and physics at the Collegium. Etching by Matthias Weber, ca. 1778. Courtesy of the Zentralbibliothek Zürich, Graphische Sammlung.

FOR ALL THE AUTHORITY THAT IT COMMANDS, "science" is a notoriously difficult concept to pin down.[26] In the age of Enlightenment, it owed its prestige mainly to the achievements of the previous century—the "scientific revolution"—and above all to the figure of Isaac Newton. Elevated by the *philosophes* to the status of a veritable demigod, Newton towered over the eighteenth century—a majestic and awe-inspiring genius who had penetrated and laid bare the secrets of God's handiwork and disclosed the existence of a law-governed universe. But not all of the sciences fitted the model of Newtonian physics. What distinguished this model was its use of the language of mathematics to express the laws of nature. It yielded a type of pure knowledge uncontaminated by the evidence of the senses, a rational mechanics that described a world of abstract objects devoid of perceptible qualities, all of them attracting and repelling one another according to invariable laws of motion. Nothing could have been further removed from such a science than eighteenth-century chemistry, which was as "dirty" in its own way as Newtonian physics was "pure."

Eighteenth-century chemistry was dirty both literally and figuratively: literally, in the sense that a chemistry laboratory was a rather messy affair, what with its noxious fumes and splattering substances, and figuratively, in the sense that it gave results tainted by subjectivity and imprecision—or, in any case, results that seemed subjective and imprecise when measured against the standard of Newtonian physics. Whereas the latter expressed itself in the universal language of mathematics, chemistry was a Babel of national idioms. It continued to identify substances with the names of vulgar speech, names that invited confusion and that contributed nothing to an analysis of the substances they labeled. The legacy of Aristotle and the influence of alchemy still weighed heavily on the understanding of chemistry, inhibiting the conceptual breakthroughs that led to modern chemistry. And until those breakthroughs occurred—until chemical reactions were conceived on the model of an equation and the nature of air and the process of combustion were correctly analyzed—chemistry as an independent branch of science scarcely existed.

To make up for this conceptual deficit, Gessner and his colleagues simply fell back on the evidence of their senses. To identify the components of a given solution, they sniffed, observed, touched, and even tasted (yes, tasted!). Essentially, their method was to reason backward from effect to cause, to infer the presence of a particular substance from its perceptible qualities or its characteristic properties. Now, to be sure, modern chemists do this, too. In modern chemistry, however, the properties that distinguish one substance from another are susceptible of being expressed quantitatively: a given quantity of a base, let us say, neutralizes a given quantity of an acid, and yields a predictable quantity of a salt; a given quantity of a metal combines with a given quantity of a reagent to yield a predictable type of precipitate. Measurements of this sort provide a corrective to the subjective bias inherent in empirical observation, but the one thing Gessner and his colleagues most conspicuously did *not* do was measure. Measurements are meaningless unless based on a coherent unit of measurement, and it was not until the development of the periodic table of elements in the nineteenth century that chemistry discovered its unit of measurement in weight.

It is worth recalling, moreover, that Gessner and his colleagues were not really "chemists" at all but university-trained physicians, and that Gessner's speciality was botany.[27] Nor could they have been university-trained chemists since chemistry had not yet established its position as a discipline within the university. The study of chemistry was merely one component of the medical curriculum at eighteenth-century universities, and it belonged to an educational system organized around the reading of textbooks rather than clinical or laboratory practice. It is not surprising, therefore, that Gessner and his colleagues proved rather less adept at making the practical maneuvers required by the "art of analysis" (*Scheidekunst*, as it was called in German) than an apothecary who lacked their Latinate erudition. Medical training did not in itself equip them to analyze the contents of the wine. But it did accustom them to a type of reasoning closely analogous to that of chemical analysis. Physicians, too, reasoned backward from effect (symptom) to cause (illness). Like chemistry, medicine was a "dirty" science, which required that a physician smell feces and inspect the color of blood. And like chemistry, it comported an element of danger: the physician exposed himself to the risk of contagion just as the chemist exposed himself to that of poisoning.

As it happened, the affair of the poisoned communion wine coincided precisely with the revolution in chemical understanding effected by Lavoisier. In a series of elegantly written theses submitted to the *Académie des sciences* in Paris during the 1770s and 1780s, Lavoisier exorcised the ghosts of alchemy and laid the foundations of modern chemistry. He disproved the ancient understanding of air as an element, developing the modern notion of a gaseous state as one of three states in which elements exist; he laid to rest the principle of "phlogiston," invented by Stahel a century earlier, and replaced it by the model of oxidation, according to which "oxygen" is the element in air that mixes with a metal during "calcification"; he established the principle of the conservation of matter, which implies that a chemical reaction involves merely the recombination of a fixed set of elements, not a metamorphosis such as alchemists had vainly striven to effect; and, perhaps most significantly of all, he set about to reform the system of naming chemical substances, replacing the arbitrary names of vulgar speech with a precise chemical nomenclature that would both name and analyze in one and the same movement. The advance in chemical understanding brought about by Lavoisier was monumental. It was one of the great foundational moments in the history of science, analogous to what Galileo and Newton had done for physics and what Darwin would later accomplish for biology. But the truth is that it had absolutely nothing to do with the procedures adopted by Gessner and his colleagues. The scientists in Zurich may have known of the controversy surrounding phlogiston, but this knowledge certainly had no impact on how they went about analyzing the wine.

So what are we to make of the "faith" placed by Hess, the Secret Council, and the newspaper editors in the results of the chemical analysis? Gessner and his colleagues may well have been scrupulous about recording the results of their empirical observations, but they were not scientists in the Newtonian sense and thus could not lay claim to the type of "pure" and objective knowledge that the Enlightenment associated with Newtonian physics. Nor did they lay claim to it. Their contemporaries simply ascribed it to them, investing them with a mantel of authority tailored to the dimensions of Isaac Newton. That mantel fitted them scarcely at all.

IV

So much for general comments. What, then, of the experiments themselves? The laboratory notebook of a chemist tends to make for rather tedious reading, and Gessner's is no exception. But so much hinges on these particular experiments that we would do well to examine them carefully.[28]

Hess brought Gessner four small glasses filled with samples of the tainted wine—one from each of the first four barrels. The first thing that Gessner did was to compare these samples with some untainted communion wine and to note the differences:

> [The untainted communion wine] was quite clear and transparent, its color was pale red and rosy, its taste full-bodied, sour [i.e., "acidic," "*säuerlich*"] and agreeable, and its odor, too, was agreeable. The tainted wine, on the other hand, had an alkaline color. In the first and second glasses, it was positively murky, somewhat less so in the third and fourth glasses, and the wine in the third and fourth glasses grew clearer when allowed to stand, its reddish color becoming somewhat yellow. The odor was sickening and in the first and second glasses it almost stank, like a mixture of garlic and bad wine spirits. The taste was disagreeable and sharp and it caused the mouth to contract.

Then Gessner turned his attention to the precipitate which had gathered in the first glass:

> It was dense, heavy and ash gray, almost like clay soil that had been dissolved. Scattered [through the precipitate] were red skin-like pieces and a few yellow seeds. I examined both [i.e., the red skin-like pieces and the yellow seeds] under a magnifying glass, and I regarded the former as being the skins of Spanish pepper / *Capsici / Physalis Alkekengi*. The latter seemed to be [seeds from] a type of iris and perhaps [from] a type of jimson weed / *Datura feros.* Now and then, the dried precipitate displayed small, shiny white parts.

This second passage contains an interesting linguistic shift. Until this point, Gessner had been writing in the third person, presenting his observations in the form of assertory propositions: "the color of the wine was murky," "its odor was sickening," etc. Then, suddenly, he shifted to the first person, as if to underscore the subjective basis of his judgment. He did not declare that the skins were those of the Spanish pepper, but that he "regarded" them as such; nor did he declare that the seeds belonged to iris or jimson weed but that they "seemed" to belong to them. If such linguistic shifts are any indication, then Gessner himself was far from sharing the illusion of scientific objectivity.

But, in any event, neither Spanish pepper, nor iris, nor jimson weed was a deadly poison. So, for the time being, not much was at stake in making a precise identification. In the next round of experiments, the stakes increased dramatically.

Now Gessner took some of the dried precipitate from the first glass and sprinkled it over hot coals:

> It began to smoke and a white stinking vapor rose from it. I collected the vapor by means of a smooth copper plate, which became covered with a white and white-gray dust. Thereupon I sprinkled white arsenic on the coals, and the same white smoke rose from it [as from the precipitate]. The smoke smelled of garlic, and on the copper plate it left a white deposit, which was somewhat thicker than that left by the precipitate.

Gessner did not spell out why, all of a sudden, he made the leap to arsenic, but, presumably, he did so because he recognized the garlic smell, the white vapor, and the white-grayish dust deposited on the copper plate as characteristic signs of the deadly poison. To confirm his intuition, Gessner repeated the procedure, this time using some of the precipitate that was still moist, heating it over coals and trapping the vapor with a smooth copper plate placed above it. It, too, left a deposit on the plate—"a broad white, somewhat grayish deposit, in which one can see silver-white shiny glimmers, as well as some silver colored specks, as if the copper had been dusted with silver." When heated over coals for the second time, the arsenic caused the copper plate to be covered with "a white . . . shiny powder."

And now the clues began coming together like the pieces in a jigsaw puzzle. One of the seeds, of whose identity Gessner had previously been uncertain, now appeared to him to belong to a type of "hyoscyamus"—*Bilsenkraut*—which was a well-known poison. And as for the Spanish pepper, it made perfectly good sense, for it was frequently used to strengthen wine vinegar. It may be surmised, concluded Gessner, that the Spanish pepper placed in the wine had yielded a strong vinegar solution, which in turn served to dissolve the arsenic.

Yet even in his conclusion—indeed, especially in his conclusion—Gessner was circumspect, advancing his interpretations of the evidence without excluding the possibility of alternative ones. "It may be surmised" [*so läßt sich muthmaßen*]: this was not the bold affirmative language employed by those who "believed" in science as an article of faith. Rather, it betrayed a certain doubt, a hesitancy born of the recognition that the truth was no less murky than the wine itself.

To clarify the truth, Gessner's colleagues, doctors Schinz and Ziegler, tried to duplicate his results. But their results were mixed. Arsenic was known to have a distinctive taste—sharp and bitter—so Schinz and Ziegler assumed that they would be able to recognize the presence of arsenic by tasting the wine. After placing a few drops of the wine on the tips of their tongues, however, both of them agreed that the taste was neither sharp nor especially bitter. Then they mixed arsenic with the wine and tasted again; they found it to be both more bitter and more nauseating than before. This seemed to indicate the absence of arsenic in the original wine sample. On the other hand, when they placed a few drops of the wine on a piece of glass and viewed the glass under a microscope, Schinz and Ziegler discerned crystals such as they associated with arsenic. And when they burned the precipitate at a high temperature, it gave off an odor which "from time to time" was "noticeably that of arsenic."

THUS DID MATTERS STAND WHEN THE MAGISTRATES in the Secret Council ordered the follow-up analysis, the responsibility for which fell to Dr. Hans Caspar Hirzel (the official town physician [*Stadtarzt*]), Dr. Johann Conrad Jahn, and an apothecary named Steinfels, whose inclusion in the team was of considerable importance because he brought to the investigation a practical experience in the "art" of analysis that the learned doctors lacked. The object of this follow-up analysis was to verify the conclusions of Gessner and his colleagues. Instead, it added new elements of confusion and heightened the mystery of the whole affair.[29]

Hirzel and his colleagues found no evidence to support the conclusion that the wine had been poisoned with arsenic. As far as they were concerned, the telltale sign of arsenic was the garlic odor that it emitted when heated. But they were unable to produce such an odor from the samples of tainted wine given to them by Hess. Having poured the wine through filtration paper, they took the paper with the sediment on top of it and heated it over coals: first they smelled the steam given off by the wine, then smoke from the burning paper, and, finally, the aromatic odor of burning plant parts—and that was all. Nor was there any hint of a garlic odor when they heated the sediment collected by Gessner, which Hess had transmitted to them along with the wine samples. Out of deference to Gessner, they considered the possibility that the wine, the paper, and the plant parts might have masked the garlic odor. So they added some arsenic to the filter paper with the sediment, and heated it again. This time the garlic odor was quite distinct. They therefore concluded that the wine, the paper, and the plants were not sufficient to conceal the presence of arsenic when arsenic was present. The wine itself had disclosed not the least trace [*keine Spur*] of the deadly poison found by Gessner and his colleagues.

On the other hand, Hirzel and his colleagues were convinced that the wine had been poisoned with "quicksilver" (i.e., mercury) or, perhaps, with "sublimate of quicksilver" (mercury oxide, in the nomenclature of modern chemistry), the report itself being rather unclear which of the two substances—the metal or its sublimate—the investigation had managed to identify. The grounds for this conviction were simple—as simple as the grounds for concluding against the presence of arsenic. If the telltale sign of arsenic was a garlic odor, that of mercury was the white sublimate that it yielded when heated. Hirzel and his colleagues took some of the sediment collected by Gessner, heated it over coals, and trapped the vapor on a copper plate. On inspection, the plate revealed a white speck, which the apothecary Steinfels identified as mercury sublimate. Then, to confirm the identification, Steinfels smeared his finger with the white sublimate and rubbed it on a coin, which turned white. And afterward Hirzel and his colleagues performed the same test on the sediment that they had collected through the filtration of the wine samples given them by Hess and obtained the same results: when rubbed with the white sublimate, the coin took on a silvery color. Hirzel was far less circumspect than Gessner in drawing conclusions from his evidence. To him, the coin test furnished "irrefutable proof" [*unumstößlicher Beweis*] that the sediment collected by Gessner contained mercury, and it also confirmed [*bestätigte*] the presence of mercury in the sediment that he and his colleagues had isolated by means of the filtration paper.

Nevertheless, Hirzel and his colleagues decided to perform one last test to confirm their conclusion. Here, too, as in the initial identification of mercury, one suspects the influence of the apothecary Steinfels (although Hirzel did not say, explicitly, that the test was Steinfels's idea), for the test betrayed a practical knowledge of chemical reactions, and it was the only test of its kind performed by any of the learned doctors in their various investigations. It was known, Hirzel's report explained, that dissolved tartar salt reacted with dissolved mercury sublimate to yield a yellow precipitate. So Hirzel and his colleagues placed a few drops of a tartar salt solution in the wine and then observed the results. What they observed was not, as they would have expected, a yellow precipitate but rather a "precipitate with a dark brown color," which gradually spread through all of the wine. But the unexpected result did not cause them to revise their hypothesis. Instead, they speculated that the dark brown color may have been caused by some of the seeds in the wine or by the presence of some other metal, which "we were unable to determine." The color of the precipitate could, therefore, be discounted, and the fact that a reaction had occurred was enough to confirm their initial conclusion. "These tests," Hirzel wrote, "assured us that mercury sublimate is the chief ingredient among the substances which were so impiously mixed into the wine, and that arsenic is not present, as its odor would have betrayed it."

But what of the potency of the mercury in the wine? To test the effect of the poisoned wine, Hirzel and his colleagues gave a few drops of it to a young dove and a few drops of untainted wine to a second dove. Both of them fluttered about quite gaily, and on the following morning they were "healthy and fresh."

Hirzel and his colleagues did not believe, therefore, that the communicants in the cathedral could have suffered any serious physical harm from the communion wine. In the conclusion to their report, they declared that the communion wine contained various plant substances as well as a quicksilver sublimate, that the plant substances exerted a narcotic and sickening effect, and that the quicksilver sublimate had a corrosive and burning effect. If, therefore, a heavy dose of the quicksilver sublimate had been present in the wine, the latter could have produced "nausea, vomiting, colic, even intestinal inflammation, narcosis, and gout." But the quantity of wine drunk by worshipers at a communion service cannot have been much greater than that given to the dove, so Hirzel and his colleagues discounted the reports of people taken ill after the communion service. Such reports, they believed, had to have some other explanation; people might have been taken ill for a variety of reasons, such as the rapid changes in the weather during the early autumn, or they might simply have imagined their illnesses, so great had been their shock and horror at the "inhuman deed."

Hirzel's report superseded that of Gessner, and its conclusions were incorporated into the official government decree read from the pulpits on Sunday, 29 September, although, just like Gessner's report, it was never published so that it was accessible to no one other than the Council members themselves. In some respects, the conclusions of Hirzel's report reduced the sinister dimensions of the crime, but Hirzel continued to speak of the "inhuman" and "godless" crime and to describe the criminal as an "arch-villain." Indeed, he added a new detail to the portrait of the villain, whom he regarded as not only wicked but also clever and cunning. The criminal, Hirzel believed, had to be clever and cunning because the crime required a good knowledge of chemistry. If the mercury sublimate had not been properly ground, and if it had not been mixed with the wine in the correct proportion, then it would simply have fallen undissolved to the bottom of the barrels. Hirzel knew this because he had tried it himself. He had mixed ground and unground portions of mercury sublimate with the wine in various quantities and discovered not only that the sublimate had to be ground but also that a particular concentration was required in order to trigger a reaction.

With his reasoning on this point, however, Hirzel became entangled in a contradiction, rather as if he were straining to fit recalcitrant evidence into a preconceived idea of the criminal and the crime. If the "arch-villain" had been trying to carry out an "inhuman" and "godless" crime and the crime had miscarried because he did not mix enough mercury in the barrels, then his "knowledge of chemistry" was faulty. But if his knowledge of chemistry was good and he deliberately mixed only a small quantity of mercury into the barrels—enough to cause a scandal but not to kill anybody—then he was not an "arch-villain" foiled in his effort to carry out an "inhuman" and "godless" crime. It is hard to see how one could have it both ways.

And what, in any case, did Hirzel mean by a "good knowledge of chemistry"? In the eighteenth century, as we noted earlier, even the very best and most experienced chemist could not predict, at a theoretical level, what quantities of different substances were required to trigger a reaction. The only way to figure this out was through a process of trial and error, such as Hirzel himself had conducted. To say of the poisoner, therefore, that he had a "good knowledge of chemistry" was to imply that he had conducted experiments beforehand, mixing mercury sublimate and wine in varying proportions until he had got the proportions right. And from this it followed that the "arch-villain" had not carried out his "godless" and "inhuman" crime in an impulsive fit of rage, but that he had carefully and painstakingly planned it days if not weeks in advance. Could the gravedigger Hartmann Wirz have been such a villain?

Chapter Three

"Not Wirz, Not the Gravedigger"

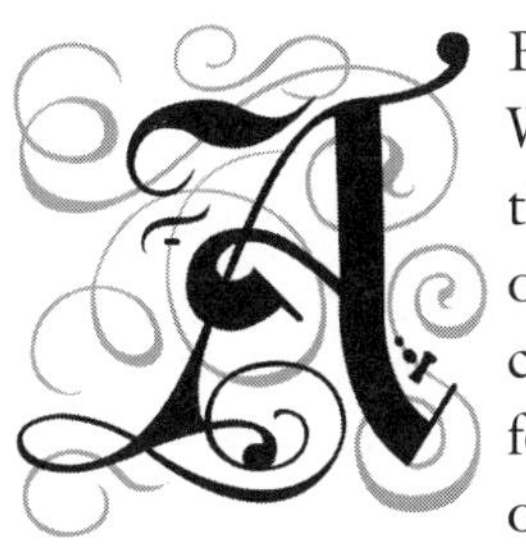

BOUT THE GRAVEDIGGER HARTMANN Wirz, one thing is certain: death was one of the most pervasive elements in his life. It shadowed him at every turn, clung to him like some cruel and sadistic tormentor. Two months before his arrest, when he was forty-seven years old, Wirz married for the fourth time: in March of the same year, he had lost his third wife; in February of the previous year, his second wife; and a little more than a decade earlier, his first wife, all of whom had died either in or soon after childbirth. Of the twenty-one children born to him by his four wives, only seven survived to adulthood, and one of his surviving sons, who served as a Swiss guard in the employ of the French monarchy, was later hanged as a deserter shortly after the storming of the Tuileries palace in August 1792. Earlier in his life, when Wirz was twenty-one, the brother closest to him in age had been beheaded in Zurich on charges of theft and bigamy. Whether as widowed husband or grieving father and brother, Wirz passed virtually all of his adult years in a state of mourning. It was as if he were being punished for a remote ancestral crime, hounded by the fates like Orestes at the hands of the Furies.[1]

Did this life of tragedy leave Wirz emotionally scarred—a man so embittered at his fate and angry with the world as to be capable of impulsive acts of irrational violence? Perhaps it did. Among his fellow citizens, Wirz had the reputation of being intemperate and explosive.[2] Generally speaking, however, the level of daily violence was much higher and the threshold of self-restraint much lower in the working-class cultures of early modern Europe than in the highly disciplined and heavily policed societies of the modern world. So we should not assume that Wirz would have stood out on account of his hot temper, and still less that such a temper would have brought him under suspicion of having committed this crime, which called, rather, for cool and level-headed planning.[3]

Nor should we assume that Wirz's contemporaries would have viewed his misfortunes in the same light as we do today. Nowadays, the sufferings endured by Wirz are almost unimaginable—at least within the framework of an ordinary, peacetime existence (we associate such experiences with extraordinary circumstances—with wars, massacres, genocides). But Wirz inhabited a world whose relation to death was far more intimate than ours—a world in which periodic famines left much of the population teetering on the brink of starvation, in which cemeteries were located at the center of towns and villages, in which public executions continued to be a common spectacle. To be sure, even by the standards of his own day, Wirz's sufferings were extreme. In itself, however, familiarity with death did not distinguish him from his fellow citizens.[4] What did set him apart was the relation of death to his work. As a gravedigger, Wirz exercised a profession that inspired widespread mistrust, if not horror, in the societies of early modern Europe; and the reputation of his profession may indeed have been one of the reasons why his fellow citizens regarded him with suspicion.

I

Early modern Europeans commonly believed that gravediggers wished to increase the number of bodies requiring burial. Thus, at times of great collective disaster such as epidemics or famines, they stood out as likely culprits, attracting suspicions that they had provoked the deaths of their fellow townsmen either through witchcraft or by poisoning the wells. In Vienna in 1562, a gravedigger and his wife were burnt at the stake; the same fate befell another Viennese gravedigger in 1679. In 1606 in Breslau, a gravedigger and his entire family were decapitated.[5] Now, to be sure, these examples come from a somewhat earlier period; no similar examples from the eighteenth century have come to light. But even so, the old prejudice about gravediggers was still alive, as one can see from several of the press reports printed in German newspapers about the arrest of Wirz. Thus a report in the *Bayreuther Zeitungen*, which wondered—half-mockingly, it is true—whether "the villain perhaps did not have enough dead bodies to bury," or a similar report published in the *Wienerisches Diarium*:

> The man responsible for the poisoning of the wine on the altar has been discovered. His name is Wirz, and he is a gravedigger, who perhaps did not have enough people to bury. He is already imprisoned in the town hall.[6]

Besides being blamed for misfortune, moreover, gravediggers were sometimes regarded as "dishonorable." Not everywhere, to be sure, and certainly not as frequently as executioners, who, especially in southern Germany, were debarred from membership in guilds and denied full citizenship rights. Yet even where they suffered no such legal disabilities, gravediggers were exposed to attacks from other artisans who imputed dishonor to them. Thus, in the early eighteenth century, gravediggers in Augsburg complained bitterly that "artisans have touched our honorable name several times, as if we belonged among the contemptible persons, such as executioners and skinners. . . . Every day we hear insulting words."[7] Because they carried a taint of dishonor, and because they often served as scapegoats, gravediggers bore some resemblance to Jews, a perennially marginal group within the communities of western Christendom and the one most vulnerable to persecution in the event of collective misfortune. Perhaps, in fact, the reader has been wondering all along when Jews would enter our story, for the poisoning of the communion wine has all the earmarks of the sort of crime for which Jews would be a likely scapegoat. The simple fact is that there were no Jews in Zurich on whom the crime could have been blamed; the Jewish community had been wiped out in the fourteenth century at the time of the plague—the victim of a massacre prompted by rumors that Jews were guilty of having poisoned the wells.[8] By going after Wirz, however, the Zurich government had the next best thing. Under the circumstances, a gravedigger was the functional equivalent of a Jew.

As a gravedigger, therefore, Wirz was in a perilous situation, but the perils to which he was exposed did not end there. They were exacerbated by his second occupation, that of bell ringer, which was also sometimes regarded as dishonorable. In Zurich, it was common for the two occupations to be linked in personal union, a link that probably derived from the physical proximity of cemeteries and bell towers. (In early modern Europe, cemeteries were located in churchyards.) But why did ringing church bells—at first glance, an innocuous activity—fall in the same category as digging graves? One reason, scholars have speculated, is that the bell ringer was bound to spend a great many hours alone in the bell tower, and in the tightly knit urban communities of early modern Europe, solitude was enough to arouse suspicions, as it did in the witchcraft persecutions of the seventeenth century, which often focused on solitary figures. And not only did the bell ringer spend many hours alone, frequently he did so at night when the rest of the community slept.[9] The night held great terror for the populations of early modern Europe. Shrouded in darkness (in a darkness thicker and more impenetrable than most inhabitants of modern cities have ever experienced), it was filled with all manner of unseen beings, populated by shades of the dead risen from graveyards, by ghosts and spirits, by witches celebrating their demonic sabbats. The Enlightenment may have mocked such superstitions, but philosophy alone could not lift the shroud of darkness—not without the real light that illuminated the night sky in the following century with the introduction of street lamps in major cities. In the eighteenth century, the bell ringer still belonged to the world of "unenlightened" night. His reputation suffered accordingly.[10]

In practice, the boundary between honor and dishonor shifted constantly depending on local struggles, which varied from one urban community to another. In Zurich, neither the gravedigger nor the bell ringer was dishonorable from the standpoint of the law—at least not in the late eighteenth century.[11] So Wirz did belong to a guild and enjoyed full citizenship rights. Indeed, he came from an eminently respectable family. His father had been a minor official in the government, Wirz himself held the rank of lieutenant in the local militia, and his fourth marriage was to the daughter of a master carpenter, a match that his father-in-law would never have allowed if the occupations of gravedigger and bell ringer had been legally defined as dishonorable.[12] Many press reports published in German-language newspapers noted explicitly that Wirz came from an "honorable" and "good" family.[13] Yet these very same reports also betrayed the persistent taint associated with gravediggers and bell ringers, for why would the authors of such reports have bothered to mention Wirz's honorable status if they had not expected readers to presume the opposite? Legal definitions were one thing, and popular prejudices quite another. The prejudices against gravediggers and bell ringers were rooted so deeply in the age-old collective fears of solitude, night, and death that an aura of something unsavory and uncanny [*unheimlich*] would have been likely to surround Wirz, no matter what his personal legal standing.

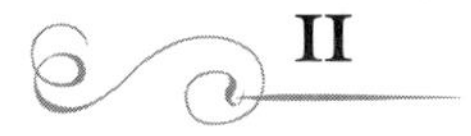

II

So the initial rumors of Wirz's guilt may have drawn their strength from the nature of his occupations. But prejudice alone could not have accounted for those rumors (Wirz was not the only gravedigger or bell ringer in Zurich), and it is not likely that the magistrates would have heeded the rumors in the absence of any other evidence or that they would have kept Wirz imprisoned on the strength of nothing more than hoary legends about gravediggers and bell ringers. As it turned out, official suspicion of Wirz's guilt rested on some very solid evidence indeed, and it was all the more difficult for Wirz to overturn those suspicions because the system of criminal justice in Old Regime Zurich—developed from the inquisitorial procedure of the late middle ages—was subject to a pronounced prosecutorial bias.[14]

The characteristic feature of the inquisitorial procedure was that all aspects of the criminal investigation, from the initial inquiry into the crime to the final rendering of judgment, fell under the direction of the state authority—in Zurich, the Small Council. After it had established the fact of a crime and it had uncovered enough evidence to warrant the arrest of a suspect, the Council would appoint two of its members to serve as investigating magistrates—"*Nachgänger*," in the idiosyncratic judicial parlance of the Zurich republic. To these men fell the task of interrogating the suspect and other witnesses. The interrogations would take place behind closed doors, not in an open courtroom, so that the public was absent from the proceedings, as were the other Council members, who followed the progress of the trial through the transcripts of the interrogations submitted to them by the investigating magistrates. On the basis of these transcripts, the Council would deliberate collectively on where to direct the investigation: which witnesses to call for further questioning, what sorts of questions to ask them, and, ultimately, whether to acquit or convict the suspect. Because it directed every aspect of the criminal proceeding, the Council functioned effectively as judge, jury, and prosecution simultaneously. But besides this all-encompassing judicial role, it performed a legislative role, too. Indeed, the two roles were so closely interwoven as to be virtually indistinguishable. In the absence of a written criminal law code or a clearly defined separation of powers, the Council both administered the law and made it at one and the same time, and this gave to it a broad discretionary authority against which a suspect was all but powerless. Denied both the benefit of legal counsel and the right of appeal in the event of a conviction, the accused was the passive object of the judgment rendered upon him, not an active participant in his own trial. Indeed, he had virtually no means of mounting a defense, for he had no opportunity to cross-examine witnesses, most of whom were interrogated in his absence. Occasionally, if an important point was in dispute, the Council members might order the investigating magistrates to arrange for a direct confrontation between the suspect and a witness, but otherwise the suspect could only guess what type of evidence the magistrates were gathering against him.[15]

It is well to remember, therefore, that in reconstructing the course of Wirz's trial, we have access to more information than Wirz did as the trial was unfolding. The judicial archive allows us to eavesdrop on the interrogations from which Wirz was absent, and to follow the thinking of the judges as it shifted in response to fresh revelations. Wirz may at times have been able to divine the nature of the case against him on the basis of the questions his judges put to him. We know precisely what reasons they had for suspecting Wirz's guilt.[16]

THE FIRST REASON FOR SUSPECTING WIRZ WAS that the evidence placed him at the scene of the crime, and that his behavior on the morning of the twelfth had been highly unusual. In the cathedral, bell ringers worked in two teams of two, each comprising a master and his assistant, who would man the tower together, taking turns ringing and sleeping until the other team came to replace them. One team was composed of Wirz and his young assistant Heinrich Pfister; the other, of a master bell ringer named Rordorf and his assistant Roduner. The investigating magistrates interrogated all four of these men, and thereby established that Wirz and Pfister were the team responsible for manning the tower from Wednesday night the eleventh until Thursday morning the twelfth. On this night, Pfister rang the bell until ten o'clock, then lay down to sleep in the tower, fearing that if he went home he might oversleep; for he was supposed to ring the first bell at five o'clock the following morning. Pfister was already sleeping when his master, Wirz, arrived some time after ten o'clock. Wirz rang the bell at eleven and then again at midnight. After ringing the midnight bell, however, he descended the bell tower and left the cathedral, abandoning his post altogether. This was not only highly irregular; it was a breach of duty. But it does not appear that Wirz abandoned his post impulsively because he had made arrangements for a third person to cover for him. That person was Roduner, the assistant of the other master bell ringer. Roduner had arrived in the tower at about 8:45 and then slept until shortly after midnight when Wirz woke him. So he saw Wirz descend into the cathedral, though he could not, as he explained to the magistrates, see what, if anything, Wirz was carrying since Wirz went downstairs without the aid of a lantern.[17]

"Without a lantern" [*ohne Licht*]. This little bit of information captured the attention of the magistrates, especially as Roduner had offered it unsolicited.[18] It was suspicious enough that Wirz had abandoned his post shortly after midnight, but what reason could he have had for going down into the cathedral enveloped in darkness? Wirz did not deny any of the facts alleged by Roduner, though he did have explanations for them. He explained his early departure from the cathedral by claiming that he had wanted to go home and rest before taking communion on the following morning. And on the morning of the twelfth, he assured the magistrates, he took communion as planned, seated alongside Roduner in the gallery of the cathedral near the tower.[19] The lantern, he explained, was in the hands of Pfister; he had left it with his young assistant, who needed it more than Wirz because he was new on the job and did not yet know his way around the cathedral.[20] Both of these explanations were plausible. Wirz's new bride confirmed that her husband had come home to sleep. Both she and Pfister testified that Wirz had attended the communion service on the following morning. And Pfister assured the magistrates that he had had Wirz's lantern.[21] Whatever the explanations, however, the fact of the matter was that Wirz had been creeping around the cathedral in the dark shortly after midnight on the morning of the twelfth. Combine that fact with the red spots on the ground in front of the communion table, which the sexton had discovered on Thursday morning, and which, presumably, had resulted from someone knocking against the wine barrels in the darkness of the night, and it is not hard to understand why Wirz appeared a likely suspect.

The second reason for suspecting Wirz was that he seemed to have a motive. Two years earlier, according to a witness named Fäsi, the Antistes, Johann Rudolf Ulrich, had summoned Wirz and had given him a severe reprimand for the sloppy and negligent manner in which he had been performing his duties. At the time, Fäsi explained, his own father, a master gravedigger and bell ringer who was now deceased, lay on his deathbed, so he was filling in for his ailing father; and he was in the bell tower on the evening after Ulrich had scolded Wirz when the latter came storming into the tower in a fit of rage, swearing oaths against "the clergy and the cathedral canons," whom he called "black heretics and priests of the devil." At first, Fäsi told the magistrates, he had protested against such language. Then he went outside to smoke a pipe, expecting that, in the meantime, Wirz's anger would subside. When he returned, however, he found Wirz lying in bed, still swearing as he had been before; and then, in his agitated state, Wirz pronounced a shocking threat, exclaiming: "I'll show a thing or two to that damn cleric, the Antistes; I'll 'pour into him' so that people will have to think of me." Thereupon Fäsi gathered up his things and headed home, telling Wirz that he could no longer remain in the presence of someone with such a "foul mouth."[22]

Fäsi's testimony about the episode in the bell tower was shocking indeed, and it weighed all the more heavily when set alongside a similar episode recounted by Roduner.

Several years earlier, Roduner told the magistrates, Wirz had planted an herb garden on the grounds of the cathedral—only to be told later that the garden had to be destroyed. He was furious at this rebuff and placed the blame for it squarely on the shoulders of "guild master [*Zunftmeister*] Scheuchzer and the Antistes Ulrich" of whom "he spoke disrespectfully."[23] If Roduner and Fäsi

FIGURE 9. Johann Rudolf Ulrich, Antistes. Mezzotint by Johann Elias Haid, 1777. Courtesy of the Zentralbibliothek Zürich, Graphische Sammlung.

were to be believed, then Wirz harbored a longstanding grudge against the leading churchman in Zurich.

But were the two witnesses credible? Wirz denied that he had ever spoken disrespectfully of Ulrich or made threatening remarks about him.[24] To clarify the matter, therefore, the judges issued an order for a direct confrontation between the suspect and his accusers, and on 21 October, with the investigating magistrates presiding, the three bell ringers were brought together in the town hall for questioning. The confrontation was the dramatic high-point of the trial, the first time Wirz had set eyes upon his former colleagues and his principal accusers since his arrest nearly a month earlier.[25]

The first scene of the drama focused on Roduner and Fäsi. The magistrates interrogated them separately, asking each to confirm his earlier testimony. Both of them did, but while Roduner's testimony was short, Fäsi's was long and detailed—longer and more detailed, in fact, than his original testimony. So before bringing Wirz into the room, the magistrates wanted to be certain that Fäsi was prepared to stand by his testimony in the presence of the suspect. A long time had elapsed since the episode in the bell tower, they pointed out to him. "Was he able to trust his memory?" "Might he not have misunderstood Wirz's words?" "Had he perhaps added certain details with the passage of time?" Fäsi dismissed such suggestions out of hand. Whoever has heard Wirz speak, he explained, would know from Wirz's "strong voice" that it is not possible to misunderstand him, especially when he falls into a state of "rage and fury." Wirz's words were indelibly imprinted in his memory. Indeed, they had shocked him so deeply that he repeated them to his mother, sister, and wife as soon as he arrived home from the bell tower; and on the following day he recounted the whole episode to the wife of the Antistes. The magistrates need only interrogate the four women to confirm that he had added no detail with the passage of time. Whatever the dangers to his own personal "security," Fäsi concluded, he was ready at any time to heed the command of the magistrates and repeat his testimony in the presence of the suspect.[26]

And so the stage was set for the confrontation with Wirz. First, however, the magistrates interrogated Wirz alone one last time, hoping to wring a confession from him by warning of the grave punishment he would incur if his statements were contradicted. "Was he not obliged to admit," they asked him, "that he had erred grievously and brought himself under suspicion of [having committed] the deed by uttering unfortunate—indeed highly punishable—words against the Antistes and other cathedral canons?" "No," protested Wirz. He considered that imputation to be "the biggest slander in the world" and a "black falsehood." "Never," he declared, "had he uttered words against anyone—let alone threats—such as could have brought him under the least suspicion of having carried out so infamous a deed."[27] No matter what manner of pressure or intimidation the magistrates brought to bear, Wirz stood his ground, defiantly rejecting the accusations made against him.

Nor did he back down when confronted by his accusers directly. After Roduner had repeated his testimony about the herb garden, the magistrates asked Wirz to respond. "The biggest and most infamous lie," he exclaimed. It had disturbed him that Scheuchzer (the guild master) had allowed him to work on the garden for so long before telling him to destroy it; it would have been less upsetting to him if the garden had been forbidden him from the very beginning. But he had merely complained about this, and his complaint concerned Scheuchzer alone, not Ulrich. And what of Fäsi's testimony? the magistrates asked him. "A total falsehood," he answered. Calling God to witness, he denied that he had ever in his entire life uttered "indecent threats" or "oaths" against Herr Antistes. But he did not deny that he had uttered threats in the bell tower on the evening after Ulrich had reprimanded him. The threats, he explained, were directed against Fäsi, whom he held responsible for the reprimand that he had suffered. He believed that Fäsi had denounced him to the Antistes. That was the source of his anger: not the reprimand as such but rather the deviousness of his coworker. Provoked by this deviousness, he had threatened revenge, warning Fäsi that a similar fate might be awaiting him, that someone might "pour into him" just as he had "poured into" Wirz. To make good his threat, Wirz said, he then went to Ulrich directly and complained of Fäsi, telling the Antistes that it was Fäsi—and not himself—who had been negligent in the performance of his duties.[28]

The confrontation between Wirz and his accusers did little to close the gap between their respective testimonies. But it did suggest to the judges a strategy for evaluating whose testimony was the most credible. Fäsi claimed to have told his own mother, sister, and wife about the episode in the bell tower as soon as he returned home on the evening in question and to have reported it to the wife of the Antistes on the following morning; Wirz claimed that he had gone to Ulrich to complain of Fäsi. To assess who was telling the truth, the judges ordered the investigating magistrates to interrogate all of the relevant witnesses.[29] When questioned, Ulrich had no memory that Wirz had ever come to him to complain of Fäsi; and under renewed questioning several weeks later, Wirz backtracked, admitting that his encounter with Ulrich had been accidental—he had merely run into him by chance, not sought him out—and that his "audience" with him had been "rather short."[30] On the other hand, all of the women bore out Fäsi's testimony. The wife of the Antistes remembered Fäsi's complaints about Wirz's behavior, and so too did the three women in Fäsi's family, all of whom had so vivid a memory of the episode that they recalled precisely what they had been doing when Fäsi returned home from the bell tower. His wife remembered that she had been sleeping and then awakened by her husband, who recounted to her what had transpired; his sister, that she had been reading aloud to their ailing father; his mother, that she had been ironing. All three of the women in Fäsi's family were able to recite, word for word, the threatening comments ascribed by Fäsi to Wirz, and the mother concluded her testimony by adding that she had thought of those comments immediately upon learning of the poisoning in the cathedral, exclaiming to herself: "Oh, my God, if he [Wirz] is not the unhappy author of the crime!" The statements made by the women in Fäsi's family fitted together like the pieces of a jigsaw puzzle (each women confirmed precisely what the others said), and they matched perfectly the statements made by Fäsi himself—so perfectly, in fact, as to be a wee bit suspicious: one could not exclude the possibility that the women had rehearsed their testimony before giving it, and that Fäsi had done his part to jog (or coach) memories grown faint with the passage of time. But the wife of the Antistes had also borne out Fäsi's testimony, and it was hard to see what possible interest she could have had in validating his version of the story.[31] All things considered, therefore, the accusations of Fäsi and Roduner seemed more credible than Wirz's denials. It was difficult for the judges to avoid the conclusion that Wirz bore a strong animus against the cathedral canons in general and the Antistes in particular.

BECAUSE WIRZ HAD A POSSIBLE MOTIVE, AND because he had been present at the scene of the crime, he seemed a likely suspect. But grounds for suspicion were not the same thing as proof of guilt. In the inquisitorial procedure, the "queen of proofs" was confession, and the best type of confession was voluntary. Failing that, however, judges had recourse to torture. Ever since the late middle ages, torture had been used in the criminal courts of continental Europe to extract confessions from recalcitrant suspects, and it continued to be used in Zurich even in 1776, despite Enlightenment polemics against it and the example of Frederick the Great, who had abolished torture in Prussia more than two decades earlier. But it was employed less frequently than in the past; and in the case of Wirz, the judges must have felt that the circumstantial evidence was not strong enough to warrant recourse to so extreme a measure. Rather than applying physical torture, they tried to break Wirz's resistance by subjecting him to a type of psychological torture—severing his ties to the outside world and plunging him into deeper and deeper isolation.[32]

Less than a week after Wirz's arrest, the judges ordered the prison guard at the town hall to refuse the prisoner all visitors. Then, only five days later, they tightened the screws again, directing the guard to remove ink, pen, and paper from Wirz's cell, and neither to accept from the prisoner nor to deliver to him any written messages or objects of any kind, which were to be confiscated immediately and submitted to the authorities.[33] Somehow—it is not clear through which channels—Wirz's wife managed to deliver to her husband a parcel of food that she had prepared. Either the guard had been negligent or he had deliberately looked the other way, perhaps out of a certain sympathy for the plight of the prisoner. In any case, the judges took this breach of quarantine very seriously—so seriously, in fact, that they warned the guard of "deadly" consequences if similar breaches occurred. The judges were resolved to plug every hole through which Wirz might be able to communicate with the outside world.[34] Shortly after Wirz had received the food parcel from his wife, however, a new problem came to light. A watchman reported seeing Heinrich Pfister, Wirz's young assistant, standing in front of the town hall for long periods, looking up in the direction of Wirz's cell. Pfister denied that he was trying to communicate with Wirz. Since his master's imprisonment, he explained, he no longer had any work and filled his idle hours by walking about the city, sometimes passing in front of the town hall.[35] This seemed a plausible explanation, but not plausible enough to reassure the judges, who remained suspicious. To ensure themselves of Wirz's total isolation, they instructed the guard to prevent the prisoner from approaching the window of his cell, lest he communicate, through gestures, with passers-by on the street below.[36]

One can easily imagine the growing sense of panic that Wirz must have felt as his isolation deepened. He had no lawyer to draft a well-turned legal brief in his behalf and no way of knowing whether his trial was going badly or well. He had only his own wits and an ardent desire to escape from his confinement. How could he persuade the judges of his innocence?

The problem confronted by Wirz (and indeed by all criminal suspects in Zurich) was that the judges fixed the agenda for the trial. Because they set the questions asked by the magistrates during the interrogations, the suspect had little or no opportunity to prompt a line of inquiry favorable to his defense. Wirz got around this problem by preempting his judges. In early October, he let it be known that he wished to speak to them, and they acceded to his request, granting him an interview on 5 October. Why exactly they granted the interview is unclear, but they may have hoped for a confession. If so, Wirz disappointed them. His goal was to wrest the initiative from his judges, not to end the ordeal of his confinement by confessing his guilt. On 5 October, for the first and last time in his trial, he held the floor, free to address any subject he pleased while the investigating magistrates sat quietly and listened.[37]

During his "protracted confinement," Wirz began, he had been plunged into "deep reflection" and had come to realize what compelling reasons he had "to praise the wise providence of God." What on earth could the prisoner have meant by this? the magistrates must have wondered to themselves. Wirz, praise the wise providence of God? Someone in such dire circumstances, whose very life hung in the balance? To explain what he meant, Wirz recounted three recent episodes in which a lucky constellation of factors had prevented him from behaving in ways that would almost certainly have compounded the appearance of his guilt. The first one concerned a doctor in Herisau whose medical cabinet included, among other things, various kinds of poison. The doctor was the friend of a general in Piedmont in whose household Wirz's sister had once lived as a servant. Since her employment there, the general had died, but she had conceived the hope that her former employer might have left her some money. To inquire about that possibility, Wirz was planning to pay a visit to the doctor. Shortly before setting off on his journey, however, he learned from the doctor that the general had died in debt, that his estate had gone to pay off the creditors, and that Wirz's sister could hope for nothing at all. Just imagine, he concluded, what "suspicions he would have drawn to himself" if he had visited the doctor as planned.

Or consider another episode, he continued, this one involving a book given to him by his elder son. The book explained how to make invisible ink, and Wirz had been eager to try his hand at making some since invisible ink had always fascinated him. But then he realized that the ingredients for the ink included a strong poison, and he changed his mind ("may God by eternally praised!"), fearing the danger to his three-year-old son, who was at the age when he was inclined to pick up everything he stumbled upon and put it in his mouth. Just imagine, Wirz concluded, "what suspicion he would have drawn to himself" if he had prepared the ink. Or consider a third and final episode, he told the magistrates—this one involving a bug ointment. Like so many others, he suffered from bed bugs. He was delighted, therefore, when he learned that Rordorf, the other master bell ringer, and his assistant, Roduner, were in possession of a special ointment designed to eliminate the pests. But Rordorf and Roduner refused to give him any, explaining that the ointment was highly dangerous and contained a strong poison. At the time, he said, the refusal had upset him, but in retrospect, he "praised God" that his request had been denied. Just imagine "what suspicion it would have drawn to him" if his coworkers had given him the ointment.

It must have been a heady experience for Wirz, a humble gravedigger, to speak without interruption before an audience of magistrates—so heady, in fact, that he got a little carried away: his tales were spun out with such an abundance of detail that the main thread of his argument was in danger of being lost. What, the magistrates must have asked themselves, was Wirz trying to accomplish by telling such elaborately-wrought tales?

His main goal, presumably, was to show that he was not an oath-swearing, impious anticlerical, as the testimony given by Fäsi suggested, but rather a God-fearing and devout Christian.[38] Besides that, however, he was also pursuing a second goal: to raise suspicions about his coworkers in the bell tower by disclosing that they possessed a poisonous bug ointment. His revelations about Rordorf and Roduner, deftly inserted in the final of his three stories, were meant to steer the investigation in a new direction, deflecting suspicions from him and widening the circle of suspects. Unfortunately for him, however, the judges interrogated Rordorf and his assistant on the subject of the bug ointment only once, then allowed the matter to drop.[39] In the end, it was not clear what, if anything, Wirz had managed to accomplish by his long, drawn-out praise of "God's wise providence."

By the following month, Wirz was at wit's end. Somehow he had managed to get hold of paper, pen, ink, and wax, and he dashed off a short note protesting his innocence and sealed it. Then one day, when he saw the mayor passing by on the street in front of the town hall, he called to him and tossed the note out the window. This was a desperate move, the main consequence of which was to cause further unpleasantness for the prison guard, who had obviously failed to remove the paper and ink from Wirz's cell.[40] To Wirz, it must have felt as if the noose were tightening around his neck.

NO MATTER HOW DESPERATE HE MAY HAVE felt, however, Wirz did not break down and confess, and in the absence of a confession it was not at all clear how the judges could prove his guilt. In other cases, reliable eyewitnesses might have substituted for a confession or justified the recourse to physical torture, but not in this case, one in which the crime had been committed under cover of darkness and eyewitnesses were an impossibility. To compensate for a lack of eyewitnesses to a crime, modern criminal investigators look for a distinctive "signature"—a fingerprint, a sample of DNA, or some other physical evidence—that serves to establish the identity of a criminal in much the same way the garlic odor or the white sublimate allowed the chemists to infer the presence of arsenic or mercury in the wine samples. The nearest thing to such methods of identification available to eighteenth-century investigators was physiognomy—a "science" whose chief advocate, as it happened, was the Zurich pastor Johann Caspar Lavater. According to Lavater, it was possible to infer the character of an individual from the silhouette of his face, and in his sermons on the affair of the poisoned communion wine, Lavater hinted that he would be able to identify the poisoner in such a manner.[41] But he did not pursue the matter any further, nor did the judges ever adopt such an approach. For all its popularity in the late eighteenth century, physiognomy was hardly reliable enough to constitute proof in a criminal proceeding.[42]

To establish Wirz's guilt, moreover, the judges needed to find evidence of poison in his possession or at least evidence of how he had come by the poison. But here too they got nowhere. Investigators ransacked Wirz's home looking for traces of poison; they found none. They combed the records of apothecaries, hoping to find evidence that Wirz had purchased poison; no evidence came to light.[43] If Wirz were the criminal, then he must have procured poison. But how? And from what source?

Back in late September, a courier from St. Gall named Schnitli had turned up in the marketplace in Zurich, boasting that he could shed light on precisely that question. He reported that several weeks earlier Wirz had stayed at an inn in St. Gall and while there had pronounced "angry words" and made purchases of "drugs." When asked what use he intended to make of the drugs, Schnitli said, Wirz had replied elliptically, claiming he needed them "at home."[44] The revelations offered by Schnitli led the judges to focus their attention on Wirz's travels and to grill him on that subject in successive interrogations. Wirz did not deny that he had been to St. Gall or that he had stayed at the inn mentioned by Schnitli. What he disputed was that he had gone there shortly before the General Day of Prayer and Repentance and that his purpose for going there had been to purchase "drugs." Just before the General Day of Prayer and Repentance, he had traveled by ship to Stäfa, a village near the banks of Lake Zurich, where he was involved in some kind of civil suit. The trip to St. Gall had taken place at the time of Pentecost, shortly after the death of his previous wife, and he had gone there to "forget his sorrow," to see his brother-in-law about arrangements for his stepchild, and to look for a new bride "suitable to his age and station."[45] When it came to the subject of his travels, Wirz spoke with assurance, giving a precise and detailed itinerary, and the judges were able to confirm the accuracy of his account by soliciting corroborating testimony from innkeepers and officials in the towns and villages where Wirz had stayed. As that testimony trickled in during the course of the trial, it became increasingly clear that Schnitli had led the judges down a false trail.[46]

So Wirz's situation was not nearly so desperate as he may have imagined it. Even as the term of his confinement lengthened and as his isolation deepened, the case against him was collapsing, undermined at its foundation by a seemingly unsolvable problem: a lack of conclusive proof. Before the judges could reach a final verdict, however, the whole affair of the poisoned communion wine took a shocking and dramatic turn.

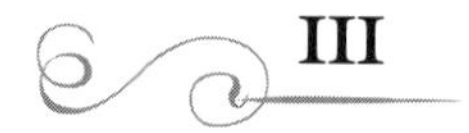

III

On Sunday morning, 13 October, shortly before dawn, a wigmaker's apprentice by the name of Heinrich Wilhelm Pauder was walking along the Limmat near the Upper Bridge when he spotted a sheet of paper, still moist with glue, stuck to the side of a shop. On the paper, he read the following:

> **NOT WIRZ NOT THE GRAVEDIGGER**
> The Treasurer [*Seckelmeister*] Orell and the Administrator [*Stiftverwalter*] Hess are guilty of the monstrous deed in the cathedral. Landvogt Füssli and Magistrate [*Stetrichter*] Ott mixed the poison with the intention of killing the Antistes, Council member [*Ratsherr*] Salomon Hirzel, and all the enemies of the French alliance, as well as half of the citizenry, and they planned afterward to make the government hereditary. The Administrator surrendered the key to the church, a second attack was planned with the help of the official [*Amtmann*] Landolt for Christmas in the Fraumünster [another church in Zurich, near the main cathedral].[47]

Immediately, Pauder took down the sheet of paper and stuffed it in his sack. Then he looked around and noticed someone hurrying away at the other end of the bridge. His first thought was to bring his discovery to the attention of the authorities, but by the time he could do so, copies of the same text had been found posted at three other locations, and news of their existence had spread throughout the city.[48]

It is hard to imagine a more incendiary libel than the one discovered by Pauder on that early Sunday morning. Instead of a humble gravedigger, a powerful faction of the ruling elite was now being accused of having plotted to poison the communion wine. To the authorities, such accusations seemed no less shocking than the original crime itself. On the very same day, therefore, the Secret Council convened in an emergency session, just as it had done one month earlier when Gessner had discovered arsenic in the wine. And as before, an air of crisis hung over the session, with the coun-

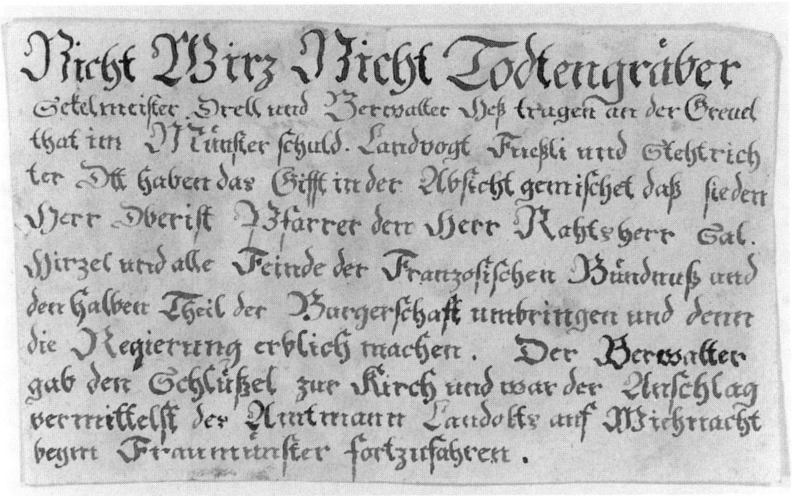
Nicht Wirz Nicht Todtengräber
Sekelmeister Orell und Verwalter Heß trugen an der Greuel
that im Münster schuld. Landvogt Füeßli und Stehtrich
ter Ott haben das Gifft in der Absicht gemischet daß sie den
Herr Oberist Pfarrer den Herr Rahtsherr Sal.
Hirzel und alle Feinde der Französischen Bündnuß und
den halben Theil der Burgerschaft umbringen und denn
die Regierung erblich machen. Der Verwalter
gab den Schlüßel zur Kirch und war der Anschlag
vermittelst der Amtmann Landolts auf Wiehnacht
beym Fraumünster fortzufahren.

FIGURE 10. One of the four handwritten libels posted in Zurich on the morning of Sunday, 13 October 1776. The text proclaims Wirz's innocence and indicts some of the leading magistrates in the state. Staatsarchiv des Kantons Zürich, A27 153, Kundschaften und Nachgänge.

cilors speaking of their "horror" and "indignation" at this "most malicious slander." The content of the slander was so "nonsensical," the councillors claimed, that few people were likely to set much store by it. Still, "the affair had become a matter of general knowledge," and the author of the libel had given evidence of so "frightening a degree of impudence" and of "such a depraved mind" that "everything possible" had to be done to capture him.[49] In a sense, the libels now became an affair in their own right, eclipsing the trial of the gravedigger Wirz, which receded temporarily into the background while investigators hunted for the author of this "most malicious slander." To accelerate the investigation, the government issued a new edict offering an additional 200 Thaler for information leading to the arrest of the libelist, and it threatened criminal penalties against anyone who made copies of the libel or failed to surrender any such copies as he or she possessed.[50]

The content of the slander was shocking indeed, but it was not nearly so "nonsensical" as the councillors claimed. They may have *hoped* that it would appear nonsensical to the citizens of Zurich, but if they had been convinced that the slander was only the expression of a single depraved mind and that everyone else would interpret it as such, then the slander would not have been likely to cause such deep anxiety. The truth of the matter was that the libel had a very clear meaning, and that most if not all of the citizens of Zurich would have been able to decipher it. The key to unlocking its meaning was the allusion to the "French alliance."

IN THE AUTUMN OF 1776, REPRESENTATIVES OF the Swiss Confederation were negotiating a renewal of a diplomatic alliance with France. The alliance enjoyed strong support from the government of Zurich, and especially from the mayor, Heidegger, who believed that the alliance was necessary to protect Zurich against the threat of Habsburg aggression. Outside the ruling councils, however, the situation was quite different. Anti-French sentiment ran strong among artisans and shopkeepers in Zurich, and for this reason alone, the treaty was unpopular. But the problem was not simply that the ordinary Zuricher disliked the French. What rankled above all was that the diplomatic negotiations had been conducted on the initiative of the government alone, without the consultation of the guilds, which represented the citizenry. Behind the controversy over the French alliance lurked a constitutional issue of great importance.[51]

The Zurich constitution was embodied in the so-called "sworn letter" [*geschworener Brief*], to which the citizenry and the government pledged an oath of allegiance in semi-annual ceremonies held in the cathedral. According to this traditional constitution, each citizen had to belong to one of twelve guilds or to the so-called *Konstaffel*, which was reserved primarily, though not exclusively, for descendants of noble families. The government was composed of three councils—the Secret Council, the Small Council, and the Large Council—which were enclosed within one another like a series of concentric circles, the Secret Council being a subset of the Small Council, and the latter a subset of the Large Council. The selection of council members took place according to a complicated system of direct and indirect elections that blocked the exercise of anything like popular sovereignty in the modern sense. As the primary electoral bodies, however, the guilds formed the foundation of the system. Twice a year, in June and December, they convened in separate guild assemblies to elect their guild masters. The elections took place by secret ballot, and by a revision to the "sworn letter" adopted in 1713, the guild assemblies also enjoyed the right to be consulted in all matters concerning war and peace. On the face of it, then, the constitution appeared to be quite democratic, but the appearance was misleading. Because certain groups of citizens—most notably, merchants and *rentiers*—were free to choose the guild to which they wished to belong, the wealthiest citizens were able to distribute family members among several guilds simultaneously and thereby dominate the guild assemblies. Increasingly, the guilds were becoming mere electoral colleges, controlled by a handful of powerful families and only loosely connected to any particular trades. Those same families established a stranglehold on the government, and artisans were pushed farther and farther from the center of power, squeezed out of the councils where they had once been well represented. In 1637, they had composed 40 percent of the Small Council; in 1790, only 6 percent.[52] Zurich had no legally defined patriciate such as existed in Bern and Lucerne, but it was becoming more and more oligarchic, and the issue of the French alliance dramatized that tendency, revealing just how far removed from ordinary Zurich citizens the ruling councils had become.

By evoking the issue of the French alliance, therefore, the libel indicted the direction Zurich politics had taken over the previous century, and it elevated Wirz to the status of a political prisoner. Behind the smoke screen of Wirz's trial, it warned the citizens of Zurich, lurked a sinister plot to destroy the republic and convert it into a patrimonial state. This was a very serious charge indeed—far more serious than any personal slander directed against the individuals named—and no doubt that was why the authorities reacted as they did and why they were so anxious to lay hold of the libelist. Two months later, at the ceremony marking the investiture of the new councils, Mayor Heidegger made no attempt to conceal his anxiety. "Our beloved fatherland," he declared, "is in a state of fermentation and crisis which can either yield to a long-abiding stability or degenerate into illness and the most dangerous and frightening movements."[53] Until this point, Zurich had managed to escape the sort of major internal revolt that accompanied similar constitutional conflicts in other Swiss cities, such as Geneva. Now, the affair of the libels seemed to portend an impending storm.

The storm broke the following year, in the summer of 1777, when the Secret Council announced the French alliance as a fait accompli and called upon the guild assemblies to approve it. Reaction to this announcement was swift and dramatic. The guilds met to formulate their grievances; spontaneous demonstrations broke out in the streets; petitions were circulated; and at least one pseudonymous pamphlet went so far as to challenge the whole electoral system, repeating the charge, first made by the libel the previous autumn, that a few powerful families were attempting to usurp the state and lay claim to it as their personal patrimony. For months afterward the outcome of the conflict was uncertain, and the atmosphere in the city remained tense until the government managed to defuse the tension by granting certain concessions and by dividing the opposition. In the end, the government weathered the storm, and the political structure of Old Regime Zurich survived intact for another two decades. But the dispute over the French alliance and the open conflict of 1777 bequeathed a legacy of mistrust, which also placed the events of the previous autumn in a new light. Looking back from the perspective of 1777, Johann Caspar Lavater was convinced that the leaders of the guild opposition had been responsible for both the libel and the poisoning of the communion wine.[54]

From the moment the libels were posted, therefore, the affair of the poisoned communion wine was both a criminal case and a political one, closely interwoven with the conflicts that rent the Zurich republic during the crisis of the late 1770s. We shall have more to say about the political uses of the poisoned communion wine later on. But we are getting ahead of ourselves, and the reader is likely to be wondering what has become of the gravedigger Wirz, whom we left languishing in the town hall.

AS WIRZ'S ORDEAL LENGTHENED, SO TOO DID that of his young bride, who suddenly found herself bereft of a husband only two months after her wedding. Wirz's arrest had come as a terrible shock to her. Indeed, it drove her to such depths of despair that her younger, unmarried sister, Anna Maria Michel, had to console her, remaining by her side for the first eight nights after Wirz's arrest. Her widowed father, a master carpenter named Michel, was given to fits of rage, venting his anger against Anna Maria—the last of his children still living at home—whom he scolded for staying away from the house for such a long period. Through his wife, Wirz was connected to a wider network of family relations, and his arrest threw their lives into turmoil. It was a hard blow not just for him but for his entire family.[55]

But was it so hard a blow as to provoke an act of revenge? The magistrates in the Secret Council seemed to have believed so, for they suspected that Michel was somehow connected to the libels. Not, however, that he had actually written and posted them. Of the deed itself they suspected a rather shadowy figure named Felix Frey. A fifty-seven-year-old bachelor, Frey had neither a fixed abode nor a fixed occupation. Sometimes he slept on a bench in a journeyman's hostel in Wiedikon, a suburb of Zurich, and there he earned a little money as a scribe, copying out congratulatory notes on the occasion of weddings and name-days for the journeymen who were unable to write. At other times, however, he drifted into Zurich, where he turned his hand to whatever odd jobs came his way, working now as a barber, now as an errand-boy. Among his customers in Zurich were Michel, whom he often shaved on Sunday mornings, and Anna Maria, who sent him to do marketing.[56] By stringing together all of these various odd jobs, Frey managed to eke out a meager living, but money did not stick to him for very long—during the course of his daily rounds, he dropped his meager earnings in the watering holes of Wiedikon and Zurich, passing from one tavern to another until his pockets were empty and he was reduced to desperate measures. Once, finding himself penniless in a tavern called the Stone Table, he tried to raise drink money by selling his shaving knife, sacrificing his future livelihood for a glass of wine or a shot of brandy, like the famine-stricken peasant who eats his seed corn to stave off starvation. As a poor and desperate drifter, Frey looked just the type to carry out a plot hatched by someone else, provided he were paid and plied with strong spirits.[57]

The magistrates in the Secret Council spared no effort to unmask that plot. To avoid publicity, they kept the direction of the investigation in their own hands, rather than delegating it to the Small Council, as was usual in a criminal case; and this time, in contrast to the initial investigation of the poisoning itself, they did not shrink from using torture. Indeed, they resorted to it almost immediately upon the arrest of Frey on 5 November, ordering the executioner "to conduct an examination [of the prisoner] under earnest flogging at the stake and to attempt to bring him [the prisoner] to make a confession."[58] The political significance of the investigation was so great and the climate in the city so tense as to justify the most extreme measures. The investigation proceeded along two lines simultaneously, one directed against Frey and the other against Michel. To prevent communication between the two chief suspects, the judges ordered them to be imprisoned separately, with Michel confined in the town hall and Frey in Oetenbach, a former convent converted after the Reformation into an orphanage and a prison.[59] Both Michel and Frey were interrogated numerous times, but the key witness was Anna Maria, who now with her father's arrest was just as isolated and vulnerable as her elder sister, Wirz's wife.[60] The judges believed that Anna Maria knew the whole truth of the plot, so they brought all manner of pressure to bear upon her. At first, they kept her under surveillance so as to keep track of every person with whom she came into contact.[61] Then they imprisoned her in Oetenbach, dispatching Johann Caspar Lavater to visit the young woman in her cell and to persuade her that it was her moral and religious duty to turn state's evidence and incriminate Frey and her father. And, finally, they tortured her—or, at least, threatened her with torture.[62] But all of this pressure was to no avail. The judges could neither coerce nor coax any revelations from her.[63] They were equally unsuccessful in their attempts to wring a confession from Frey, who protested his innocence despite being repeatedly bound to a stake and "earnestly flogged."[64] After a week of frenetic interrogations, therefore, they gave up. The testimony of twenty-nine witnesses, some of it extracted under the threat of torture, had failed to prove the guilt of either Michel or Frey. The judicial investigations had reached an impasse.[65] Finally, on 16 November, the prison cells in the town hall and in Oetenbach began disgorging their prisoners. The Small Council ordered the release of both Michel and Frey, exonerating Michel completely while condemning Frey (somewhat illogically) to lifetime banishment from the city of Zurich; and at the same time, the Council ordered the release of Wirz, who emerged from his cell a free man after nearly two months of confinement. Having failed to lay hold of either the poisoner or the libelist, the government had to content itself with a type of symbolic execution. With no convicts to send to the scaffold, it ordered the public hangman to burn copies of the libel instead.[66]

To put matters right, the Small Council awarded Wirz his back pay. After so long an ordeal, however, Wirz had scores to settle, not least with Roduner, whose testimony had almost cost him his neck. One evening, shortly after returning to work, Wirz, in effect, "poured into" Roduner in the bell tower and would have throttled him if another bell ringer had not been there to intervene. For this, Wirz was suspended from work for four weeks and docked his pay, but that was all.[67] Thereafter, virtually all mention of him vanishes from our sources, and it is likely that he passed the remainder of his days in peaceful obscurity, digging graves and marking the passage of the hours in the bell tower of the cathedral.[68] In the end, someone else would suffer the fate that had been hanging over Wirz's head during the long autumn months of 1776.

Chapter Four

The Enlightenment in German-Speaking Europe

ITH THE RELEASE OF WIRZ FROM prison, the narrowly juridical aspect of the affair had reached an impasse. For the time being, no new suspects were arrested, the investigation ground to a halt, and the whole business lay dormant for several years before it sprang back to life in a bizarre epilogue, which unfolded in the first half of 1780. More about that epilogue later. In the meantime, however, what of the significance attributed to the affair by the wider public both in and outside of Zurich?

From the very outset, as we have already seen, German newspaper editors snapped up the sensational story of the poisoned communion wine, often pilfering reports from one another to satisfy the curiosity of their readers. This brought the story within the "public sphere" of German-speaking Europe, inspiring comment, reflection, and debate, which flared up intermittently over several years even as the judicial affair in Zurich had seemed to peter out. This public debate, touched off by the mysterious events in Zurich, centered on questions of fundamental significance to the Enlightenment [*Aufklärung*]—questions of such fundamental significance, in fact, that the debate may well be described, metaphorically, as a judicial process in its own right. In the absence of compelling evidence, the trial of the gravedigger Wirz was relatively brief; but long after Wirz had departed his cell in the town hall, the Aufklärung itself was being called upon to defend itself in the court of public criticism.

We shall turn our attention in the next chapter to the debate inspired by the affair of the poisoned communion wine—"the Enlightenment on trial." But first we would do well to get our bearings and to map the wider terrain upon which our story will now be unfolding. The reader will no doubt have noticed that I spoke above of the "Aufklärung." The use of the German term is deliberate, and it is meant to call attention to the peculiar features of the Enlightenment in German-speaking Europe. Traditionally, research on the Enlightenment has been subject to a Francocentric bias, identifying the Enlightenment with the *philosophes* and locating its geographic center in Paris. This makes it all the more important to examine those features peculiar to the Aufklärung, for if we are to understand why the affair of the poisoned communion wine had such wide resonance in German-speaking Europe, we need to begin by defining the context in which the affair was received.

I

The first and most distinctive feature of the Aufklärung was its relation to theology and to Christianity in general.[1] From Leibniz to Lessing, the *Aufklärer* grappled with issues of Christian theology—theodicy, original sin, eternal damnation, predestination, vicarious satisfaction, the doctrine of the Trinity, the divinity of

Christ, the status of Biblical text, and the nature of revelation, sacraments, miracles, prophecies, resurrection, angels, and the devil. They examined such issues in a critical spirit, challenging the orthodox dogma of the established Protestant churches—Lutheran and Reformed—but they undertook this critique without, for the most part, severing their ties to Christianity, for which they retained a deep, earnest, and abiding respect. Nothing could have been farther removed from them than the mocking and contemptuous hauteur of a Voltaire, who looked down upon Christianity as little more than a colossal and pernicious hoax, a pack of lies imposed by wicked priests on gullible people. Unlike the philosophes, most of the Aufklärer were, or at least considered themselves to be in one form or another, Christians. This implied no contradiction, and it helps us to make sense of the fact (which is so striking when set against the situation in France) that many of the leading figures in the Aufklärung were clergymen themselves and, if not clergymen, then sons of clergymen. While the French Enlightenment developed in opposition to the Catholic Church, the Aufklärung developed within the established Protestant churches of German-speaking Europe, its goal to reform—rationalize—Christian theology and Christian worship rather than to abolish them.

To be sure, the deep and intimate connection of theology to the intellectual life of German-speaking Europe was not a peculiarity of the Aufklärung alone. It continued into the nineteenth century, through the Romantics and Schelling to Hegel and, finally, to the Young Hegelians—Strauss and Feuerbach—who brought the project of critiquing religion to a close. How to interpret this phenomenon is far from clear. Surveying the history of German philosophy in the wake of Strauss and Feuerbach, the young Marx lamented that the Germans had taken so long to topple God from his celestial throne and observed that in the meantime the French had been toppling their kings and getting on with the business of revolution.[2] Something of this lament has found its way into the oft-cited argument about Germany's "special path" [*Sonderweg*] to modernity, which imputes the misfortunes of German history to the timidity and cowardice of a bourgeoisie more prone to seek accommodations with the powers-that-be than to strike out boldly on the path of revolution. This explanatory thesis is now largely discredited.[3] But facts stand even if the explanation for them is inadequate, and it is a fact that the Aufklärung was more conciliatory toward the established churches and more preoccupied with theological issues than was true of its counterpart in France. D'Holbach may have been a native German, but his spiritual home was in Paris.

Whatever the explanation, then, the Aufklärung was far less secular than *lumières*. And this basic contrast, so characteristic of the difference between the intellectual life of France and that of Germany, applied not only to Aufklärer and to philosophes in the narrow sense but to the literary market in general. As late as the 1770s, when theological works accounted for no more than 5 or 10 percent of domestic French literary production,[4] they continued to make up nearly one-quarter of the new titles announced in the semi-annual Leipzig book fair catalogues.[5] By this date, the German literary market was already beginning to break out of the mold of the traditional scholarly book trade. The production of books in German had long ago eclipsed that of books in Latin, and total book production was growing by leaps and bounds. It is not possible, therefore, to dismiss the strength of demand for theological works in Germany as the mere vestige of a scholarly book trade [*Gelehrtenbuchhandel*], more resilient in Germany than it was in France. The scandal of the poisoned communion wine burst upon a broad German-speaking public both accustomed to and deeply concerned about debates on issues of theology.

II

I have said that the Aufklärer were Christians.[6] To the orthodox, however, Christianity was inextricably tied to certain mysteries—the Creation, the Incarnation, the Trinity—the truth of its revelation grounded upon the performance of miracles and the fulfillment of prophecies. It was no easy matter, therefore, to cleanse

Christianity of its mysterious and miraculous "impurities," and the risk was always great that the project would miscarry and that it would end by throwing out the Christian baby with the impure bath water. In effect, Leibniz and his followers in the early eighteenth century had recognized this point and had stopped short at demonstrating the possibility of revelation. The truths of revelation, Leibniz conceded, could not be proved but neither could they be disproved: they were above reason, not contrary to it. But the prudence and circumspection characteristic of Leibniz no longer satisfied the Aufklärer of the next generation, members of the theological school known as "Neology," which spanned the period from the 1740s to the 1770s. Not content to demonstrate the possibility of revelation, the Neologians set about to critique its contents. Could a particular article of faith stand the test of reason? If so, it was in; otherwise, it was out. And what, exactly, was the nature of this test? Essentially, it was morality, practical reason understood in a eudaemonistic fashion. Critiquing Christianity from the standpoint of practical reason, the Neologians discarded the doctrines of original sin, eternal damnation, and vicarious satisfaction; and they vigorously championed the principle that pagans, too, could be virtuous and hence justified in the eyes of God. The main tendency of Neology was to present Christ as a teacher of morality and to reduce Christianity to a system of moral philosophy, a school of virtue whose basic precepts could be apprehended as truths of reason. The result of this radical reduction was a religion worthy of the Aufklärung, one that apostles of humanity could embrace without embarrassment. But was it still Christianity?

To the orthodox, the answer to this question was an emphatic "No." They regarded Christian revelation as a cohesive and unitary system of beliefs, so they did not think it possible to pick and choose from among those beliefs, behaving toward revelation like diners at a smorgasbord who kept those morsels that suited their taste and discarded the rest. Discard the doctrine of original sin and what was left? It was absurd to think that God had condemned his only begotten son to suffer on the cross if the crucifixion had not been necessary to redeem the sins of fallen humanity. And it was equally absurd to think that God had become flesh in the person of Jesus Christ if pagans could be as virtuous as Christians and the core of Christ's teachings was nothing more than the moral reason of humanity. The main line of defense against this type of attack was an historical argument of the sort advanced by Lessing in his *Education of Humanity* (1780).[7] Lessing speculated that Christianity might be regarded as a stage in the evolution of mankind. In the age of Christ, mankind was not yet ready to apprehend basic truths—the existence of one God, the immortality of the soul, morality—as truths of reason. So God presented them in the form of revelation, backed up by miracles, which appealed more to the senses than to reason. But even this historical argument did not address the underlying objections of orthodox critics, for it implied that Christianity, though necessary in the past, had ceased to be so in the present, and that its basic truths could now be taken up [*aufgehoben*] in the philosophy of the Aufklärung. It is not hard to understand why orthodox critics remained unsatisfied and why they continued to suspect that Neology was a Deist wolf in sheep's clothing, which, having gained entry to the sheepfold, would soon devour the Christian flock

Then, as the orthodox saw it, a single event (which coincided exactly with the scandal of the poisoned communion wine) laid bare the true form of the Aufklärung: the publication in three installments of Reimarus's *Fragments on Natural Religion* (1775–1778), arranged by Lessing shortly after the death of the author. During his lifetime, Reimarus had not dared publish the work, which denied any preeminence to Christianity, dropped all Neological pretense, and embraced natural religion thoroughly and without reservation. Its posthumous publication was thus calculated to produce an explosion, for it seemed to confirm the view that the Aufklärung was on a slippery slope heading inexorably toward the abandonment of Christianity.

The publication of Reimarus's *Fragments* inaugurated the first round of an epochal battle. In the subsequent rounds, the stakes rose even higher as the charges leveled against the Aufklärung grew more and more damning. Reimarus's work had given orthodox critics the opportunity to tar the Aufklärung with the brush of Deism. Then, in a series of short works published in the early 1780s, the philosopher Friedrich Heinrich Jacobi argued that the Aufklärung led not just to Deism but also to atheism—or, to be more precise, to the doctrines of Spinoza, of which, as Jacobi claimed, Lessing had professed himself to be an adherent shortly before his death. According to Jacobi, the core of the Aufklärung resided in the principle of "sufficient reason." If applied consistently, this principle led to a thoroughgoing determinism, which excluded freedom of the will and hence morality, and it ended in the abyss of "nihilism," from which the only escape was a leap of faith—*salto mortale.*[8]

Finally, to compound all of the charges laid against the Aufklärung, came the French Revolution. Initially, most of the leading men of letters in Germany hailed the advent of the Revolution as a triumph of the Aufklärung.[9] But once the Revolution began to radicalize, the association of Revolution and Aufklärung yielded a new set of indictments, saddling the Aufklärung with responsibility for Jacobinism, regicide, and terror. By the 1790s, the list of accusations laid at the doorstep of the Aufklärung had grown so long that it was as if the Aufklärung itself provided the answer to the origin of evil in the world—the very problem with which Leibniz had been grappling in his *Theodicy* nearly a century earlier.

Beginning in the late 1770s, therefore, and extending for nearly two decades to the late 1790s, the Aufklärung was on the defensive. Not all of the charges leveled against it stemmed from the ranks of the orthodox. Many of them came from within. But whatever their source, the result was to cause the Aufklärung to turn back on itself, to interrogate its own limits and possibilities, to engage in a process of self-clarification, which amounted, in effect, to the critique of critique. As an expression of this reflexive turn, one event stands out with particular clarity: the famous essay competition sponsored by the Berlin Academy in 1780 on the question whether it was expedient to deceive the people. Even to ask such a question was to betray the most profound doubts about the direction of the Aufklärung. Prompted by no less a figure than Frederick the Great, the *roi philosophe*, the essay competition invited respondents to examine the potentially harmful consequences of unfettered critique, and it raised the possibility that errors born of prejudice might, in some cases, be more conducive to virtue and happiness than truths established by the clear light of reason. Following the essay competition, a massive public debate broke out in Germany. In journals and in scores of books and pamphlets, men of letters argued over the nature of Enlightenment, the distinction between "true" and "false" Enlightenment, and the appropriate limits, if any, to the exercise of critique. The famous essay "What is Enlightenment?" published by Immanuel Kant in the *Berlinische Monatschrift* in 1784 belonged to this vast debate, and so too in a certain sense did the Kantian *Critiques.* For what indeed was the critical philosophy if not an expression of the reflexive turn—an attempt to define the limits of reason by critiquing the categories of the understanding?[10]

Putting the basic point more abstractly (and in the language of Hegel), one may say that the Aufklärung was raised to the level of self-consciousness at the moment that it was about to pass out of existence. Nothing of the sort occurred in France, perhaps because there the Enlightenment never did pass out of existence. Instead, it was taken up into the Revolution so that Voltaire and Rousseau were enshrined in the Pantheon at the same time that Kant was fighting a rearguard action to defend the authority of reason.[11] The reflexive turn was thus a unique characteristic of the Aufklärung in its last phase. The scandal of the poisoned communion wine fell at the very beginning of this phase, coinciding as it did with the publication by Lessing of Reimarus's *Fragments.* But as we shall see, the debate it inspired anticipated issues addressed later by the likes of Jacobi and Kant. So it may be regarded as a link in a chain, as one step in an ongoing process of self-clarification. The scandal in Zurich coincided with the early twilight of the Aufklärung, when the Owl of Minerva was preparing to spread her wings.

III

Thus far, we have considered two distinctive features of the Aufklärung: its preoccupation with theology and its reflexive turn. But there was a third feature, equally distinctive and fundamental to understanding how the scandal of the poisoned communion wine was received. This was the particular importance of the written word, and especially of print, to the system of communication in eighteenth-century Germany.

Not, of course, that print was unimportant elsewhere. It provided a medium of diffusion for the philosophes, too, whose works began to materialize in print around mid-century. And, indeed, it is hard to think of a more perfect expression of *philosophie* than the monumental *Encylopédie*, which Diderot brought to completion in the late 1760s. But the French Enlightenment began in the Parisian salons of the 1720s, in the witty and irreverent conversation between *gens de lettres* and *gens du monde*. There it acquired its characteristic tone, which it never lost, for even the printed works of the philosophes retained the light air of esprit and badinage characteristic of elegant conversation in Parisian society. Because Paris was France, and because the philosophes knew one another personally, frequented the same salons, drank at the same cafés, and strolled in the same parks, the French Enlightenment has lent itself especially well to a diffusionist model of analysis: first conversation among the philosophes in Paris, then the materialization of philosophie in print, and, finally, the conquest of the public.[12]

Germany, on the other hand, had no center comparable to Paris, so the diffusionist model applied by historians to the French Enlightenment has only a limited purchase on German realities. In the 1770s, Kant resided in Königsberg, Mendelssohn in Berlin, Lessing in Wolfenbüttel, Herder in Bückeburg, Jacobi in Düsseldorf, Möser in Osnabrück, Merck in Darmstadt, Wieland in Weimar, Bodmer in Zurich, Zimmermann in Hanover, Semler in Halle, and Schlözer in Göttingen. The only thing that held together this far-flung intellectual world was the written word: personal letters, to be sure, but also print and especially printed journals, such as the *General German Library* [*Allgemeine deutsche Bibliothek* or *ADB*], which its editor, Friedrich Nicolai, presented explicitly as a journalistic attempt to compensate for the lack of a capital city.[13] As a review journal whose stated goal was to review every single work published in Germany, the *ADB* has been compared to the *Encyclopédie.* Like the latter, it was a massive collective undertaking for which Nicolai had to mobilize an army of hundreds of collaborators.[14] But unlike Diderot, who was able to solicit contributions from philosophes in Paris, Nicolai had to raise his army of collaborators from among scholars scattered across the length and breadth of the German-speaking world. The list of those who contributed reviews to Nicolai's journal provides a map of the German (Protestant) republic of letters, and the *ADB* itself formed the arena—a journalistic equivalent to the *palais royal* or the *café de la régence*—in which the reviewers were able to meet.[15] In France, the printed word was an extension of the spoken word, one link in a chain of communication that ran from conversation to writing to print. In Germany, on the other hand, print was not so much an extension of speech as a substitute for it. Rather than merely amplifying conversation, it provided one of the principal sites at which conversation took place. "Writing," observed the Freiherr von Knigge, a German author of the late eighteenth century, "is the public communication of thoughts, printed conversation, audible discourse directed at every member of the public who is willing to listen, a discussion with the world of readers."[16]

I am not arguing, therefore, that print mattered more to Germany than it did to France—only that it mattered in different ways, that its function was not the same in the one context as it was in the other, and that this difference of function is critical to understanding the distinctiveness of the Aufklärung. The distinctive function of print for the Aufklärung found its clearest statement in Kant's classic essay, "What is Enlightenment?" To Kant, the goal of Aufklärung was independent thinking—"man's emergence from his self-imposed immaturity"—and it required, as he put it, that the "public use of reason" be free. What did Kant mean by the "public use of reason"? He meant "that use which man, as scholar, makes of his reason before the entire reading public" [*vor dem ganzen Publikum der Leserwelt*].[17] In Kant's usage, "public" referred to the reading public, not to a small circle of like-minded friends gathered in a café, and "the public use of reason" could find expression only on the printed page, not in oral communication, because one of the main requirements of reason, as Kant saw it, was that it be universally accessible and only print could in principle satisfy that requirement. Seen from the Kantian perspective, print was not something merely added to the Aufklärung, it was constitutive of it: it was the very medium in which Aufklärung unfolded.[18]

Print was the medium in which Aufklärung unfolded, provided, that is, that censorship did not impede its production and distribution. The truth of the matter is that censorship was still very much a force in eighteenth-century Germany.[19] But it was less of a force in Germany than it was in France. For one thing, the Aufklärung benefited from the political fragmentation of the old Reich, which prevented the implementation of a cohesive system of censorship and surveillance. (The authorities in Zurich prohibited all reporting on local events, so Zurich newspapers printed not a single word on the subject of the poisoned communion wine. But the authorities in Zurich had no power to prevent other German-language newspapers from covering the story and reporting whatever they pleased.) Besides benefiting from political fragmentation, moreover, the Aufklärung also received support (in the sense of benign neglect) from Frederick the Great, the King of Prussia, who occupied the throne of the largest Protestant state in the Reich from 1740 to 1786. To be sure, Frederick did not dismantle censorship as such—indeed, the much vaunted tolerance of the roi philosophe had very narrow limits when it came to political matters—but as a free-thinker in his own right, he turned a blind eye to the circulation of works that challenged orthodox religious dogma.[20] And it was for this reason that Kant paid tribute to his sovereign, identifying the age of the Aufklärung with the "century of Frederick."[21]

Until the death of Frederick the Great, therefore, what Kant took to be the essential condition for the Aufklärung was if not fully then at least partially realized. By the 1770s, Germany had, as we noted earlier, become the leading newspaper producer in all of Europe, covered by a blanket of daily news sheets that stretched from Hamburg to Leipzig and from Frankfurt to Berlin. At this time, too, Germany was seeing a veritable explosion in the production of journals, of which Nicolai's *ADB* was only the most famous.[22] And, most significantly of all, the German book trade was fast assuming the characteristic form that would survive into the twentieth century, the form that would make of it a model of efficiency for all the nations of Europe. From Leipzig, which had established itself as the undisputed center of the German book trade, new publications were now swiftly disseminated across all of German-speaking Europe, thus creating the broad outlines of a national literary market nearly a full century before the creation of political unity under Bismarck.[23]

AND SO THE STAGE WAS SET FOR THE AFFAIR OF the poisoned communion wine to become the object of a "public" debate. The main protagonists in the debate were Friedrich Nicolai, one of the leading figures in the Berlin Aufklärung, whose journal, the *ADB*, we have already mentioned, and Johann Caspar Lavater, a pastor in Zurich, whom we mentioned earlier as the author of works on physiognomy, and who was becoming, during the 1770s, one of the most prominent and outspoken defenders of Christianity in German-speaking Europe. The enmity between these two ideological opponents had a long history (and it would have a long future, too). On Nicolai's side, it went back several years to 1769, when Lavater had issued a public challenge to Moses Mendelssohn, defying the Jewish philosopher to refute the "proofs" for Christianity and to accept conversion if he were unable to do so. Nicolai seems never to have forgiven Lavater the public offense directed against Mendelssohn, whom he regarded both as a kindred spirit and a personal friend.[24] For his part, however, Lavater came to regard Nicolai as the ringleader of a sinister clique—the *Nicolaiten*—

bent on the destruction of Christianity.[25] With the affair of the poisoned communion wine, the enmity between them found a new object, and the rift between them deepened; but it did not deepen so far as to block communication. However much they may have been estranged ideologically, these two archenemies were enmeshed in the same networks of communication. Their circles of correspondents overlapped, and so too did the books and journals which they read. In pleading their respective cases, both of them were appealing to the same court of opinion: the public sphere created by the widespread circulation of the written word.

Chapter Five

"And God Fell Silent": The Enlightenment on Trial (I)

TO ENGLISH-SPEAKING READERS, JOhann Caspar Lavater is known, if at all, as the author of works on physiognomy. Yet such a view hardly does justice to so complex and multifaceted a figure. Who, then, was the pastor from Zurich, one of the chief protagonists in the public debate on the affair of the poisoned communion wine?[1]

I

Johann Caspar Lavater styled himself a defender of Christianity, which he believed was under attack from the various theological schools of the Aufklärung. Before becoming a critic of the Aufklärung, however, Lavater himself had come under its influence. Born in 1741, the thirteenth son of a well-respected Zurich physician, he belonged to a generation of students whose chief mentor

Figure 11. Johann Caspar Lavater, deacon at the St. Peter's church in Zurich. Copper engraving by Johann Heinrich Lips. After the painting by Johann Heinrich Wilhelm Tischbein, 1781. From: Johann Caspar Lavater, *Essay sur la physiognomie*, vol. 2 (The Hague, 1783). Courtesy of the Zentralbibliothek Zürich, Graphische Sammlung.

was Johann Jakob Bodmer, the elder statesman of the Aufklärung in Zurich, an author of international renown and a professor at the main institution of higher learning in Zurich, the Carolinum.[2] Of all the Protestant churches in Switzerland, the Zurich church was the one most open to the modern theological currents flowing from Germany; and this opening was largely the work of clergymen who, like Lavater, were former pupils of Bodmer.[3] While waiting for a vacant benefice, moreover, Lavater became entangled in a political conflict and ran afoul of the authorities in the late 1760s. So his family thought it wise for him to absent himself temporarily from Zurich, and he set off on a journey to Germany. There he made the acquaintance of many of the leading Neologians and formed friendships with them, some of which endured long after he had grown intellectually estranged from them.

This estrangement began around 1768, almost as soon as Lavater had returned from Germany. Even as it deepened, however, he was still far from the camp of the orthodox. He continued to reject (esoterically, if not exoterically) such orthodox doctrines as predestination, eternal damnation, and vicarious satisfaction, and he kept aloof from confessional rivalries since he believed that no visible church corresponded perfectly to the invisible church and that members of all Christian denominations could be justified in the eyes of God—including even Catholics, toward whom Lavater was a good deal more tolerant than both orthodox Protestants and a great many self-professed Aufklärer such as Nicolai. Temperamentally, Lavater was emotional, tempestuous, and passionate—to his enemies, an "enthusiast" [*Schwärmer*]. The coolly analytic tone of the Aufklärung alienated him profoundly. But about such an attitude there was also nothing intrinsically orthodox. If anything, it revealed a kinship with the Sturm und Drang, and above all with Rousseau, whose secular critique of civilization Lavater transposed into a religious and eschatological key. In one of his early works, *Perspectives on Eternity*, Lavater projected the Rousseauian ideal of transparency onto the heavens, imagining a type of direct and intuitive communication among the elect in which a "pantomimic and physiognomic" language would supplant the falsifying language of the spoken word.[4] Very much in the spirit of Rousseau, Lavater seems to have interpreted the Fall in terms of a loss of transparency, to have displaced it, as it were, from the Garden of Eden to the Tower of Babel. And although he was no social revolutionary and never entertained the possibility that mankind could overcome the loss of transparency by remaking the social contract, neither was he so otherworldly as to defer all hope of redemption to the end of time: his defense of physiognomy rested on the premise that some rough relation between seeming and being, outer and inner, existed even among flesh-and-blood human beings in the here and now.[5] Whatever else he may have been, Lavater was no orthodox critic of the Aufklärung.

But a critic he undoubtedly was. The main focus of Lavater's criticism was the vision of a transcendent God developed by the Aufklärung. To Lavater, God was not some distant and remote deity, the mere creator of a universe built to operate according to natural laws. He was, on the contrary, a living, vibrant force whose presence in the world human beings could experience directly, and He was inseparable from Jesus Christ—Christ not as a mere teacher of morality, but as God become flesh—who alone brought the divine within the range of human experience. Against the rationalist Aufklärung, therefore, Lavater deployed what amounted to a kind of religious empiricism: he appealed to sensory experience [*Sinneserfahrung*], to the direct enjoyment of God [*Gottesgenuß*], and above all to miracles [*Wunder*], which provided tangible evidence of a divine force in the world. Nothing could have been more remote from Lavater's religious vision than the tendency of the Aufklärung to regard miracles as mere disruptions of natural law and to relegate them to a distant past—to a Biblical epoch that had passed out of existence once and for all. Lavater was firmly convinced that miracles could, and indeed did, occur constantly. If they seemed to occur less frequently today than in the past, this was only because man had become so jaded and his religious sensibility so atrophied that he was no longer able to perceive them. To make this point convincingly, however, Lavater had to find miracles. So he set off on a wild goose chase, pursuing every lead he got wind of, and became the dupe of virtually every charlatan, quack, and impostor—from Swedenborg to Gassner to Cagliostro to Mesmer—who enjoyed a brief moment of celebrity in the last decades of the eighteenth century. Lavater's credulity produced snickering among his enemies and embarrassment among his friends, but it did not detract from the power that his religious vision exercised over many of his contemporaries. That vision looked both backward and forward: backward to Pietism, with which it shared a yearning for a direct, personal connection to God, and forward to the Romantics, who castigated the modern "philistine" for having lost the childlike sense of wonder and who lamented the disenchantment of the world in much the same spirit that Lavater criticized the Aufklärung.

Romanticism, Pietism, empiricism, Rousseau, Sturm und Drang, and even, to some extent, the Aufklärung of his youth—Lavater's thought was located at the confluence of virtually all the major currents of eighteenth-century intellectual life. That so many powerful and opposing currents were able to flow into one single stream, and that Lavater's thought was able to contain them without bursting, is itself something of a miracle. But contain them it did, and this made of Lavater both one of the most eclectic and one of the most perfect exemplars of his century. He embodied his age in all of its contradictions.

It is no wonder, then, that Lavater became a celebrity in Germany, an object of fascination even to those who were otherwise ill disposed toward his religious outlook, and that from the 1770s onward, countless German visitors to Switzerland came calling at Lavater's house, hoping to meet the renowned Zurich pastor. Nor is it any wonder that Lavater's enormous network of correspondents embraced both friends and foes alike, and that, indeed, friends and foes were often indistinguishable, for Lavater was such a bundle of contradictions that he both attracted and repelled the very same people. As a young *Stürmer und Dränger*, Goethe fell under the spell of Lavater's effusive, radiant, and charismatic personality, only to grow disenchanted later on as Lavater became more and more insistent on "converting" him to Christianity. By the mid-1780s, Goethe's youthful infatuation had given way to outright rejection.[6]

And finally, because he was such a celebrity in Germany, Lavater's works were also lucrative objects of commercial speculation, a prize coveted by publishers who wished to turn a profit. Lavater preached two sermons on the poisoning of the communion wine: the first, as ordered by the Small Council, on 29 September; the second, two months later, on his own initiative. Other pastors, too, preached sermons on the poisoning of the communion wine, two of which were printed.[7] But Lavater's sermons were not only printed, they spawned a veritable frenzy of competition among booksellers. Three editions of his first sermon and two of the second were printed in Switzerland before the year was out. Then in 1777 a bookseller in Augsburg published an edition of the first sermon, and a bookseller in Frankfurt published editions of both the first and the second.[8] But still the market was not saturated, for the Frankfurt bookseller declared that he had been able to sell "1,500 copies of the sermons in the space of four weeks, despite the large quantity of copies produced by others."[9] Lavater was displeased with the Frankfurt edition, which he regarded as faulty. So in February 1777 he turned to the Leipzig publisher Philipp Erasmus Reich, the leading publisher in all of Germany, who was in the process of bringing out a luxurious edition of Lavater's *Physiognomik*.[10] No sooner had Reich decided to produce an edition of Lavater's sermons than he began receiving inquiries about it. Johann Georg Zimmermann, an author and physician in Hanover, wrote to Reich, congratulating him on his decision. His copy of Lavater's sermons, the only one in Hanover, had "been torn from his hands," Zimmermann explained. He asked Reich to send him a half dozen copies of the new edition, adding: "There is demand [for the sermons] everywhere."[11] Lavater supplied Reich with corrected copies of his two sermons, along with a copy of his "True History of the Communion Poisoning" (the same one published in Wieland's *Teutscher Merkur*), and a poem called "The Undiscovered Criminal," all of which Reich included in his edition.[12] And, eventually, after some delays, the edition appeared, just in time for the Leipzig Easter fair, when booksellers from all over the German-speaking world came together to purchase and swap new publications.[13] By May 1777 at the latest, thousands of copies of Lavater's sermons had been diffused through the channels of the German book trade.

Lavater had the ear of the German public. Few among his contemporaries were better placed to launch a public debate than he.

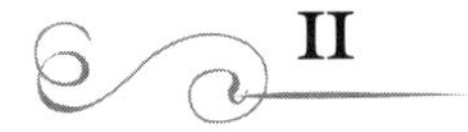

II

The debate on the affair of the poisoned communion wine took place through the medium of the written word. Indeed, it could scarcely have occurred otherwise, as I argued earlier, for the simple reason that German intellectuals were scattered so far afield. Yet one cannot read the published version of Lavater's sermons without recalling that they had their origins in the spoken word. The cadence of the language, the nature of the rhetoric both carried the traces of an oral performance. Initially, Lavater was not addressing himself to an anonymous public dispersed across German-speaking Europe—he was preaching to his congregation, deploying the power of Christian oratory to communicate directly with the worshipers in his church.

Lavater's first rhetorical move when he ascended the pulpit on the morning of Sunday, September 29, was to profess himself unworthy to speak in the name of the Almighty on so mournful an occasion. The deed was so dreadful and so monstrous that it seemed almost to defy the power of language. And so Lavater addressed himself to God, appealing for divine inspiration:

> Only one little spark! Not for my sake but for the honor of thy name, for the sake of thy scorned religion, thy profaned temple, thy desecrated sacrament! (7)

Yet still Lavater felt overwhelmed by the enormity of the task, crushed by the weight of responsibility that rested on his shoulders. How to speak of the unspeakable? How to evoke the unimaginable?

Essentially, Lavater's rhetorical strategy consisted in the use of hyperbole. Was the crime so dreadful as to be above normal language? Then the only solution was to raise language to its uppermost limits, to pile superlatives—"the worst," "most monstrous"—one upon the other, until they reached a rhetorical summit:

> And so it has come about that I must speak before a Christian congregation of the most unchristian, the most inhuman, the

> most outrageous, and the most unspeakable deed that has ever been committed or that ever will be committed. (4–5)

And if even hyperbole fell short? The printed text is full of dots, dashes, and exclamation marks, a whole repertoire of typographical signs that calls to mind the sermon as bodily performance, and that allows the reader to imagine Lavater standing at the pulpit, grimacing, sighing, raising his hands toward the heavens—supplementing the inadequacies of the spoken word by the "pantomimic and physiognomic" language that he had described in his *Perspectives on Eternity.*

With their high rhetorical peaks and their wild emotional swings, Lavater's sermons sounded an ecclesiastical echo of the Sturm und Drang. Now raging against the iniquity of the criminal, now conjuring the wrath of God, they stormed from one topic to the next as if driven by some blind and overweening force. For all that they raged and stormed, however, the sermons made a number of important points (one hesitates to call them "arguments"), which would be taken up within the wider debate in Germany. Lavater did not develop these points in any systematic fashion (no sooner had he alighted on one subject than he took wing and flew off to another), nor did he present them as distinct and separate points, so great was his aversion to the analytic mode of thought. To isolate them, we need to remove them from the onward rushing stream of Lavater's rhetoric and rearrange them in the kind of order—systematic, analytic—that Lavater's rhetoric worked to undermine.

THE FIRST OF THESE POINTS CONCERNS THE nature of evidence. Lavater took it as a solid and irrefutable fact that the wine had been poisoned. But how could he be so certain? What sort of evidence was convincing to a Christian apologist who believed in the literal truth of the Bible and the reality of miracles? The answer, as it turned out, was the testimony of "impartial" scientists:

> Not only plant parts with narcotic powers, not only nauseating seeds—poison! . . . Poison, deadly, corrosive, torturing poison,

> was found in the holy wine—found by the most judicious, the wisest, the most experienced, the most impartial physicians and scientists [*Naturforschern*]. (18)

Is it surprising that Lavater appealed to the testimony of "impartial" scientists? Only if one assumes that Christianity stood in opposition to science. But such an assumption fails to do justice to the complex relation between science and religion. Gessner, who performed the first analysis on the wine, was a friend of Lavater. Far from viewing Christianity as an adversary, he was a pious Christian, and he placed his scientific research within a religious frame, regarding it as an act of devotion, as a paean to the wonders of the divine creation.[14] Conversely, Lavater defended Christianity from the standpoint of what I have called "religious empiricism," appealing to miracles as evidence for the truth of his religious faith, so his religious outlook was not at all incompatible with that of science—especially that of a "dirty science" such as chemistry (physics might have been a different matter), which relied so heavily on sensory experience. Miracles were to God what the smell of garlic was to arsenic.[15]

It made perfectly good sense, therefore, that Lavater would invoke the authority of science. But science could establish only the fact of the crime, not its meaning. To interpret the meaning of the crime, Lavater turned to an analogic mode of reasoning, to the type of exegetical practice that Christian theologians had traditionally employed in order to seek meaning in the relations between the Old Testament and the New. Adapting this practice to the interpretation of a contemporary event, Lavater related the poisoning to the crucifixion of Christ:

> O, Jesus Christ! What does this mean if not that thy blood is being trampled under foot? What does it signify if not that thou art being crucified anew?[16]

From here it followed that the poisoner was a second Judas, and to clinch the analogy, Lavater advanced as evidence that both the betrayal of Christ by Judas and the poisoning of the wine had fallen on a Thursday (22).

Of course, this type of evidence only clinched the analogy provided that one accepted the analogic mode of reasoning and provided above all that one accepted the starting point—namely, that the blood of Christ had been spilled. The truth is that many of Lavater's fellow clergymen would have had their doubts about the starting point. Zwinglians had always interpreted the communion wine symbolically rather than literally, claiming that it *signified* the blood of Christ, not that it *was* the blood of Christ. During the Reformation, much actual blood had been spilled over just this issue. It is little wonder, however, that Lavater should have found such a position uncongenial, preferring instead a literal interpretation of the sacrament, which was closer to Catholicism than to Protestantism. The miracle of transubstantiation, the sense of God as physically present in the world, fitted quite well with Lavater's religious outlook. Indeed, it fitted far better than did Zwinglian Protestantism, which had driven the divine from the world by emptying reliquaries, smashing idols, and reinterpreting the sacrament of communion.[17]

But if, as Lavater so firmly believed, God was not simply a distant being in some remote ethereal realm, if He was physically present in the world and intervened in human affairs, how to explain His silence in the face of so monstrous a crime? And Lavater did go to great lengths to conjure up the enormity of the crime. He depicted, in vivid and lugubrious detail, how the criminal had stolen into the cathedral in the dark of night bearing "death and destruction," how he had made his way to the table where "the supper of love, reconciliation and grace" lay prepared, and how, finally, after having accomplished his devilish work, he had wiped his mouth contentedly, smelled the poisonous odor on his finger, and thrilled silently at the thought of the impending doom: "Tomorrow! Tomorrow! What a day it will be! A day of pain and lamentation, of mockery and wantonness! And I, I have brought it forth in darkness" (12–13). To place poison [*Gift*] in the cup of life—the cup from which Christians drank the antidote [*Gegengift*] to sin—was a crime of devilish perversity (21). It defied rational explanation (neither revenge nor greed could account for it),[18] and in its unmitigated wickedness, it was worse than anything recorded in all the annals of human history, "a crime without parallel" [*Verbrechen ohne seines gleichen*], a crime at which even pagans and Jews would recoil in horror (16–17). Why, then, had the ground not given way beneath the feet of the poisoner, swallowing him up and dragging him down into the bowels of hell? Why had God not smitten him with a lightening bolt from the heavens? Of the thousands in attendance at the celestial court, why had not one roused himself to action and hacked the poisoner to bits with his glistening sword (12–13)? After evoking the iniquity of the crime, Lavater was moved to exclaim: "May the heavens turn red! May the earth tremble!" (10). And yet, as he acknowledged, nothing of the sort had occurred: neither had the heavens turned red nor had the earth trembled. Instead, there was only silence—eery, deafening silence. "This crime is so horrific," Lavater declared, "that nothing is more inconceivable to us than the silence [of God]" (16).

To make matters worse, Lavater doubted that Wirz was guilty. Indeed, he seems to have believed (although it is not clear why) that the criminal was still roaming about within the walls of the city, and that he may very well have been among the workshipers in his congregation. Yet even so, God delivered no sign, gave no indication of who had committed the atrocity, allowing the criminal to mock his would-be victims and to do so with impunity. The mere thought of such mockery was almost too much for Lavater to bear:

> Oh, God, lord God . . . appear! Arise, thou judge of the world! Punish the wicked according to their just deserts! Lord! For how long shall the godless exult? . . . They persecute the just and fall upon them with gnashing teeth, and they declare: the Lord sees not, the God of Jacob takes no notice! Oh, God! Please do not keep silent! Be not so still! . . . Why dost thou remain silent when the godless wish to devour the pious? Hath thine hand been cut off? . . . Awaken, awaken! Show thy power! . . . Awaken as in days of yore! (31–33)

Repeatedly throughout his first sermon, Lavater addressed himself to God in this way, now questioning the grounds of His silence, now beseeching Him to break it; and by doing so, he revealed a great deal about his religious outlook which he would probably have been loath to admit and of which he may have been only partially conscious. The cornerstone of Lavater's religious outlook was the belief in miracles [*Wunderglauben*], which he presented as the expression of a firm faith in Jesus Christ. But his despair at God's silence suggests, on the contrary, that he was subject to the most horrible doubts, consumed by the terrible, gnawing fear that the Aufklärung may have been right, and that God was no longer so near as in the Biblical epoch ("the days of yore"), that the age of miracles had, in fact, come to a close. Rather than expressing the strength of his faith, therefore, Lavater's belief in miracles was the sign of its weakness. Such a faith had no firm ground at all, requiring ever-new proofs to keep doubt at bay. It never came to a stable resting place, and it sent Lavater careening between moods of elation at the signs of God's presence and moods of despair at His apparent absence. By the end of his sermon, he seemed to be nearing a mood of the very blackest despair. To stave it off, he called on God in a tone at once defiant and reproachful:

> Far be it from thee to keep silent! Should not thou, judge of all the world, judge righteously!? Show that thou art the living, holy God! And that thou wilt not allow the godless to raise his head and the mocker to mock, else thy thunder strike him down, his tongue grow stiff, and his sneering lips turn blue. (46–47)

In his relentless quest for the evidence of God's presence in the world, Lavater had backed himself into a corner, trapping himself in a position from which he was all but accusing God of an act of betrayal. For a pastor and an apologist of Christianity, this was a frightening position indeed. What paths of escape lay open to him?

Lavater spurned the two most obvious solutions to his predicament. He did not attempt to vindicate the idea of divine justice by appealing to some future day of reckoning, consoling himself with the thought that the criminal would suffer punishment in the world-to-come.[19] Nor did he attempt to solve the problem of God's silence by playing down the gravity of the crime. It was true, he acknowledged, that the attempt at mass murder had miscarried, since, as he believed, no one had died as a result of the poisoning. From the standpoint of morality, however, failure altered nothing at all. Lavater's ethics were, as philosophers would say nowadays, "intentionalist" rather than "consequentialist" (in this respect, at least, he was impeccably Protestant—and also, one might add, Kantian). So the only relevant point was that the criminal had wanted to wipe out an entire Christian congregation, that his goal had been to kill innocent communicants, who had come to the cathedral in a spirit of piety and humility to partake of the sacrament of their Lord. To mitigate the evil of such a crime, or, still worse, to act as if it did not exist, was an evasion: moral evil remained no less a problem for the absence of physical evil.[20]

Lavater attempted to solve this problem—in effect, the classic problem of theodicy—by performing a feat of dialectical juggling. On the one hand, he described the crime as a singular act of unparalleled wickedness, refusing to mitigate or play down its gravity in any way; on the other hand, he sought to generalize its meaning, interpreting the crime as the symptom of an underlying illness whose spread, if unchecked, could imperil all of humanity. But he was not really agile enough to keep both terms of his dialectic in the air simultaneously, so he brought them into play one at a time. His first sermon tended to stress the singular aspects of the crime; his second, its more general meaning.[21]

AS THE PROOF TEXT FOR HIS SECOND SERMON, Lavater selected a passage from the book of the prophet Nahum (3:1): "Woe to the bloodthirsty city full of lies and wanton violence." The book of the prophet Nahum recounts the bloody destruction of the city of Nineveh, presenting the destruction as a just punishment visited by God upon a wicked and impious people. By taking such a text as the starting point of his sermon, Lavater was raising the rhetorical tone yet again, striking a note so shrill that the most bombastic passages in his first sermon seemed almost restrained by comparison. And besides heightening the rhetorical tone, he was also broadening his subject matter. What was at stake now, he implied, was not just a single crime and a single criminal but the moral character of an entire city.

Zurich, a latter-day Nineveh? Lavater did not press the analogy so far as to indict the whole city of Zurich without distinction. He was careful to exempt the "just" and "equitable" magistrates, who had made a good faith effort to capture both the poisoner and the libelists.[22] When it came to the other citizens of Zurich, however, he saw little to praise. He railed at their "frivolity," "depravity," and "irreligion"—their growing "lack of conscience" and their "forgetfulness of God," which was growing worse by the day, spreading like a "cancer" through the body of the city.[23] Lavater did not pinpoint the source of this "cancer," but he did gesture toward it, speaking darkly and ominously of the "manner and the character of our age" (53), and in so doing, he foreshadowed an accusation that he would make explicitly three years later in a speech before the Zurich synod: that the poisoning of the communion wine gave evidence of a general decline of Christian faith, the chief cause of which was the wide dissemination of works by such dangerous authors as Lessing (a "crude" and "overt" Deist) and Gotthilf Steinbart (a "refined" and "covert" Deist).[24] Seen in this light, the crime reflected the impiety and unbelief not just of a single criminal, or even for that matter of the city of Zurich, but of the entire age. In effect, Lavater was trying to exonerate God by blaming the Aufklärung.

And he was also trying to make out a case for seeing the poisoning of the communion wine as an object lesson in the perils of impiety, as a kind of wake-up call addressed to the city of Zurich in order to rouse it from its complacency. No, Zurich was not yet so wicked as the city of Nineveh, nor had it suffered anything like the same punishment as its Biblical predecessor. But the signs of its moral and religious decay were everywhere. Not a few citizens, Lavater asserted, had treated the poisoning of the communion wine with lighthearted indifference, laughing it off as if it had been nothing more than a bit of innocent mischief.[25] And on top of that came the libels, whose allegations were so preposterous that they could only have sprung from a spirit of the most insolent mendacity (61–

62). In light of such signs, Lavater felt called upon to warn his fellow citizens of their impending doom. He referred to the prophet Nahum, but he was casting himself in the role of a Jeremiah, admonishing his compatriots to heed the lesson embodied in the worst crime in all of history. If they did so, they could still find their way back to God; if they did not, they were doomed (53).

As Lavater presented it, the chief lesson of the crime was that Christianity and virtue, like impiety and vice, were inextricably connected. If religious faith decayed, then so too did the ground of morality, hurtling man into an abyss—a moral void—in which he was all but helpless before the temptations of evil. This decay did not occur in a single instant, however; it was a process. One transgression begat another, and so on, in a downward spiral until man became so alienated from God that he fell into the hands of the devil:

> Merely abandon prayer. . . . You will soon become capable of vices of which you were previously incapable and you will become acquainted with crimes, the mere thought of which now make you tremble. Merely begin to regard divine worship and religion with indifference, then to speak of them with a half contemptuous tone. [Merely begin] to laugh with the jester, then to joke yourself. . . . Your joking will soon become mockery; your mockery, scornful derision; your derision, blasphemy; your blasphemy, acts of desecration, profanation . . . poisoning of the most holy. (46)

Not even the poisoner of the communion wine, therefore, was born to his crime. At first, Lavater argued, the criminal would have trembled at the mere thought of so monstrous a crime. His first transgression must have been relatively minor—say, the torturing of an insect. Then perhaps he became so bold as to poison the animal of a neighbor, moving from there to the poisoning of a fellow human being:

> And so, little by little, he worked himself up to the most dreadful of all deeds, dashing ahead with giant strides from one sin to the next, from one depraved act to another. (44)

Before the criminal had committed this most dreadful of all deeds, it was likely that no one else in Zurich could have imagined such a thing. Indeed, the very imagining of it would itself have been a crime. But the commission of the deed had dramatically altered this situation. What had once been done was now imaginable, and what was imaginable could, in principle, be done again, raising the specter of an infernal cycle, with one crime leading to another until no one in Zurich could partake of the holy sacrament without quivering. Would it ever again be possible to drink from the cup of life without fearing that it was a cup of death? One thing and one thing only, Lavater argued, could ward off this terrifying prospect and halt Zurich's quickening slide into the abyss of crime:

> [The religion of Christ] alone can preserve us against vice and atrocities, both in the light of day and in darkness. It alone can teach us virtues which eclipse all—even the most despicable—vices. It alone raises our souls above the temptations of sin and arms us against the blandishments of infamous desires. It alone makes us into just, good, holy and godly men. It alone strengthens us in all our weaknesses, consoles us in our distress, restores us in our suffering. It alone is our life in the face of death, our joy in the future! (47–48)

From whatever angle one approached it, the poisoning of the communion wine remained deeply disturbing; but the horror of the crime could be redeemed—transformed, as it were, from a curse into a blessing—if its general significance were understood aright and if the people of Zurich embraced that understanding in a spirit of humility and gave it effect by weaving it into the fabric of their daily lives. Such a crime did not contradict the goodness of God. Indeed, it manifested it, for it led to the apprehension of a universal truth on which the virtue and happiness of mankind depended. Whoever poisoned the communion wine was *both* a singularly wicked criminal and a representative of all humanity, his fall into sin *both* an unparalleled example of evil and an allegory of the human condition: remove the foundation of Christian faith, and we are all, potentially, poisoners of the communion wine.

From the most shockingly anti-Christian of all crimes, Lavater had managed to wrest a sweeping vindication of the Christian religion. What were his many foes in the ranks of the Aufklärung to make of such a conclusion?[26]

NOW, THE AUFKLÄRUNG DID NOT, FOR THE MOST part, deny the ethical value of Christianity. (In this respect, as we saw earlier, it was quite different from its French counterpart.) Nor, of course, did it speak with one voice on so large and momentous an issue. On one particular point, however, unanimity prevailed. Wolffians, Neologians, Deists, Spinozists—all rejected the traditional Christian doctrine of original sin. They viewed the doctrine as an affront to reason and an insult to the dignity of man; and having discarded it, they could no longer accept Christianity as the indispensable antidote to man's inherent sinfulness, as the unique source of salvation for a corrupt humanity that was otherwise helpless before the temptations of evil. However much their views of God and Christianity may have differed, they were all committed to the principle that pagans—and even atheists—were capable of virtue, that man as a rational being could determine his own will according to the dictates of morality. Lavater's sermons challenged this principle; they called it fundamentally into question, and they did so in a published form, which was tantamount to throwing down the gauntlet. One year after their publication, Friedrich Nicolai took up the challenge.[27]

III

If Lavater had become by the 1770s one of the leading critics of the Aufklärung in German-speaking Europe, Friedrich Nicolai had a strong claim to being its most influential defender.[28] Not that Nicolai was a great original thinker or an eminent scholar. Unlike most of the leading figures in German intellectual life, he had never gone to university; and his posthumous reputation has suffered tremendously because he managed during his long life to cross swords with all the philosophic and literary giants of the late eighteenth century—from Kant and Goethe to Fichte and Friedrich Schlegel—who avenged themselves on Nicolai by spreading the picture of him as the representative of a shallow and simple-minded Aufklärung.[29] But this image is not only unjust, as we shall see presently; it also misses the main point. What made Nicolai so enormously significant is that he embodied the connection between Aufklärung and print. At once a bookseller, a journal editor, and an author in his own right, he contributed more than any of his contemporaries to "publicizing" the Aufklärung, to bringing it out of the lecture halls of universities and into the marketplace of ideas. Precisely because he was a bookseller, moreover, and not a scholar, he had a keen sense of how to package ideas for the marketplace and he wrote in a language that appealed to a broad middle-class public. His satirical novel *The Life and Opinions of Master Sebaldus Nothanker*, which popularized the ideas of the Neologians, became the most widely disseminated German novel of the entire eighteenth century and contributed far more to spreading the values of the new rationalist theology than all the works of Semler, Teller, and Jerusalem combined.[30] As we noted earlier, however, print was important to the Aufklärung, not only—or even mainly—because it provided a vehicle for the spread of its ideas, but because it created the conditions for the "public use of reason," for an ongoing debate among widely scattered interlocutors. Whatever his role as an agent of diffusion, therefore, Nicolai's most important achievement was to have edited and published the *ADB*, which was, during the 1770s, the leading review journal in Germany. When he began the journal, Nicolai set himself the goal of producing reviews of every single work published in Germany. The volume of literary production in Germany was growing so rapidly that the goal proved to be unattainable, but the *ADB* realized a lofty goal even if it fell short of the one that Nicolai had set himself. In the preface to the first edition of the *Critique of Pure Reason*, Kant wrote: "Ours is the true age of critique and to critique everything must submit."[31] The *ADB* extended the practice of critique to virtually all fields of modern literary production.

With its vast army of collaborators, the *ADB* was a mammoth collective undertaking, and as its editor, Nicolai was like a general leading his troops into battle. This position gave to him a great deal of power, which he deployed during the 1770s to launch a campaign against Lavater.[32] He wrote and published in the *ADB* critical reviews of Lavater's *Physiognomik*.[33] He arranged for the publication of a bitingly satirical work by Lichtenberg—*The Defense of Two Israelites Who Were Moved through the Force of Lavater's Proofs and that of Göttingen Sausage to Accept the True Faith*—which ridiculed Lavater for his naive and simple-minded attempt to convert Moses Mendelssohn.[34] And in 1777, just after the affair of the poisoned communion wine had burst on the scene, he published another satirical polemic—*Considerations on the Belief in Miracles* . . .—which pilloried and lampooned Lavater for his credulity.[35] To one of Nicolai's correspondents, it seemed as if the intellectual life of Germany had become a great battlefield disputed by two competing armies with Lavater and Nicolai at their heads.[36] With the publication of Lavater's sermons, however, Nicolai entered the lists himself, descending from his general's tent to skirmish directly with his archenemy.[37] Ostensibly, Nicolai's response took a modest form: an anonymous twenty-seven page review of Lavater's sermons published in January 1778 as a supplement to the *ADB* from the last quarter of the previous year. But the form belied the content, for what Nicolai wrote was, in fact, a radically new interpretation of the entire affair of the poisoned communion wine, undertaken, as he put it, from the perspective of "natural reason."[38]

IV

To move from Lavater's sermons to Nicolai's review is to pass from one stylistic universe to another. Gone are the hyperbole, the dashes and exclamation marks, and the wildly bombastic rhetoric. Nicolai wrote crisply, clearly, and lucidly. Instead of dashing about from one topic to the next, he laid out his argument and then pursued it, step by step, until he reached his conclusion, carrying the

FIGURE 12. Friedrich Nicolai. Oil on canvas by Anton Graf, ca. 1783.

reader along by the rigor of his logic rather than the force of his passion and the vividness of his metaphors. So striking was the contrast that one wonders whether Nicolai may not have been making a deliberate rhetorical move in forsaking rhetorical extravagance, whether he was not, in other words, practicing the rhetoric of antirhetoric. In any event, Nicolai found Lavater's stylistic pyrotechnics deeply offensive—they produced more heat than light—and he objected especially to Lavater's imprecations against the monstrous criminal and his appeals for divine vengeance, which breathed such a spirit of hatred and vindictiveness as to be unseemly for a Christian pastor (638).

As against this spirit of hatred and vindictiveness, Nicolai cast himself in the role of a "friend of humanity" (643). The claim to this lofty title was highly significant, for it set up a second fundamental contrast, beyond the stylistic one, between Nicolai and his adversary by implying that Lavater was an enemy of humanity. For his own part, of course, Lavater would never have accepted the legitimacy of such a contrast (he described physiognomy as a "science dedicated to furthering the love of humanity"), but if Lavater's religion were not, at bottom, misanthropic, if it did not despise humanity and take a dim view of human nature, how else could one explain his global condemnation of the city of Zurich and his imputation of wickedness to virtually all of its citizens? Surely, Nicolai argued, the "good city of Zurich" did not deserve such a sweeping indictment (641). And even if some of its citizens were not exactly paragons of virtue, it did not follow that they were guilty of having reared a monster because there were no grounds for assuming that the monster came from Zurich (642). Lavater had introduced this assumption as if it were self-evident, but it was not self-evident at all, and if one discarded this assumption, if one severed this critical link in the chain of Lavater's argument, then the entire argument fell apart. One could no longer claim that irreligion in Zurich provided the soil for evil to grow and that the Aufklärung was responsible for the crime because it fostered irreligion. One was left with a singularly monstrous criminal, to be sure, but the broader implications of the crime fell away.

Or was one left with a singularly monstrous criminal? Within the first six pages of his review, Nicolai had already overthrown Lavater's main argument, toppling the interpretative edifice that Lavater had built upon the crime. But then, to make his victory complete, Nicolai lowered his sights so as to strike at the very foundation upon which the argument had been raised. It was not just that Lavater was wrong about the meaning of the crime, he was wrong about the crime itself: wrong that a monster had crept unseen into the cathedral on the night before the communion service, wrong that anyone had attempted to commit mass murder, and wrong, in fact, that the wine had been poisoned. To Nicolai, the whole official version of events was shot through with so many inconsistencies, invalid assumptions, and logical flaws as to be utterly unconvincing. And he set about to demonstrate his point by examining every tidbit of evidence at his disposal and by applying to it the principle of systematic and thoroughgoing doubt, accepting nothing as true unless it could be clearly and irrefutably proved. The result was a spectacular work of demolition, a destructive tour de force worthy of Descartes.

TWO BASIC PRINCIPLES GUIDED NICOLAI AS HE worked his way through the evidence available to him from the published accounts of the affair. The first was that evidence, even seemingly hard physical evidence, was not unambiguous, and that it was susceptible of multiple interpretations. The second was that testimony, even if came from a perfectly respectable witness, should not be taken at face value because it was likely to embody a certain bias and because, in many cases, witnesses may have had an interest in validating a particular version of events. The first amounted to a mistrust of what we might call naive empiricism. The second could be summed up in the standard question: *Cui bono*?

Applying these principles, Nicolai began at the beginning. The first piece of evidence cited in the published accounts concerned the moisture on the floor of the cathedral and the smeared cup discovered by the sexton upon his arrival in the cathedral on the morning of the communion service. All the published accounts presented these facts as deeply suspicious, with the implication that the moisture came from wine spilled by the poisoner as he was fumbling about in the darkness of the cathedral, and that the smeared cup contained poison intended for the Antistes, whose life was spared thanks to the sexton, who noticed the smeared cup and ordered his daughter to wash it. But it had never been established that the moisture was spilled wine—it could just as easily have been urine from some stray cats or dogs that had found their way into the cathedral. And why assume that an intruder had smeared the cup with poison during the night when it was equally plausible that the sexton's maid had simply overlooked the stain when she had been preparing the cups on the previous evening (644)? None of these facts would have come to light, moreover, if Hess, the cathedral administrator, had not decided to undertake an investigation, for the sexton himself had not found them suspicious enough to warrant any mention.

And why in fact did Hess initiate an investigation? That the wine used in the communion service had been appallingly bad could scarcely be doubted. The evidence on that point was so overwhelming as to be incontestable. But bad wine was not necessarily poisoned wine. When a similar incident had occurred in a church in France, Nicolai explained, the authorities there had not leapt to the conclusion of foul play—they made arrangements to purchase their wine from a different vintner. Nor, in the immediate aftermath of the communion service, did the authorities in Zurich suspect any type of criminal activity. Hess had thus acted entirely on his own initiative, and that he had done so was a matter of no small importance. Indeed, it compromised the credibility of his investigation because Hess was an interested party. As the man responsible for the wine cellar, he stood to gain from the conclusions of his investigation, which alleged that the wine in the cellar was not at fault. And the same was true of the principal witnesses—the cellar master, his two assistants, and the sexton—all of whom would have found themselves in a compromising position if it had come to light that they had knowingly delivered bad wine to the cathedral for the communion service. Once the many complaints about the poor quality of the wine had reached their ears, they would probably have declared that the wine had looked fine to them on the previous evening even if, as Nicolai suspected, they had never bothered to inspect it at all. The sexton may very well have been a fine and honorable fellow (Nicolai disclaimed any wish to impugn his integrity), but his reputation alone should not have shielded him from serious questioning and legitimate suspicion (646–648).

To Nicolai, Hess's investigation seemed so badly compromised that virtually all of its results were subject to question. One of its main findings was that only the wine contained in the four wooden barrels in the cathedral appeared tainted, whereas the wine used in the Predigerkirche appeared fine. This was significant, according to Hess's report, because all of the wine came from the same source—from a single keg in the wine cellar of the convent. But Nicolai doubted that this was so. He believed (although it is not clear why) that there were several kegs in the wine cellar, and that the cellar master and his assistants would either have forgotten which keg supplied which church or lied about it to create the impression that all of the wine had come from the same source. In itself, therefore, the contrast between the wines did not signify anything. And neither did the contrast between the wine contained in the barrels and the little bit of wine left in the vessels used to transport the wine on the evening before the communion service. This contrast, too, was cited to support the conclusion that something had to have happened to the wine in the barrels when it was sitting in the cathedral during the night. From the end of the communion service until the inspection of the carrying vessels, however, enough time must have elapsed for someone (the cellar master? his assistants? the sexton?) to deposit untainted wine in the vessels. The mere possibility that someone had tampered with the evidence vitiated its significance, but even if one ruled out such a possibility, the evidence signified little because Nicolai considered that several carrying vessels must have been lying in the cellar and that no one is likely to have remembered precisely which vessel had transported which wine to which church. Of all the samples of untainted wine to which the tainted wine from the barrels had been compared, only one seemed to Nicolai to warrant any further comment: the sample taken from the tin cans. Nicolai accepted that the wine in the cans and the wine in the barrels must have come from the same keg in the cellar, and that the former was less murky and less offensive than the latter, because the communicants themselves had noticed the contrast. But what did that signify? The barrels were made of wood, the cans of tin. So it would have been perfectly plausible to attribute the poor quality of wine to moldy wood (which, in fairness, Hess too had considered). At this point, if not sooner, an impartial investigation would have come to an end.

But Hess pushed on, delivering samples of the tainted wine to Gessner and his colleagues; and this, as Nicolai realized, was the decisive moment in the whole sequence of events, for it led to the "discovery" of poison, which was the hinge on which everything else turned: "From this moment forward, the entire affair appeared in a new light" (648). In order to carry his work of demolition to completion, therefore, Nicolai had to apply the principle of systematic doubt to science itself, thus challenging the authority of Gessner and his colleagues, which Lavater had accepted unquestioningly. At first glance, this may seem paradoxical: Lavater accepting the authority of science, and Nicolai challenging it. But it is less paradoxical than it seems. Strictly speaking, "the authority of science" was redundant when considered from the perspective of the Aufklärung. In an age in which, as Kant said, everything had to submit to critique, the only authority that merited respect was the authority of reason itself. In practice, this ideal was far from realized—a great many people (Lavater, for example) continued to give their unquestioning assent to authority that had no other basis than its own authority. But that only meant, as Kant would have said, that the age was an "age of Enlightenment" rather than an "Enlightened age"—in other words, that Enlightenment was a process and that the process still had far to go. Nicolai was advancing the process by making science itself an object of critical scrutiny. Even scientists, he implied, could get things wrong.

To Lavater, it had hardly seemed possible that Gessner and his colleague might have been wrong, because they were, as he said, "impartial" [*unpartheyisch*]. With its implications of fair-mindedness and unprejudiced judgment, "impartial" was a key word in the language of the Aufklärung, and Lavater's invocation of the value of impartiality is a measure of its importance and the breadth of its diffusion. On this point, if nothing else, Lavater and Nicolai agreed.[39] The main point of disagreement was not the value of impartiality as such, but whether Gessner and his colleagues were impartial. Nicolai denied that they were. Indeed, he did not see how it was possible for them to be impartial in light of the circumstances, even if one allowed, as Nicolai was prepared to do, that they were men of good faith with no conscious wish to deceive.

Consider the circumstances in which Gessner and his colleagues set to work. When Hess arrived at Gessner's house with the samples of wine, both the moisture in the cathedral (presumed to be spilled wine) and the smeared cup discovered by the sexton had established the "fact" that an intruder had been in the cathedral during the night; the testimony of the cellar master, his assistants, and the sexton had established the "fact" that the wine had been perfectly fine on the previous evening; and the testimony of all those who had tasted the wine had established the fact (which was indeed a fact) that the wine in the wooden barrels, though not that in the tin cans, had been of dreadfully poor quality. All of this appeared to add up to a simple and almost inescapable conclusion: someone had done something bad to the wine in the barrels during the night. So Gessner and his colleagues were, as Nicolai put it, "predisposed to find something harmful in the sediment of the wine" (649). And indeed they did: they found what they were looking for.

Nicolai had not seen Gessner's report, which was never published. But he guessed (rightly, as it turned out) that the presence of arsenic had been inferred from the smell of garlic emitted when the sediment of the wine was burned. This raised two possibilities: either bias may have been operating at the level of perception itself, so that Gessner and his colleagues had only imagined the garlic odor, or it may have been operating at the level of interpretation, causing Gessner and his colleagues to reach an overhasty conclusion on the strength of ambiguous evidence because they were convinced that poison had to be present and arsenic seemed a likely candidate. Other substances, Nicolai observed, give off a garlic odor, too: garlic, for example (650).

In any event, the second team of chemists found no evidence of arsenic; instead, it found evidence of mercury. So striking a contradiction raised doubts about the reliability of both results (651). And further doubts arose when one considered that the wine contained a whole host of different plant parts, many of which were not poisonous at all. It was hard to understand why anyone wishing to commit mass murder would have dropped plant parts into the wine barrels, for these could have had no other effect than to enhance the likelihood that the wine would attract suspicion (659–660).

And finally, Nicolai wondered how it was possible for poisoned wine, if it contained either arsenic or mercury, to have had no noticeable effect on the health of those who had drunk it. To be sure, there had been numerous complaints of illness. But these, Nicolai hastened to point out, had come only after the revelations of poisoning. So the only thing they proved was the power of the imagination to conjure up physical ailments (652–653, 655).

Taken together, the scientific evidence was so contradictory and so vitiated by bias that it added up to virtually nothing. Once the authorities in Zurich had accepted the conclusion of poisoning, however, the whole investigation was shifted onto the wrong track. From then on, it concentrated exclusively on the question who had committed the crime, not whether the crime had been committed. And once it had taken this wrong turn, it could no longer double back and re-examine its starting point in an impartial light because, in the meantime, all of the pieces had fallen into place. Hess's original investigation now made sense in light of the chemical analysis, just as the latter made sense in light of the former. The result was a kind of closed interpretative circle, a cohesive self-confirming system whose various elements validated one another. Nicolai's achievement was to have broken open the circle, prying apart its various elements so that they could be held up individually to critical scrutiny. For all of its apparent commonsense simplicity, this was an impressive achievement indeed, executed in a series of deft critical moves, that should put to rest, once and for all, the unflattering image of Nicolai as a shallow and simpleminded Aufklärer. Indeed, it raises the question how Nicolai ever acquired such an image in the first place.

The main charge against Nicolai has always been that he failed to make the transition to critical philosophy and that he never got beyond a simple appeal to what he and others called "healthy human understanding" [*gesunder Menschenverstand*]. According to this view, "healthy human understanding" was like a yardstick: it took itself to be the measure of all things and judged the world accordingly. But it could not take the measure of itself, and this meant that it was "dogmatic" in much the same way as the religious orthodoxy whose prejudices it denounced.[40] Now, it is perfectly true that Nicolai misunderstood Kant's critical philosophy, which he condemned for depreciating the value of experience. In two satiric novels, directed more against Kantian epigones than against Kant himself, he poured scorn upon followers of Kant whose remoteness from the world [*Weltfremdheit*] made them unfit for any useful function in society, and he had the temerity to ridicule the obscurity of Kantian jargon (nothing was more uncongenial to an Aufklärer like Nicolai than obscurity) as if he were grappling with an intellectual adversary no more formidable than Lavater.[41] For this, Kant never forgave him, avenging the offense by spreading the view of Nicolai as an intellectual simpleton and a mercenary bookseller.[42] In his review of Lavater's sermons, however, Nicolai showed that he was quite capable of using reason critically. He demonstrated, in effect, that science did not have an unmediated access to the world of phenomena, that it apprehended phenomena through a priori categories, and that, therefore, not only religion but science too was subject to "prejudice" [*Vorurteil*]: in the case of religion, a prejudice in favor of external authority, which led to dogmatism and fanaticism; in the case of science, a prejudice in favor of its own empirical method, which, if not rectified through critical self-reflection, led to a dangerous confusion between provisional judgments and definitive ones, between subjective interpretation and objective knowledge.[43] Of course, Nicolai did not make the point using anything like these terms. Such words as "phenomenon" and "a priori" had no place in his vocabulary, which was that of a self-taught bookseller rather than a university professor. Nor was it Nicolai's objective, in his short review of Lavater's sermons, to offer a "transcendental" critique of "pure reason." His goal was to critique a particular empirical judgment, not the faculty of judging as such. But for all the differences in style and objective, the fact remains that nearly three years before Kant announced the "Copernican revolution in philosophy," Nicolai was using reason to expose the limits of scientific understanding.

NOW THAT THE OFFICIAL VERSION OF EVENTS had been demolished, the question arose what to put in its place. As Nicolai interpreted the evidence, two stubborn facts regarding the wine in the barrels still required explanation: its poor quality and the strange assortment of plant parts and other ingredients it contained. Of these, the first posed little difficulty: the bad wine was simply bad wine. Normally, however, even bad wine did not contain Spanish pepper, iris, jimson weed, and glue. The problem, then, was how to account for so bizarre a collection of ingredients. In the final part of his review, Nicolai turned his attention to solving that problem, advancing his own hypothesis to replace that which he had destroyed.

Nicolai speculated that several of the ingredients could plausibly be identified as additives frequently used in the wine cellars of vintners in order to restore the quality of bad wine.[44] He advanced this hypothesis somewhat gingerly, being careful to observe the type of epistemological modesty that he found so conspicuously wanting in Lavater. No expert on the subject himself, he referred the reader to a manual on wine additives entitled *The Wine Doctor*. The procedures described in the manual, if not the manual itself, would almost certainly have been known to the cellar master (they were the tricks of his trade), and as a cellar master in a cathedral, he would have had ample opportunity to practice them since it was well known that churches seldom purchased wines of high quality for use in the communion service. In light of this fact, it seemed significant that several of the additives cited in the manual resembled substances identified by the chemical analyses performed by the scientists. This, Nicolai was prepared to admit, did not prove the hypothesis of wine additives—only direct empirical verification could do that. But direct empirical verification was no longer possible because the wine samples no longer existed. Under the circumstances, the only test possible was that of plausibility—whether the hypothesis was able to account for the relevant evidence, and whether it was able to do so more convincingly than the alternative explanation of poisoning. Suppose, then, that the cellar master had deposited additives in the keg in the cellar of the convent. What consequences followed?

The cellar master was a simple artisan, not a learned scientist, and practiced the art of his craft in a more or less mechanical fashion, performing a set of techniques first acquired during his apprenticeship without understanding exactly how those techniques worked. Imagine his shock and dismay when he learned after the communion service that a team of university-trained and erudite physicians had discovered poison in the wine he had prepared. He knew that he had not intended to poison anyone, but would others believe him? Under the circumstances, it would have been perfectly understandable if he had given false testimony about the wine, claiming that he had inspected the wine on the previous evening and found it normal (662–663). Such behavior may not have been very laudable; but it was comprehensible—and it was far more rational than the behavior required by the alternative hypothesis, that of a monster who set out to massacre 1,200 innocent worshipers without "the slightest motive" (661).

Where did all of this leave Lavater and his sermons? Nicolai had not mentioned his archenemy since the first pages of the review but now returned to him, buoyed by the sense that he had scored a resounding and unmistakable victory. And with obvious relish, he drove home his victory by throwing one last sardonic dart, perfectly aimed to pique Lavater's wounded pride. Just think, Nicolai said, what embarrassment Lavater could have spared himself if he had not allowed his overheated imagination to get the better of him; then he would not have been exposed to the mockery of his enemies, who had wondered why he had not been able to identify the criminal by his physiognomy. How indeed could Lavater have recognized the comparatively innocent and honorable cellar master when he was seeking "the diabolical physiognomy of a black villain"? But, alas, he had made himself ridiculous by pursuing his fancies. "It was not the first time," Nicolai concluded, "that in their desire to find the ideal and the extraordinary, Lavater and others like him had overlooked the natural and the ordinary" (663). Yes, God had kept silent. There had been no reason for Him to speak.

NICOLAI MUST HAVE BEEN RATHER CONTENT with himself because two months after publishing his review in the *ADB*, he issued it separately as a pamphlet under the title "A Few

Doubts Concerning the History of the Communion Wine Poisoning. . . ."[45] Then, he sat back and waited for the reaction, which was not slow to materialize.

From their widely scattered locations across the German-speaking world, friends and allies of Nicolai lavished praise and congratulations on the journal editor who had descended onto the field of battle and who had fought so valiantly for the good cause. From Halle, one of the main strongholds of Neology, Johann Eberhard saluted Nicolai for his pamphlet, declaring that it was "superb," and that he was in full agreement with its conclusions; and he added that his cousin, to whom he had given a copy, had passed a "thoroughly enjoyable afternoon" reading it.[46] From Bremen, Konrad Heinrich Runge, a pastor who had himself penned polemics against Lavater, published a short piece in which he went so far as to claim that the poisoning of the wine had never existed anywhere other than "in the imagination of Lavater."[47] And from Basel, Isaac Iselin, a contributor to the *ADB*, wrote to Nicolai to say that "from the beginning I have seen the whole affair in the same way as yourself." Even in Zurich, moreover, Nicolai's pamphlet seems to have found considerable favor. Thus Iselin reported to Nicolai that he had met Zurichers who "are quite content with your judgment of the poisoning of the communion wine." This was not true of all Zurichers, to be sure. Some of them, Iselin explained, were quite upset, not least the authorities themselves, who reacted to Nicolai's pamphlet by ordering the leading bookseller in the city, the firm of Orell, Gessner, and Füssli, to withdraw it from sale.[48]

And yet the attempt of the authorities to suppress the pamphlet was in itself a tribute to its persuasiveness, an implicit admission that Nicolai had raised significant doubts about their conduct of the investigation and that his pamphlet would damage their standing in the eyes of the citizenry if allowed to circulate. In a letter to a pastor in Schaffhausen, Lavater himself complained bitterly of his fellow citizens, who "frequently express their approval of this nonsensical twaddle [i.e., Nicolai's allegations]."[49] In the aftermath of Nicolai's pamphlet, therefore, Lavater must have endured some painful and humiliating moments. It was bad enough that so many of his fellow citizens judged Nicolai the victor on the battlefield of ideas; what must have wounded Lavater more than anything was that Nicolai had skewered him with the poisoned sword of ridicule, exposing him not only to condemnation but also to laughter. Once, on the occasion of an annual dinner attended by the cathedral canons and the students of the Carolinum, Lavater found himself seated opposite the theology professor Leonhard Usteri, who let it be known that he endorsed the conclusions of Nicolai's pamphlet. According to the journal of Lavater's cousin Anna Barabara von Muralt, Usteri gave Lavater such a "malicious smile" and became so "coarse" in his speech that Lavater stood up and moved to another corner of the room rather than become embroiled in a bitter argument. Reading Muralt's description of the scene, one can all but hear the peals of laughter that echoed behind Lavater's back as he beat an embarrassed retreat from the table.[50]

But what of Lavater's numerous allies and Nicolai's equally numerous enemies? Perhaps the most striking thing about the favorable reaction to Nicolai's pamphlet is that it spanned the ideological spectrum and united the public, regardless of personal predilections. Johann Georg Zimmermann in Hanover, an expatriate Swiss physician, was an intimate friend of Lavater (in their letters, he and Lavater addressed one another with "thou" and "thine"), and he played an important role in the preparation of the *Physiognomische Fragmente*. Still, Zimmerman hailed Nicolai's achievement. "For having removed this disgrace from our age and from my nation," Zimmerman wrote to Nicolai, "you have earned immortal honor and eternal gratitude."[51] Indeed, even Herder, one of the leading figures in the Sturm und Drang, who had broken definitively with Nicolai in the early 1770s, and whose writings Nicolai had attacked in the pages of the *ADB*—even he could not deny the power of Nicolai's argument. Writing to Lavater in the summer of 1779, Herder wondered why Lavater had not bestirred himself to make a response:

> Have you read the Berlin piece about the poisoning of your communion wine? What do you make of it? Is nobody answering? If

> there are other circumstances that put the matter in a different light, I'd like [to know about them]; for at present the appearances are on the side of the "doubter."[52]

"Appearances are on the side of the 'doubter'" was putting it mildly. A short review of Nicolai's pamphlet published in the *Hamburgischer unpartheyische Correspondent* put the case more strongly, and the *HC*, it is worth recalling, was not only the most widely disseminated German newspaper of its age, it was also the newspaper of record, the *New York Times* of eighteenth-century Germany:

> The impartial examination undertaken in this pamphlet establishes the likelihood—and, indeed, the virtual certainty—that the supposed poisoning has a very natural and innocent explanation, which removes the ground for all accusations. How, one may ask, does this concern us after so much time has elapsed? In fact, it concerns us a great deal; for besides the Swiss, did not the entire public of the civilized world [*das ganze gesittete Publikum*] shudder at the wickedness of such a deed? And is it not a duty in such cases to warn the public against leaping to a hasty and emotional [*schwärmerisch*] judgment, and, above all, to warn it against forming the unnatural suspicion of an inhuman crime, until such time as a rational and rigorous investigation has excluded all other possibilities?[53]

On the face of it, the reaction to Nicolai's pamphlet seemed to conform perfectly to the eighteenth-century ideal of the "public use of reason": the superior argument had triumphed before an impartial and critically reasoning public not because it bore the imprimatur of the established church or because it was able to appeal to venerable and illustrious authorities but simply by virtue of its intrinsic rationality. To all appearances, the affair of the poisoned communion wine was now dead and buried, and Nicolai had written its epitaph: the last word belonged to the Aufklärung.

Or did it?

Chapter Six
Radical Evil: The Enlightenment on Trial (II)

WHY WAS NO ONE ANSWERING THE "doubter"? Herder had asked in his letter to Lavater. The truth is that Lavater was already at work on an answer. He had obtained copies of all the chemists' reports; he had written directly to the scientists themselves, soliciting their opinion of Nicolai's claims; and he had secured copies of the original report submitted by Hess to the Secret Council, the minutes of the Council session that followed Hess's disclosures, and the testimony of the witnesses interrogated by the investigators.[1] Armed with the necessary information, he then launched his counterattack, which took the form of a handwritten letter to his friend Johann Joachim Spalding in Berlin.[2] That Lavater chose this form rather than print may be significant. It may imply that Nicolai's attack had stung so deeply as to make Lavater wary of exposing himself to ridicule for a second time: once bitten, twice shy. On the other hand, the choice of Spalding as a correspondent was hardly the opening gambit of a man who wished to shy away from battle. Although a friend of Lavater, Spalding was also a contributor to the *ADB* and a prominent Neologian in Berlin.[3] By addressing his response to Spalding, therefore, Lavater was firing directly into the enemy camp. His response was bound to circulate among Spalding's friends and colleagues, and it was almost certain to come to the attention of Nicolai. What form did it take?

Much of the response was little more than a reaffirmation of the authority of science, which completely missed the argument of Nicolai's critique. Holding fast to his naive empiricism, Lavater wondered how it was possible to doubt the existence of a suspicious sediment attested by "eyewitnesses," the presence of substances "seen" by scientists, and the reality of poison "found" by them. In fact, Nicolai had never doubted any of this; he was perfectly willing to accept that the scientists had seen the things that they claimed to have seen. His point was that seeing, in itself, was not enough. Lavater simply sidestepped this point, reasserting that the scientists were the "most prudent and the most competent physicians," and that "they had no interest in the affair either one way or the other," as if Nicolai had imputed to them nothing more than bias in the ordinary sense of "interest." Either the a priori component of scientific understanding was incomprehensible to Lavater, or he pretended not to understand it.

When it came to Nicolai's alternative explanation, however, Lavater was able to make a number of telling points. First, Lavater argued, it was rather odd that additives whose function was to restore the quality of the wine had produced precisely the opposite effect—they had turned clear wine murky instead of making murky wine clear, they had worsened the taste of the wine instead of improving it, and they had given it an odor so disagreeable as to be nauseating. This alone was enough to raise doubts about Nicolai's explanation. Even if one granted, however, that the cellar master had simply botched the operation by mixing the additives in the wrong proportions, or that the additives had sat in the keg for so long as to produce the opposite of the desired effect, Nicolai's explanation was still unable to account for the most important evidence—namely, that yielded by the comparisons of the various wine samples. Lavater accepted Hess's account, which claimed that the wine used in the Predigerkirche also came from the keg in the cellar of the convent. He did not see, therefore, how one could reconcile Nicolai's explanation with the fact, attested by countless witnesses, that the wine from the Predigerkirche had none of the disagreeable qualities perceived in the wine taken from the wooden barrels in the cathedral. Nicolai's explanation required tampering at the source; the comparison of the wine samples made tampering at the source seem impossible. And finally, what of the comparison between the wine in the tin cans and that in the barrels, which revealed the same contrast as the comparison between the wine in the cathedral and that from the Predigerkirche? Even Nicolai admitted that the wine in the tin cans and that in the barrels came from the same keg in the cellar. He then attempted to account for the contrast between them by speculating that the wood in the barrels may have been moldy—afterward, he never mentioned the contrast again, passing over it as if it had already been ruled out of court and shown to be irrelevant. But it was hardly irrelevant. Indeed, it raised insuperable difficulties for the hypothesis of wine additives. Grant, for the moment, that the wood was moldy. Even moldy wood could not account for all of the various substances in the wine, which, had they been wine additives, would have been present in the original keg and would therefore have shown up in all of the wine samples: not only in the one taken from the barrels, but also in those taken from the tin cans and the Predigerkirche. The real appeal of Nicolai's argument, Lavater insinuated, was not its intrinsic rationality. What guaranteed it such widespread assent was that it expressed what everyone *wished* to believe, denying the reality of a crime whose wickedness was deeply disturbing.[4] Meanwhile, however, all of the evidence continued to point to the conclusion that substances had been dumped into the wine barrels during the night when they were sitting under the baptismal stone in the cathedral.

To Lavater, this conclusion was so clear, self-evident, and irrefutable that denying it was nothing less than a "suppression of truth." That the denial came from someone who professed "love of humanity" made it all the more outrageous, for what could be more hypocritical than for an enemy of truth to pose as a lover of humanity? These were fighting words, far more serious and accusatory than anything contained in Nicolai's review, which had only mocked Lavater for having been the dupe of his own fertile fantasy.[5] The implication was that Nicolai was not only wrong, but willfully wrong—that something about the truth revealed in the affair of the poisoned communion wine was so unsettling that it had to be "denied out of existence" [*weggezweifelt*].[6] In his letter to Spalding, Lavater did not spell out what, precisely, Nicolai was so bent on "denying out of existence." The answer lies in a series of sermons Lavater delivered over a period of six months in 1777, which were published the following year shortly after the appearance of Nicolai's review: *Sermons on the Existence and the Effects of the Devil.*[7]

I

In March 1777, roughly four months after his second sermon on the affair of the poisoned communion wine, Lavater began a cycle of sermons on the temptation of Christ.[8] The main argument of the sermons was that the temptation marked an important stage in Jesus' apprenticeship as a man, bringing him closer to mankind by exposing him to the same evils that bedeviled all humanity. After the temptation, Jesus was able to understand how difficult it was for humanity to escape the snares of the devil, and humanity was able to recognize in Jesus the figure of a man subject to the same trials and tribulations as all others, and to exclaim with Pontius Pilate: "*Ecce homo.*" In preaching on such a subject, Lavater knew full well that he was swimming against the current. The "spirit of our philosophy," the "spirit of the eighteenth century," "the prejudices and the taste" of the age—all were disposed against any talk of things "miraculous" and "unusual," especially when such talk concerned Satan, whose very existence fashionable philosophers were inclined to doubt.[9] But such doubt only made it all the more important to represent the devil as he is and to explain his true nature, lest mankind be caught unawares and fall victim to his seductions.

Essentially, as Lavater saw it, the nature of the devil was to take pleasure in the sufferings and misfortunes of humanity, to spread evil out of what Lavater called "*Schadenfreude*."[10] It is difficult (and perhaps thankfully so) to find an adequate translation for *Schadenfreude* in English.[11] Even in German, however, the word is not unambiguous. In colloquial German, it often means little more than a kind of mischievous delight, the perverse pleasure of seeing a rival discomfited or someone high and mighty receive his comeuppance. But what Lavater meant by it was something altogether more sinister and also purer—a delight in the suffering of others uncontaminated by anything so base and mundane as revenge or envy. The devil, explained Lavater, performed evil for the sake of evil, just as God performed good for the sake of good. He was thus the mirror image of God, and diabolic *Schadenfreude* was just as pure in its negativity (although, admittedly, not as powerful) as was divine love in its positive character.[12] As presented by Lavater, in fact, the opposition between diabolic *Schadenfreude* and divine love looked uncannily like the oft-mentioned opposition between Sade and Kant, which, it has been argued, represented two poles in the dialectic of reason—Sadian characters breaking the moral law for the sake of breaking it, and the Categorical Imperative demanding the observance of the law out of a pure sense of duty.[13] But, of course, Lavater would have been shocked at such a comparison, not least because the dialectic between Kant and Sade unfolded, as it were, within human reason. For his part, Lavater vigorously rejected any suggestion that the devil might be little more than an allegory or symbol of the evil in man. He was, just like God, a physical presence in the world, and he appeared to man in all manner of physical disguises (not just in the caricatured disguises represented in art), which is why his ruses were so difficult to unmask and why so many unsuspecting victims succumbed to them. Victims of the devil were not diabolic by nature, but once they became agents of the devil, they could perform unspeakable deeds (like the poisoner of the communion wine, whom Lavater fully expected to find with the mark of Satan upon his forehead). It was a matter of no small importance, therefore, when fashionable philosophers sought to play down the physical reality of the devil or when they performed deft exegetical maneuvers on the Word of God to get around the textual evidence for the existence of the devil. They may have fancied that they were explaining Scripture by purifying and rationalizing it, but really they were not explaining anything at all—they were explaining away. And what, indeed, was the object of this "explaining away" [*Wegerklären*] if not the suppression of a disturbing and uncomfortable truth?[14]

Re-reading Lavater's letter to Spalding in the light of his sermons on the devil, we can now begin to understand what he was driving at. The disturbing and uncomfortable truth that Nicolai was bent on "denying out of existence" was the reality of diabolic *Schadenfreude*. He shared the "prejudice and the taste" of his age, which could not abide anything so seemingly irrational as the existence of the devil. When confronted with evidence to the contrary, therefore, he did not seek to explain it—he explained it away. He suppressed the truth, pure and simple, and so played into the hands of the devil, whose future victims would fall all the more easily into his net because they had been led to doubt the reality of the devil's existence. Far from being a "friend of humanity," as Nicolai claimed to be, he was, in effect, a friend of humanity's archenemy.

That Nicolai was an accomplice of the devil was a bit much to swallow, and even Lavater himself never made the accusation explicitly—he merely hinted at it. Still, Lavater found a measure of support in an anonymous review of Nicolai's pamphlet published in the *Frankfurter gelehrte Anzeigen* (*FGA*) in March 1779. The *FGA* was the leading organ of the Sturm und Drang; its publisher, Johann Conrad Deinet, was a personal friend and admirer of Lavater.[15] The support thus came from a friendly quarter, and its objective was to make out the best possible case for the Zurich pastor in the wake of Nicolai's attack. Even the best possible case did not go so far as to dispute the persuasiveness of Nicolai's critique, which, the reviewer admitted, had raised serious doubts about the official version of events. Nor did it endorse the rhetoric of Lavater's sermons, which the reviewer, like Nicolai, found somewhat intemperate. But whatever the intemperance of Lavater's rhetoric and the persuasiveness of Nicolai's critique, the reviewer considered it wrong—and indeed dangerous—to exclude the very possibility of such a crime as the poisoning of the communion wine:

> Such a deed requires almost too much wickedness to be admitted in the absence of very strong and indubitable proof. Herod's Slaughter of the Innocents was a monstrous deed! But this tyrant had a conceivable motive [*begreiflichen Bewegungsgrund*]. He labored under the illusion that spilling the blood of children who had given offense to no one was necessary to secure his throne. Indeed, wherever one finds bloodbaths . . . one discovers the same mistaken policy: that it is necessary to be wicked for reasons of self-interest and self-protection. And the same reasons underlie false religious zealotry. . . . But what ground or motive can a citizen have to execute 1,200 people by poisoning? It cannot be vengeance—all the communicants cannot possibly have offended him. It must be the purely inconceivable delight [*unbegreifliche Lust*] of seeing 1,000 people perish, feasting one's eyes upon a spectacle without parallel, playing the part of the Destroying Angel in a house of worship, finding unnatural pleasure in the thought of rewarding pious devotion with death. Such a deed without any advantage, without any motive of revenge, is not conceivable [*nicht begreiflich*]. And nevertheless—yes! On many occasions, deadly arsonists have set fire to an entire town, simply because they had received some punishment from the magistrate, and so condemned to the flames not merely their presumed persecutors but all the inhabitants of the town.[16]

In most instances, the reviewer was saying, evil sprang from the imperfections and limitations of human understanding—from what Leibniz would have called "metaphysical evil"—and such evil was "conceivable": men performed wicked deeds because they misconstrued their true interest. Still, the prevalence of this type of evil did not preclude the possibility of diabolic evil, however "inconceivable" it may appear. Both types of evil were possible.

None of this, to be sure, redeemed Lavater's most extreme charge, which claimed that Nicolai was suppressing the truth. But the review in the *FGA* suggested a reformulation of the charge in more defensible language: that Nicolai was not so much suppressing the truth as betraying his prejudice. For what was it if not a prejudice, albeit a prejudice of reason, to suppose that the crime had to have a rational explanation? Nicolai may have fancied that he occupied a position above the fray, from which he could judge impartially and expose the prejudices of others, but he, too, was subject to prejudice. His prejudice was that no one could have committed a crime so dreadful as the poisoning of the communion wine because such a crime could only have sprung from what was "inconceivable"—from pure, uncontaminated, disinterested *Schadenfreude*.[17]

II

Since we are on the subject of prejudice, this may be an appropriate moment for the author to reveal his own biases. I confess, as the reader may already have suspected, that I find Nicolai a far more congenial figure than Lavater. The Berlin Aufklärer, ally of Mendelssohn and Lessing and intrepid crusader against superstition and fanaticism, has, I believe, a far better claim to being a "friend of humanity" than his Zurich antagonist with his belief in miracles, his self-righteousness, his appeals for divine vengeance, and, as we shall see in the next chapter, his rather unpleasant role in local Zurich politics. But despite my preference for Nicolai, it is difficult for me to deny that Lavater and especially his anonymous ally in the *FGA* may have made an important point—or, at least, hinted at it. I do not mean, of course, the point about Nicolai being an accomplice of the devil (which we may discreetly put to one side). The fundamental point has to do with the prejudice of reason, which deserves a close examination.[18]

Consider the following statement of principle made by Nicolai in his review of Lavater's sermons:

> [N]ot a single possible motive [*Veranlassung*] can be adduced which could move a man to commit so devilish a crime, for it is not thinkable [*es läßt sich nicht denken*] that even the most wicked man would commit a crime both so unspeakably repugnant and so dangerous for its author, unless he had a direct and strong motive [*unmittelbare starke Veranlassung*].[19]

Because the criminal had to have had a motive, the crime as described in the official version was "unthinkable." This was a prejudice in the literal sense of a "pre-judgment" [*Vorurteil*]: It formed Nicolai's starting point and gave him the criterion by which to judge the plausibility of competing explanations. If an explanation provided an adequate account of motive, then it was plausible; otherwise, not. But such a procedure was tautological; in effect, it predetermined the outcome by its starting point and so trapped Nicolai in a vicious circle as closed and self-validating as the one that he had so brilliantly managed to crack. Nicolai had excluded the possibility of the devil, so he could not explain diabolic evil. He was, therefore, predisposed to explain it away. What other move could he have made?

Nicolai's predicament calls to mind the phrase that Hegel cited (incorrectly, as it turned out) from Goethe's *Faust*: "They have got rid of the Evil One—evil remains" [*Den Bösen sind sie los, das Böse ist geblieben*].[20] Eventually, to resolve this conundrum, Kant made the radical move of locating evil in human reason alone [*extra hominem, nil malum*], severing all connection between moral evil and physical evil, and granting to the former an ontological status denied to it by the Leibnizian tradition, which had treated evil only as a defect—a *privatio boni*. With this move, Kant not only detached the problem of evil from the framework of theodicy, he introduced an anthropological Manichaeanism, displacing the cosmic principles of light and dark onto man himself so that the battle between good and evil took place between two competing dispositions [*Gesinnungen*] within human reason: the one prompting man to obey the moral law out of a sense of duty, the other prompting him to give priority to considerations other than that of duty. But Kant did not arrive at this anthropological conception of radical evil until the 1790s.[21] Writing in the 1770s, Nicolai was still closer to Leibniz than he was to Kant—or, rather, he was somewhere in between. He could no longer conceive of the devil, but neither did he have any conception of radical evil as a potential inherent in man, so he fell back on what he called "natural reason."[22]

Essentially, what Nicolai meant by "natural reason" was the doctrine of "sufficient reason," or rather a weak version of that doctrine—what we might describe as a doctrine of "necessary reason." Generalizing the conclusions of the modern natural sciences, such a doctrine held that there must be some condition or set of conditions for everything that happens such that in the absence of that condition or set of conditions, the thing could not occur. From this standpoint, to conceive of anything was to explain where it came from, to understand it as the consequence of a set of conditions or a sequence of causes; and it followed, if one pursued the doctrine rigorously and systematically, that an uncaused cause or an unmoved mover was, quite literally, inconceivable. Now, to be sure, Nicolai never bothered to interrogate the wider implications of such a doctrine (which raised some rather troubling doubts about the rationality of the belief in God), least of all in his review of Lavater's sermons, the goal of which was limited and practical. Within the limited framework of his review, however, Nicolai did apply the doctrine rigorously and systematically, and that was why he dismissed the possibility of the crime as presented in the official version of events: such a crime was inconceivable because it seemed to spring from an unmoved mover—from a criminal who lacked, as the reviewer in the *FGA* aptly described it, a *Bewegungsgrund* (literally, "a ground of motion").[23]

The main problem with this type of argument was that it landed Nicolai (and not just Nicolai) in a place where he almost certainly did not wish to be: in a position uncomfortably close to that of the much-reviled Saint Augustine. To Nicolai and his comrades, scarcely anything could have been so detestable as the Augustinian doctrines of predestination and hereditary sin, which denied the possibility of human freedom, and which held that fallen humanity could not, by its own efforts, avoid sinning: *non posse non peccare*. In their view, Augustine bore the main responsibility for having converted the religion of Christ into the grim, dour, and misanthropic religion of the modern Church. And against this perverted form of Christianity, they took up their cudgels to defend human dignity and human freedom. (When Nicolai implied that Lavater was an "enemy of humanity," he was echoing the standard accusation made by Neologians against Augustine.) But what became of human dignity and human freedom if one applied the doctrine of sufficient reason as rigorously and systematically as did Nicolai in his review of Lavater's sermons? How could one maintain that man was free and that he could behave morally on his own initiative if one excluded as inconceivable the very possibility of an unmoved mover, of an action without a "ground of motion." Strictly speaking, of course, Nicolai's review excluded only the possibility of diabolical immorality, not of morality as such. But the two things were logically connected since morality would be meaningless if man were not free to choose its opposite. So it could be argued (and Friedrich Heinrich Jacobi would soon make an argument of this sort) that the doctrine of sufficient reason negated the possibility of morality, and that it did so because it led to a naturalistic determinism as thoroughgoing in its own way as the theological doctrines of predestination and hereditary sin developed by Augustine.[24] Even Lavater held out the possibility that man could resist the temptations of evil by choosing to place his faith in God.

Eventually, as with most of the problems raised by the Aufklärung, it fell to Kant to work out a solution, which he presented as an answer to the third antinomy of reason.[25] According to Kant, both the doctrine of determinism and that of human freedom were true, so that man was both, as it were, free and unfree: as a phenomenal being, located in time and space, he was subject to the laws of causality; as noumenon, he was free of those laws and his reason could determine his will, thus providing the necessary condition for the experience of moral obligation (which Kant took up in *The Critique of Practical Reason*). With the distinction between phenomenal and noumenal, however, Kant had entered a realm into which Nicolai was either unwilling or unable to venture.

SO WHAT DO THE VARIOUS CONTRADICTIONS IN Nicolai's position add up to? And what of the larger significance of his debate with Lavater?

To say that Nicolai's critique of Lavater rested on prejudice is not necessarily to imply that the content of the prejudice was wrong or that it led inevitably to erroneous conclusions. Occasionally, as some of the most prominent figures in the Aufklärung were prepared to concede, prejudices may turn out to be true—or at least useful—and the overall persuasiveness of Nicolai's account is testimony to the heuristic value of his prejudice in favor of rational explanation: his account was almost certainly closer to the truth of what had happened in the cathedral than was Lavater's alternative.[26]

But the debate between Nicolai and Lavater was only partly about what had happened in the cathedral. As it unfolded, it became, in fact, two debates—or, if one prefers, one debate operating on two levels. On the most basic level, its object was the event in the Zurich cathedral, its goal to clarify the mystery surrounding that event. On another level, however, its object was interpretation as such, its goal the self-clarification of thought, and on this more formal level, Nicolai's prejudice did appear as an error: a provisional judgment that he treated unreflectively as if it were certain and indubitable. During the course of the debate, of course, neither Nicolai nor Lavater distinguished explicitly between the two levels of the debate. But the distinction between the form of a prejudice and its content was central to the theory of prejudice developed by the Aufklärung, and in view of such a distinction, it is quite possible to maintain that Lavater was simultaneously both right and wrong: right on one level about the prejudice of reason as a formal error of thought; wrong on another about the wine's being poisoned.[27]

Let us put to one side, therefore, the question who won the debate. The main point is that Nicolai did not have the last word—that for all of its persuasiveness, his critique was itself subject to critique inasmuch as it, too, embodied a certain prejudice unacknowledged by Nicolai himself. Critiquing prejudice was one of the central goals of the Aufklärung, but we can now see that it was not (if I may be permitted one last military metaphor) a one-shot affair. It was a process, open-ended and continuous, and it embraced not only those who identified themselves with the Aufklärung but also its self-styled opponents. Wittingly or unwittingly, Lavater was participating in it as soon as he decided to respond to Nicolai's review, for it was impossible to expose the prejudice of reason otherwise than through rational argument. The critique of Enlightenment belonged to the process of Enlightenment.[28]

Whether such a process ever comes to an end, whether it ever reaches a final resting place that does not itself rest upon prejudice—the equivalent, in terms of critique, to an "unmoved mover"—that question I leave to professional philosophers.

Chapter Seven
The Sword of Justice

BY NOW, I FEAR, THE READER IS LIKELY to be feeling a bit dizzy: from the poisoning of the communion wine to the third antinomy of reason was a steep climb, indeed! It is time that we return to the nether regions of the Zurich plain.

While the battle was raging between Lavater and Nicolai, the affair of the poisoned communion wine had died down in Zurich. In 1780, however, it rose, phoenix-like, from the ashes and became entwined with one of the most spectacular and horrific treason cases of the late eighteenth century: the affair of "unhappy Pastor Waser." I say "horrific" because the trial and condemnation of Waser truly horrified the German-speaking public. To many contemporaries, Waser seemed to have been the victim of a judicial murder, a sacrificial lamb slaughtered on the altar of raison d'état. The execution of Waser shattered the complacent belief that such a brutal and cynical act of repression could no longer occur in an age of Enlightenment, let alone in Switzerland, the land of William Tell, republican virtue, and free, self-governing citizens.

Before the execution of Waser, Switzerland was the object of a veritable cult among the educated classes in Germany. Afterward, some of its former admirers would have been inclined to agree with Goethe, who had his doubts about the myth of Swiss liberty, and who gave expression to those doubts when he passed through Switzerland in 1779, one year before Waser perished beneath the executioner's sword:

> The Swiss are said to be free. Free, these prosperous burghers in their walled cities? Free, these poor devils surrounded by rocks and cliffs? Oh, what one can make people believe, especially if one adds an old fairy tale preserved for all time in spirits! Once upon a time they rid themselves of a tyrant and for that moment they were able to imagine that they were free. Then, by a remarkable sort of rebirth, the beloved sun created out of the rotting corpse of the persecutor a whole swarm of little tyrants. The Swiss continue to recount the old fairy tale, indulging in the illusion that once upon a time they had made themselves free and remain so today.[1]

Who was the "unhappy pastor Waser"? And how, in 1780, did he suddenly come under suspicion of having committed a crime, the investigation of which had lain dormant since Wirz's release from prison more than three years earlier? To answer these questions, we need to say a few words about Waser's career and the historical context in which it took shape.[2]

I

As a theology student in the 1760s, Waser belonged to the same generation as Lavater and passed through the same school, absorbing the influence of Bodmer, who was professor of history at the Carolinum. In both of the young theology students, the elder Bodmer inspired a passionate "patriotism," a commitment to the commonweal, whose goal was to expose and redress corruption and abuses of power.[3] Unlike Lavater, however, who strayed from this youthful commitment, gradually becoming a supporter and apologist of the oligarchic elite, Waser remained faithful to it. During his short life, he suffered repeated hardships on account of his convictions.

Waser's problems began in 1770 just as soon as he received his first appointment as pastor in Riesbach, a parish just outside the walls of the city of Zurich. The early 1770s coincided with a period of dire economic conditions throughout Switzerland and much of Germany.[4] A series of abnormally cold years led to failing harvests and widespread famine, the effects of which strained the limited capacity of the local poor relief in Waser's parish. His compassion stirred by the suffering of his parishioners, Waser pressed the local officials of the district to increase tax revenues for the support of the indigent. When he discovered evidence that the officials were misappropriating those revenues, he brought his discovery to the attention of the two *Obervögte*, the governors who oversaw the administration of Riesbach from their residence within the walls of the city. After reviewing the evidence presented to them by Waser, the governors agreed that funds had been misappropriated, but they were lax in meting out punishment and did little to rectify the underlying problem. So, eventually, Waser took his case elsewhere, appealing over the heads of the Obervögte to the committee on poor relief of the city of Zurich. For this act of insubordination, however, he was severely punished. In 1774, the Small Council suspended him from his ministry and refused to overturn the suspension, despite Waser's repeated requests for reinstatement. Debarred from exercising his profession, the young pastor moved back to Zurich with his wife, whose dowry provided the couple with its only means of support.

In Zurich during the late 1770s, Waser shifted his attention to "statistical" studies devoted to the population of the canton. At the time, statistics was a burgeoning field of study. It enjoyed a great deal of prestige on account of its quantitative method, the value of which had proved itself so dramatically in the natural sciences (though not yet in chemistry, as we noted earlier), and it dovetailed with the concerns of cameralists and enlightened administrators, who needed reliable information on economic and demographic trends in order to introduce necessary reforms. In itself, therefore, "statistics" was not a subversive discipline, nor did Waser undertake his statistical studies in a subversive spirit. Initially, in fact, he enjoyed the patronage of the Zurich elite. He became a member of the *Physikalische Gesellschaft*, whose founder, Johannes Gessner, had been one of Waser's professors at the Carolinum. Far from discouraging Waser, Gessner took the young pastor under his wings. He recognized that Waser had a good head for figures and a tremendous capacity for work, and he hoped that Waser's studies would be of considerable utility to the government. The main problem was that information useful to the government could also prove compromising if it were made public. One of Waser's demographic studies uncovered evidence of a stagnating and even declining population in certain rural districts.[5] To Waser (and indeed to cameralists in general), it was axiomatic that a growing population was good, that it was both cause and symptom of economic prosperity. So the evidence of a stagnating and declining population demanded an explanation, which Waser believed he had found in the trade in mercenaries practiced by the Swiss cantons. With this, Waser was touching upon a very delicate subject indeed, for the trade in mercenaries was not only a useful safety valve for disposing of excess population, it was a major source of fiscal revenue. Yet Waser condemned the lucrative trade without restraint, documenting with hard statistical evidence the population losses it caused; and he drove home his point with anecdotes such as the following, which appeared in the introduction to a study provocatively entitled, "Swiss Blood, French Money":

> With the General Stuppa in attendance, the Marquis de Louvois, the War Minister of Louis XIV, is supposed once to have said to his king: "Sire, if you had all the gold and silver paid by yourself and by your royal ancestors to the Swiss, you would be able to pave the highway from Paris to Basel with Thalers." Whereupon General Stuppa declared: "Sire, that may well be so; but if it were possible to collect all the blood shed by our nation for you and your royal ancestors, one could build a navigable canal from Paris to Basel."[6]

Add to all of this the fact that the storm over the renewal of the French alliance had only recently subsided, and it is little wonder that the authorities in Zurich tried to silence Waser. In this, however, they failed. Undeterred by the prohibition placed on most of his writings in Zurich, Waser published them abroad in the journal edited by the Göttingen professor August Ludwig von Schlözer, *Correspondence on Historical and Political Matters.*[7] He delivered to Schlözer some of his most incendiary works—the one on the Swiss trade in mercenaries with France ("Swiss Blood, French Money"), his demographic study of Zurich, and a short work on the war treasury in Zurich, which revealed how taxes intended to defray the costs of armaments for poorer citizens had been diverted to other, less laudable ends. And to these works from his own pen he added the transcript of two speeches delivered before one of the guild assemblies in 1777 by a Zuricher named Johann Bürkli, who had denounced the French alliance and accused the government of having violated the "fundamental laws" of the Zurich constitution. It is hard to imagine a more defiant gesture than the publication of works such as these, which appeared, one after the other, in Schlözer's journal during the early months of 1780.[8] At stake in this act of defiance was nothing less than the principle of "publicity," whose immense significance to the educated classes in German-speaking Europe calls for a brief explanation.

II

Earlier, in discussing the Aufklärung, I emphasized just how important theological issues were to the German public. Interest in theology was indeed a constant feature of the entire period. Gradually, however, the range of public debate began to expand so that it came to embrace not only theology but politics, too.[9] The decades of the 1770s and 1780s saw the creation of a series of political journals, such as the one edited by Schlözer in Göttingen, whose self-appointed function was to make the state and its policies objects of public scrutiny by disseminating information on political matters—much of it, like Waser's studies, in statistical form. To Schlözer and a great many of his contemporaries, the practice of publicity alone seemed to provide a powerful weapon against despotism. Their belief was that such a practice, if implemented systematically, would yield a regime of transparency; that in such a regime, the prince would be led, willy-nilly, to make his policies conform to the dictates of reason as embodied in public opinion; and that, therefore, all arbitrary acts of the prince's will would cease, giving way to a "state of law" [*Rechtsstaat*] even in the absence of representative assemblies, estates, or other intermediary powers. Such a belief might seem rather fanciful—even magical—but it was widespread, and not only in Germany. In 1781, one year after Waser's statistical studies appeared in Schlözer's journal, Necker, the French finance minister, took the unprecedented step of publishing a balance sheet of royal finances, the famous *Compte rendu*. At the time, Necker was under attack from various quarters for having implemented a program of reform. With the *Compte rendu*, therefore, he was attempting to fend off his attackers by appealing for the support of "public opinion." Such an appeal marked a dramatic repudiation of the traditional principle that affairs of state were secrets of the king—*arcana imperii*—rather than matters of public concern.[10]

So the idea of publicity was, so to speak, in the air. But not in Zurich—or, in any case, not among the ruling oligarchy in Zurich, who were committed to maintaining the secrecy of politics, especially after the guild protests of 1777. By publishing his statistical studies in Schlözer's journal, therefore, Waser was not only exposing abuses of power as he had done when he had served as a pastor in Riesbach in the early 1770s—he was challenging the very nature of politics in Old Regime Zurich, opposing the principle of publicity to that of secrecy. This challenge called forth a swift and brutal response.

ON THE MORNING OF 17 MARCH 1780, GENdarmes arrived suddenly at Waser's apartment and led him, still clothed in his dressing gown and slippers, to the town hall, where he was placed under arrest. Here, Waser may well have occupied the same cell in which Wirz had been imprisoned three-and-a-half years earlier, but he did not remain there for long. Reserved mainly for prisoners under investigative arrest or those whose social status demanded special consideration, the town hall offered conditions of imprisonment far less onerous than those of the infamous tower of Wellenberg, the Zurich Bastille, which was located on an island in the Limmat. Sensing the danger to which he was exposed, Waser seized the opportunity offered him by the comparatively lax conditions in the town hall, and on 20 March, three days after his arrest, he made an attempt at escape. First, he stopped up the keyhole in the door to his cell so that the guard standing watch would not be able to hear him. Then he constructed a makeshift rope from his bed sheet. And finally, after fastening the rope to the leg of a heavy oak table, he lowered himself out of the window of his cell into the Limmat, which flowed alongside the town hall. Unfortunately for poor Waser, the rope broke, sending him plunging into the river, and the noise of his fall alerted the guard so that he was quickly fished out of the water by a nearby barge. Several days later, twelve heavily armed gendarmes came to escort Waser to the Wellenberg, where he was consigned, bound in chains, to a dungeon and placed under constant surveillance.

With Waser's imprisonment, however, the authorities had to confront a different sort of problem. True, Waser had been silenced. But coming so soon after the guild conflicts, his imprisonment could easily have backfired, converting Waser into a martyr in the eyes of his fellow citizens. From the standpoint of the authorities, therefore, it was vitally important to saddle Waser with additional crimes so as to blacken his reputation, and to represent him in the most sinister light possible. To this end, they ordered a search of Waser's house, hoping that it might yield evidence compromising to the prisoner—and indeed it did. It turned up documents taken by Waser from the archives, one of which, the so-called *Kyburger Brief*, was especially compromising because it provided support for territorial claims made by the Habsburgs on a rural district of the canton. Why the *Kyburger Brief* was in Waser's possession is not

FIGURE 13. Wellenberg, prison tower built in the thirteenth century, destroyed in 1838. Etching by Johann Balthasar Bullinder the elder, 1772.

altogether clear. In his perilous position, Waser may have retained it with the intention of blackmailing the authorities. Whatever his real intention, however, the authorities put the worst possible construction upon it, using the discovery of the document to present Waser as both a traitor and a thief. And finally, to damn Waser completely, they reached into their portfolio of unsolved cases, dusted off an old dossier, and threw it at the prisoner: in April 1780, with Waser imprisoned in the Wellenberg, they began spreading the accusation that Waser had been complicitous in the poisoning of the communion wine.

Were there any real grounds for suspecting Waser as an accomplice in the poisoning of the communion wine? The main evidence to support such a suspicion was that Waser had his own key to the cathedral, where he went occasionally to conduct astronomical observations from one of the cathedral towers. (Waser dabbled in the natural sciences at the same time that he pursued his statistical studies.) Because the sexton had found no sign of a break-in on the morning of the communion service, it was assumed that the poisoner must have possessed his own key. Add to this Waser's well-known grievance against the civilian and ecclesiastical authorities (who had suspended him from his ministry), and it was possible to claim that he had poisoned the wine as an act of revenge. But the authorities did not, in fact, go to any great lengths to pin the crime on him. The subject of the poisoned communion wine came up briefly during Waser's second interrogation on 13 April 1780. On this occasion, the investigators simply asked Waser point-blank whether he had been involved in the poisoning. When he vigorously protested his innocence, declaring that "he hope[d] for the sake of God never to have been under suspicion on this account and never to have given any cause for such suspicions," they allowed the matter to drop.[11]

It is difficult to escape the conclusion, therefore, that the accusation of Waser's participation in the poisoning sprang from a rather cynical maneuver on the part of his judges, who scarcely believed the accusation themselves. Whether or not they believed it, however, the accusation seems to have succeeded in discrediting the prisoner. Many decades later, Johann Heinrich Füssli, the well-known publisher and successor to Bodmer as professor of history at the Carolinum, recalled with obvious embarrassment how the government of Zurich had proceeded against Waser. "More than anything," Füssli wrote, "what envenomed the hatred . . . against Waser was the absurd suspicion that he had poisoned . . . the bread [*sic*] of the holy communion." According to Füssli, the whole business of the poisoning had been nothing more than an "old wives' tale spread by Lavater," which had made Zurich "the laughing stock of all of Germany," but "it served singularly well to consummate his [Waser's] ruin."[12]

And, indeed, no one could have applied himself more diligently to ruining Waser's reputation than Lavater, who viewed the prisoner as both a traitor and a dangerously unbalanced individual. Writing to Goethe in early April 1780, Lavater expressed his belief that Waser had played some role in the poisoning, and he added with obvious anticipation: "Next Thursday he [Waser] will be questioned in the presence of the executioner on the subject of the poisoning."[13] Later, after Waser had denied playing any role in the poisoning, Lavater admitted that the circumstantial evidence against the prisoner was too weak to warrant any further questioning, but he continued to harbor suspicions. "If he [Waser] is not the poisoner of the communion wine," Lavater wrote to Goethe on 12 May, "then I shall never again in my life give room to any suspicion, however likely."[14] In his former classmate and clerical colleague, Lavater seems to have discerned the physiognomy of the satanic figure he had been seeking in vain since autumn 1776. And now that he had found him, he was eager to confront him directly.

III

At ten o'clock on the morning of 27 May, while the judges were engaged in their final deliberations on Waser's fate, Lavater set off for the Wellenberg in order to visit the prisoner in his cell, and he stayed there for several hours, later recording his conversation with Waser in a work entitled *Waser's Last Hours*, copies of which circulated in manuscript. *Waser's Last Hours* is a disturbing text. Bad enough that Lavater accepted the "pastoral" task of preparing a former colleague for execution, urging the prisoner to cleanse his soul by confessing to all the crimes imputed to him by the magistrates. The really disagreeable thing is that Lavater exploited the occasion for his own self-promotion, styling himself as the magnanimous consoler who extended the hand of Christian love to a poor and reprobate criminal and who was even prepared to admit his own (admittedly, rather trivial) faults into the bargain. And yet, for all its disagreeable aspects, *Waser's Last Hours* contains an element of drama (call it sordid drama), which Lavater strove to heighten: two former classmates, whose lives had taken such divergent paths, reunited in the gloomy dungeon of the Wellenberg—the one an internationally renowned defender of Christianity, the other a fallen man contemplating the prospect of his imminent end.[15]

Roughly midway through *Waser's Last Hours*, the conversation came round to the subject of the poisoned communion wine.[16] Waser was prepared to confess himself a sinner—indeed, "the greatest of all sinners"—but never, he proclaimed, had he lost his "faith in God and Jesus Christ," nor had "God allowed him to fall so far" as to commit the crimes imputed to him:

> People have wanted to saddle me with blasphemies and crimes of which I have never dreamed and which I despise from the depths of my soul. Nothing caused me so much pain as this. People wanted to make me out to be the most monstrous criminal, even though, in my whole life, I have never knowingly given any cause for people to suspect me of an irreligious deed or blasphemous sentiments against religion.

To Waser's astonishment, Lavater then confessed that he, too, had shared such suspicions, although he claimed that his suspicions had now been removed, and for this, he pronounced himself guilty, magnanimously begging forgiveness in a spirit of contrition and self-abasement that, so the reader is given to understand, stood in contrast to the stubborn pride of the incorrigible Waser:

> Yes! I, too, was so unfortunate as to have harbored such suspicions. Indeed, on one or two occasions, I mentioned to others that you might have had a part in the abominable atrocity to which you have alluded. Not true—Forgive me! I am ashamed. Now all suspicion has been completely extinguished in me, and so far as it lies in my power, I shall smother every spark of such suspicion in others.

With this, the discussion might have come to an end. But instead, Waser disclosed what he thought of the whole poisoned wine business: "Truly, Herr Deacon, I believe that there is nothing to the affair at all, that it was all just a great big mistake. I cannot imagine any man so villainous." This was rather like waving a red flag before a raging bull. Now, suddenly, instead of administering pastoral care to a man in the antechamber of death, Lavater spoke excitedly and passionately, as if he were sitting opposite the "doubter" from Berlin (and perhaps, indeed, he may have forgotten himself for just a moment and imagined Nicolai imprisoned in the Wellenberg—oh, what sweet *Schadenfreude* that would have been!):

> It is no less certain that I am sitting here than it is that the most abominable of all deeds occurred. The five finger prints left on the table cloth of the communion table are no mistake! The witnesses! The libels! They are certainly no mistake. It is all real.[17]

Waser had no wish to provoke Lavater's rage over this issue. So he backed off, conceding that "no, it was not a mistake at all, it was all real." But by now, Lavater had worked himself into such a fury that he was unstoppable:

> And a deed perfectly in the spirit of Satan! All-knowing, merciful God! It is thus certain that there lives in our midst a man who flings himself at the throats of the innocent and performs deeds of which even the most blasphemous would judge themselves incapable! A man without conscience and without humanity! Take pity on this most infamous of men and take pity on our fatherland, which nourishes such a monster in its womb.

And so it ended—the discussion on the subject of the poisoned communion wine, which was not really a discussion at all but an harangue delivered by Lavater.

While Waser endured this harangue, the judges were rendering their verdict, which the tower guard communicated to Waser in the presence of Lavater shortly after eleven o'clock. The deliberations had been contentious—only a slim majority voted to convict—and the final verdict dropped all mention of the poisoned communion wine. Still, Waser was condemned of high treason and ordered, in the words of the official judgment, to be "delivered over to the executioner, who shall bind his hands in front and then lead him to the usual place of execution, where a sword shall be used to sever his head from his body, such that a wheel may pass between them and he may thus fully atone for his crime and give satisfaction to the secular court and to the laws."[18] Later, on the same afternoon, Waser was brought before the town hall, and his condemnation was read aloud. From there he was led out beyond the walls of the city, where a crowd had formed to witness his execution. According to those witnesses, Waser bore himself with dignity, maintaining his composure until the very end. But he did not play his part according to the script that Lavater had proposed to him several hours earlier. Fearing a sudden movement of sympathy in favor of Waser, Lavater had urged the condemned man to address conciliatory words to the crowd of spectators, some edifying remark such as: "Stay true to your calling," "Trust the magistrates," or "Beware the unhappy consequences of vengeance."[19] When the time came for Waser to pronounce the words suggested to him by Lavater, however, he kept silent. Then he mounted the scaffold, placed his head on the block, and, as the executioner raised the sword of justice, cried out, "Lord Jesus, I die for you."

IN THE AFTERMATH OF WASER'S EXECUTION, Lavater bent his efforts toward justifying the verdict of the magistrates, denouncing the character of the condemned man in a published sermon and in countless letters to correspondents.[20] But Lavater's defense of the verdict was submerged in a veritable torrent of pamphlets and journal articles that expressed outrage and indignation at the injustice committed against a respected man of letters. In Göttingen, Schlözer was so furious upon learning of Waser's fate that he resolved to devote an entire issue of his journal to exposing "the terror of oligarchic despotism."[21] Within the compass of this book, we could not possibly survey all of the angry responses to Waser's execution, so let us take our leave of the "unhappy pastor Waser" by considering just one of those responses, the epitaph to

Waser written by Friedrich Nicolai in a letter to a correspondent in Basel. Looking back over the events in Zurich during the previous four years, Nicolai discerned a coherent pattern in which all the elements fitted together:

> When one reads Bürkli's speeches in Schlözer's *Correspondence* and considers how cruelly the authorities behaved toward the man who made them known, one feels confirmed in what I have long believed: that the whole foolish story of poisoning in 1776 was merely thrown at the people, like a decoy to a whale, in order to divert its attention from the alliance with France and from the question raised by the alliance whether the Council has the right on its own to make decisions in matters of war, peace, and foreign alliances, or whether the decision belongs to the Council and the people together. Waser's fate is meant to provide a terrifying example, making clear to others that death awaits anyone who raises the question anew. Thus do those with power behave in republics, and thus do they behave in monarchies.[22]

In the light of Nicolai's conspiracy theory, two final observations spring to mind. The first is that Nicolai's theory fitted quite well in an age haunted by the specter of Jesuits, philosophes, Masonic plots, and Illuminati. In the eighteenth century, conspiracy theories proliferated with wild abandon, and if they found such fertile soil in the age of Enlightenment, this was in no small part because the ideal of publicity espoused by Schlözer and Waser was so far from being realized. To rulers immured in secrecy, one could ascribe all manner of sinister designs, giving free rein to a conspiratorial fantasy unchecked by the possibility of verification. Perhaps, one might counter, the ideal of publicity is intrinsically incapable of being realized. If so, that would explain why all ages, and not just the Enlightenment, have given rise to conspiracy theories: however bright the light of publicity shines, man retains an ineradicable element of opacity, and perfect transparency, as Lavater would have said, belongs only to the elect in the next world. Such, indeed, was the lesson of the French Revolution, which spawned no end of conspiracy theories, in spite (or perhaps because) of its commitment to enforcing transparency. But for all that the ideal may be unrealizable, publicity has existed in greater and lesser degrees. In Old Regime Zurich, it existed scarcely at all. Its absence fostered the sort of suspicion to which Nicolai gave expression.

The second observation is that conspiracy theories are not necessarily wrong, and that Nicolai's may well have contained a kernel of truth. Not, of course, that the authorities stage-managed the whole affair of the poisoned communion wine from the beginning—that implication of Nicolai's theory seems too far-fetched to be believed. The kernel of truth wrapped in an otherwise incredible theory was that the affair of the poisoned communion wine had been useful. It gave the government an accusation to throw at Waser, it gave the guild opposition a language with which to denounce the government, it gave Lavater a stick with which to beat the Aufklärung, and it gave Nicolai the opportunity to ridicule Lavater. Whatever actually happened on 12 September 1776, the affair of the poisoned communion wine served a variety of functions for a range of different people. No wonder that it lived such a long life.

Chapter Eight
The Search for Truth

HAT DID ACTUALLY HAPPEN IN the cathedral in Zurich on 12 September 1776? So far, we have passed in review the interpretations of others, watched as contemporaries struggled to apprehend the truth of what had transpired on that fateful day. It is now time to hazard my own interpretation. Here, for what it is worth, is my reading of the available evidence.

At bottom, the case for poisoning stands or falls on the results of the chemical analyses. On this point, Nicolai was absolutely right. And he was right, too, that the results were contradictory, that preconceptions on the part of the scientists compromised their accuracy, and that, therefore, the scientific evidence is not convincing. Add to all of this the dove test performed by Hirzel (of which Nicolai was unaware because the scientific reports were never published) and also the strong likelihood that none of the communicants died as a result of poisoning, and only one conclusion seems possible: the wine was not poisoned.

But mysteries persist even if one discounts the explanation of poisoning. The wine in the barrels, though not that in the tin cans or that used in the Predigerkirche, contained a variety of substances, identified by Gessner as seeds and plant parts, as well as a thick glue-like sediment. Gessner was an expert in botany, so his identification of plants carries more weight than his identification of arsenic. But even if he were wrong about which seeds and plant parts were in the wine, the fact remains that a number of strange substances tarnished the wine in the wooden barrels, which had a foul odor, a repulsive taste, and a murky color absent from all the other wine samples. So the wine in the barrels must have undergone some kind of transformation between Wednesday night and Thursday morning. Nicolai's alternative explanation—that of wine additives—cannot account for this because it requires tampering at the source (i.e., in the wine cellar), nor is it likely that moldy wood alone could have produced so dramatic a transformation. It is difficult to escape the conclusion, therefore, that someone dumped some highly disagreeable "stuff"—not poison, just "stuff"—into the wine barrels during the night when they lay exposed and unguarded in the nave of the cathedral. But who was that someone? And what motive could he have had for behaving as he did?

My own suspicion is that the someone was our old friend gravedigger Wirz, and that his motive was *Schadenfreude*—not the diabolic sort, to be sure, but ordinary and prosaic *Schadenfreude*, that mischievous delight which comes from performing a prank such as placing a tack on the teacher's chair. I believe, moreover, that if I had the opportunity to present my thesis to Friedrich Nicolai, I could persuade him of it. Nicolai was a reasonable fellow, so he would admit that Wirz could have performed the deed (he was in the tower on the night in question and abandoned his post shortly after midnight), and that such a deed was perfectly "conceivable." Wirz hated clergymen and the Antistes Ulrich above all others. On this point, the testimony of witnesses is fairly strong. No doubt the resentment felt by Wirz had been accumulating over the years. But for how long could it continue to build without triggering an explosion? Eventually, Wirz could endure the situation no longer. He decided to take revenge—and not only that, but to take in the spectacle of his revenge. When questioned on the matter, Wirz testified that he had attended the communion service in the gallery of the cathedral, and none of the other witnesses contradicted him. Imagine, then, Wirz's secret delight as he sat, expectantly, in the gallery on the General Day of Prayer and Repentance, surveying the scene stretched out beneath him. Oh, what joy he must have felt to observe his black-coated tormentors squirm and to see the pained expression on the face of the Antistes as it dawned on him that something had gone terribly wrong! Now, to be sure, such an account does presuppose a high degree of irreverence toward one of the most sacred rites of the Church. But such irreverence is hardly inconceivable. Not only anticlericalism but acts of desecration had a long history in the popular culture of medieval and Renaissance Europe, culminating in the Reformation, which was nothing if not a great frenzy of desecration: Protestant crowds overturned altars, smashed images, trampled communion wafers, and left human excrement on holy-water basins.[1] Once I had explained all of this to Nicolai, he would concede that my explanation was more plausible than his, although he would hasten to add that my explanation, too, is far from being proved—and on that score, he would be right.

But if I laid out this same explanation before Lavater, his reaction would be altogether different. Probably, I would not even have the opportunity to complete my explanation—Lavater would cut me off beforehand and then subject me to an harangue of the sort he delivered to the "unhappy Pastor Waser," repeating the usual litany of "proofs" in support of his contention that the wine had been poisoned. In the light of such "proofs," he would argue, my explanation could only have sprung from a wish to suppress the truth and to trivialize evil, and it was, therefore, a kind of "revisionism" (he would not, of course, have used that word exactly), which was all the more appalling because it was being practiced upon the most monstrous crime in all of history. I can all but hear Lavater's angry voice ringing out at me, and I can picture him grimacing and sighing and raising his hands to the heavens. As I imagine the scene, I feel uneasy, for some very troubling associations come flooding into my mind, and it begins to dawn on me that there may be reason in Lavater's folly.

LIVING AT THE BEGINNING OF A NEW MILLENnium, we have just emerged from the bloodiest and most violent century in all of history. Its record of atrocities haunts our collective memory; its vast anonymous graveyards stretch out before our mind's eye—the rows of crosses laid out upon the battlefield of Verdun, the mangled bodies entombed beneath the rubble of Hiroshima, the prison camps of Siberia—as if to mock our most cherished hopes for the future of humanity. Such horrors challenge rational understanding, and none more so than the supreme horror in a century of horrors: the systematic murder of millions of European Jews.[2] In the wake of the Holocaust, who would be so bold as to deny on principle man's potential for the type of moral depravity described by Lavater? Take away the devil, and Lavater's account of diabolic *Schadenfreude* seems chillingly prescient.[3]

Prescient, and yet strangely out of harmony with much of twentieth-century thought. What distinguished Lavater's notion of diabolic *Schadenfreude* was its uncompromising radicalism. It posited an absolute foundation for evil, declaring, in effect, that it was impossible to dig any deeper, that the devil marked the unsurpassable limit to rational thought because no antecedent cause drove him to commit evil deeds, which he performed simply for their own sake—out of *Schadenfreude*. Whether in its Christian or its secular form, however, this kind of radical approach to the problem of evil has lost virtually all of its currency. It comports ill with those currents of philosophy usually subsumed under the heading "postmodern," whose distinguishing characteristic is precisely that they are antifoundationalist.[4] It makes no sense at all when judged from the standpoint of psychoanalysis and the social sciences, which have ensnared modern man in such a tight web of impersonal forces and drives that he has all but vanished as a responsible moral agent, whether for good or for ill.[5] Hence the paradox of our current situation: on the one hand, unprecedented horror; on the other, a growing incapacity to conceive of radical evil. That anyone—even

Hitler—might be capable of performing an evil act freely and knowingly simply to exult at the suffering of others has become well-nigh unthinkable.[6]

Faced with this paradox, Lavater would very likely feel vindicated—but not only (or even mainly) because the horrors of the twentieth century lend credence to his notion of diabolic *Schadenfreude*. He would feel vindicated, I think, because he would regard such a paradox as an illustration of the moral perils that result from the prejudice in favor of rational explanation. He had warned about those perils in the eighteenth century, arguing that a thoroughly rational picture of man and the world undermines the human capacity to experience *both* wonder and outrage, that it leads *both* to forgetfulness of God and to moral evasion. And here, in our current situation, he would find the proof that his warning had been justified. Explain evil in rational terms alone, and you do not explain it at all; you explain it away. *Tout comprendre, c'est tout pardonner.*

Looking back from the standpoint of the present, I do not think that we can avoid conceding to Lavater the power of his insight. But does that mean that we have come to the end of the debate and that Lavater gets the last word? Not necessarily. The problem with Lavater's position is that it, too, is one sided. If Nicolai was predisposed to explain evil away, Lavater was predisposed to find it—and find it he did, even where it may not have been present at all. Lavater's position thus presents its own danger, not that of moral evasion, but that of fanaticism. Not all acts of bloodletting, not even the most appalling episodes of modern warfare, are traceable to some sort of radical evil: most soldiers really are just cogs in the wheel of some gigantic military machine; most criminals really do commit their crimes for reasons of greed or personal vengeance or on account of poverty or because passions becloud their judgment. To assume otherwise is, whether literally or figuratively, to *demonize* them. The point, then, is not that Nicolai speaks to us today as from another world and that across the war-scarred landscapes and the vast graveyards of the twentieth century his voice can no longer reach us. However un-self-critical it may sometimes have been, his spirited defense of reason is still worth heeding, but so, too, are the admonitions of Lavater. And listening to the debate between them from the standpoint of the present, we are especially well placed to discern the synthesis toward which their debate was moving—a synthesis that preserves the commitment to rational explanation and yet remains ever attentive to the limits of reason. Most crimes lend themselves to the type of analysis offered by Nicolai; a few rare exceptions do not.

Did the affair of the poisoned communion wine belong to the category of exceptions? I doubt it. My account of what occurred in the cathedral differs from Nicolai's in some points of detail (it rejects his position on the matter of the wine additives), but it is much closer to his account than it is to Lavater's, for the motive of revenge I am imputing to Wirz has nothing to do with radical evil. In my account, *Schadenfreude* does not function as the ultimate determining ground of Wirz's action; it is itself simply an emotional response to mounting frustration—to frustration such as a somewhat intemperate and explosive member of the urban working class might very well have felt after laboring for decades under the stern, moral supervision of the reformed Protestant clergy. Most of us, I think, can understand such an emotion; some of us (not too many, I hope) may even identify with it, experiencing a little bit of vicarious *Schadenfreude* at the distance of more than two hundred years.[7] If I am right, then all the evidence lends itself quite well to a rational explanation, one that is different from Nicolai's in certain respects but that nevertheless belongs to the same universe of discourse. Basically, Nicolai's interpretative position is mine too, except that Nicolai embraced his position as a prejudice and I am adopting it as a conclusion. It is possible, however, that my conclusion is mistaken; and if the affair of the poisoned communion wine yields any lesson, it is undoubtedly the danger of reaching an overhasty conclusion. Rather than attempting to tie up all the loose ends, therefore, I would like to close this book, in the spirit of the Enlightenment, with a confession of fallibility.

IN THE MEMOIRS THAT HE WROTE SEVERAL decades after the affair of the poisoned communion wine, Friedrich

Nicolai looked back fondly on the conversations he had once enjoyed in the company of his close friends Moses Mendelssohn and Lessing. He described the conversations as a kind of playful exercise in thinking in which the three friends would take turns arguing different sides of a single question. Everyone, Nicolai recalled, was "skeptical in a high degree" so the conversations never arrived at any final conclusions. But they were no less valuable for being inconclusive. The value of the conversations lay less in the "sum total" of "philosophic truth" they uncovered than in the "development of mental powers," in the fostering of a kind of intellectual empathy. From this "exchange of ideas," explained Nicolai, "I learned very early how to transpose myself into the manner of thinking of others" [*mich in die Denkungsart Anderer zu versetzen*], "to clarify my own thinking," and "to become less one-sided."[8] Conceived in this way, conversation was the royal road to intellectual progress, but not because it culminated in anything so grand as Absolute Knowledge—a synthesis in which thought and world were definitively reconciled. Such a goal was foreign to the spirit of the Enlightenment. Nicolai and his fellow travelers set themselves a more modest goal: not to pin down the truth, as it were, but to surround it, to converge upon a subject from as many perspectives as possible, to multiply the angles of approach so as to overcome their own one-sidedness. At the time that Nicolai described his conversations with Lessing and Mendelssohn, both of the latter had long since died and Nicolai himself was an old man, overtaken by a new generation of philosophers who scorned his vision of Enlightenment as the relic of a bygone era. In the end, however, the Enlightenment commitment to the cultivation of empathy through conversation has outlived its own historical epoch. It lives on in all the disciplines of the humanities, and especially in the discipline of history, which pursues its own version of truth by entering into dialogue with the past. To search for the truth about the affair of the poisoned communion wine is to extend a conversation begun by Nicolai and Lavater in the eighteenth century, a conversation as open-ended as the process of Enlightenment itself.

Notes

ARCHIVAL SOURCES FREQUENTLY CITED IN THE NOTES HAVE BEEN identified by the following abbreviations:

BPUN	Bibliothèque Publique et Universitaire de Neuchâtel
GRP	Geheimen Rats Protocoll
KN	Kundschaften und Nachgänge
LUB	Leipziger Universitätsbibliothek
RM	Ratsmanuale
SPKB NN	Staatsbibliothek Preußischer Kulturbesitz (Berlin) Nachlaß Nicolai
StAZ	Staatsarchiv des Kantons Zürich
ZBZ	Zentralbibliothek Zürich

Unless otherwise noted, all of the translations from the German are my own.

Introduction

1. Johann Caspar Lavater, *Zwo Predigten bey Anlaß der Vergiftung des Nachtmahlweins, nebst einigen historischen und poetischen Beylagen* (Leipzig, 1777), p. 22.

2. As a self-governing city state whose political constitution gave a central importance to guilds, Zurich bore some resemblance to the imperial cities of the German Reich. In many of the imperial cities, however, and especially in those located in southern Germany, such as Augsburg, the Reformation had bequeathed a legacy of religious division that led to a divorce between confessional identity on the one hand and the identity of the political community on the other. Not so in Zurich. Here, church and state were closely intertwined and the identity of the political community was inextricably bound to the reformed Protestant faith—hence the political threat posed by the poisoning of the communion wine in Zurich. On the divorce between confessional identity and political community in the Reich, see R. Po-Chia Hsia, *Social Discipline in the Reformation: Central Europe 1550–1750* (London and New York, 1989), pp. 73–88, 183. On communion as a ritual of social cohesion in the rural Protestant communities of early modern Germany, see David Warren Sabean, "Communion and Community: The Refusal to Attend the Lord's Supper in the Sixteenth Century," in *Power in the Blood. Popular Culture and Village Discourse in Early Modern Germany* (Cambridge, 1984), pp. 37–60.

3. Johann Caspar Lavater to Johann Joachim Spalding, Zurich (undated), ZBZ FA Lav Ms. 49i. Lavater reported to Spalding that the mayor, Johann Conrad Heidegger, had taken communion in the main cathedral on 12 September 1776.

4. Usually, the responsibility for criminal investigations belonged to the Small Council; the Secret Council, a select group composed of twelve leading magistrates, launched investigations only in the event of state crimes or other exceptional circumstances. It is significant, therefore, that the Secret Council launched the investigation into the poisoning of the communion wine. After doing so, it delegated the conduct of the investigation to the Small Council, but later it took control of the investigation back into its own hands and excluded the Small Council entirely, presumably because it wished to maintain secrecy in so delicate and explosive a case. The Secret Council convened only in extraordinary circumstances, not at regular intervals, and from mid-September until late November every one of its meetings was related either directly or indirectly to the affair of the poisoned communion wine. The Small Council convened thrice weekly so it was bound to spread its attention more widely than the Secret Council. To judge from its official register of proclamations, decisions, and verdicts, it devoted roughly 40 percent of its deliberations during this two months' period to matters related to the affair of the poisoned communion wine. StAZ BII 1074, GRP, pp. 56–71; StAz BII 974, RM, pp. 71–148.

5. Not a single mention of the affair appears in Bruno Fritzsche et al., *Geschichte des Kantons Zürich*, vol. 2, *Frühe Neuzeit—16. bis 18. Jahrhundert* (Zurich, 1996). On the other hand, Karl Dändliker (*Geschichte der Stadt und des Kantons Zürich*, vol. 3, *Von 1712 bis zur Gegenwart* [Zurich, 1912], p. 72) alludes to it briefly in his discussion of the trial and execution of Johann Heinrich Waser.

In his exhaustive three-volume study of Swiss Protestantism in the eighteenth century (*Der schweizerische Protestantismus im 18. Jahrhundert* [Tübingen, 1923–1925], vol. 1, p. 547 and vol. 2, p. 548), Paul Wernle mentions the affair of the poisoned communion wine only twice, and the first time he gets the year wrong, placing the affair in 1775 rather than in 1776. Martin Hürlimann (*Die Aufklärung in Zürich. Die Entwicklung des Züricher Protestantismus im 18. Jahrhundert* [Leipzig, 1924], p. 206) mentions the affair parenthetically in his discussion of a speech given by the Zurich pastor Johann Caspar Lavater at the synod of 1779. In general, the works most likely to mention the affair are those devoted to Lavater, who played such an important role in it. Thus one finds brief allusions to the affair of the poisoned communion wine in Horst Weigelt, *J. K. Lavater. Leben, Werk und Wirkung* (Göttingen, 1991), p. 39; Klaus Martin Sauer, *Die Predigttätigkeit Johann Kaspar Lavaters (1741–1801). Darstellung und Quellengrundlage* (Zurich, 1988), pp. 191–192, 427–432; and O. Guinaudeau, *Etudes sur J.-G. Lavater* (Paris, 1924), p. 397. The affair also comes up briefly in studies devoted to the trial and execution of Johann Heinrich Waser: Rolf Graber, "Der Waser-Handel. Analyse eines soziopolitischen Konflikts in der Alten Eidgenossenschaft," *Schweizerische Zeitschrift für Geschichte* 30 (1980), p. 340; and Hans Martin Stückelberger, *Johann Heinrich Waser von Zürich* (Zurich, 1932), pp. 46–48, 92. Additionally, Graber mentions the affair in his study devoted to clubs and societies in Zurich during the second half of the eighteenth century: *Bürgerliche Öffentlichkeit und spätabsolutistischer Staat. Sozietätenbewegung und Konfliktkonjuktur in Zürich 1746–1780* (Zurich, 1993), p. 133.

6. "Von gelehrten Sachen," *Hamburgischer unpartheyische Correspondent* (16 January 1779).

7. On the self-critique of the German Enlightenment, see Werner Schneiders, *Die wahre Aufklärung. Zum Selbstverständnis der deutschen Aufklärung* (Freiburg and Munich, 1974). For a fuller treatment of the themes taken up in this paragraph, see chapters 4–6, below.

8. Consider, for example, the history of western jurisprudence since the middle ages, which reveals at least two dramatic shifts in standards of evidence: first, the replacement of the Germanic ordeals by the practice of extracting confession under torture, which coincided with the spread of the inquisitorial procedure in the late middle ages; second, the abolition of torture during the Enlightenment. That anyone could seriously have credited a confession extracted under torture may be hard for us today to imagine, but for hundreds of years, confession—whether coerced or voluntary—counted as an absolutely certain proof of guilt in the law courts of continental Europe. On shifting standards of evidence in western jurisprudence, see John H. Langbein, *Torture and the Law of Proof: Europe and England in the Ancien Régime* (Chicago, 1977); and Edward Peters, *Torture* (New York, 1985).

9. In one sense, to be sure, this book does not resemble a detective story so much as a meta-detective story—a detective story about a detective story—since

it is trying to get to the bottom of how others tried to get to the bottom of a mysterious crime. To assess the efforts of others in this regard, however, I am obliged to make my own efforts to clarify the mystery. As a result, the book is both a detective story and a meta-detective story.

10. Carlo Ginzburg, "Clues: Roots of an Evidential Paradigm," in *Clues, Myths, and the Historical Method*, trans. John and Anne Tedeschi (Baltimore, 1989), 96–125. The study of a criminal case also evokes parallels between the historian and the judge—a theme developed by Ginzburg in a more recent work devoted to a contemporary terrorism trial in Italy: *The Judge and the Historian*, trans. Anthony Shugaar (London, 1999). On the relation between the historian and the judge, see especially Natalie Zemon Davis, *The Return of Martin Guerre* (Cambridge, Mass., 1983).

Chapter One

Murder in the Cathedral

1. On the architectural history of the Zurich cathedral, see Daniel Gutscher, *Das Grossmünster in Zürich. Eine Baugeschichtliche Monographie* (Bern, 1983). Of course, the appearance of the cathedral had changed since the sixteenth century, but the changes were minor compared with those of the nineteenth and twentieth centuries, which attempted, in the general spirit of Historicism, to restore (cynics might say "reinvent") the medieval cathedral. Today, the cathedral has stained glass windows (one of which represents the infant Jesus and the Virgin Mary!) and an organ built in 1874, the nave is cluttered with rows of wooden pews, and the pulpit no longer occupies a central position at the far end of the nave, having been shifted onto a side column so that the preacher does not face the congregation directly. A contemporary visitor to the cathedral would have difficulty imagining what it looked like two centuries ago.

2. Although foreign policy no longer reflected confessional rivalries, Zurich remained a Protestant polity. A decree of 1755 established automatic loss of citizenship and banishment from the land as penalties for conversion to Catholicism, and marriage to a Catholic was also subject to legal penalties. Dändliker, *Geschichte der Stadt und des Kantons Zürich*, vol. 3, p. 19.

3. On the practical—that is, moral—function ascribed to the sermon by Enlightenment theologians, see Alfred Ehrensperger, *Die Theorie des Gottesdienstes in der späten deutschen Aufklärung (1770–1815)* (Zurich, 1971), pp. 133–141; and Sauer, *Predigttäatigkeit*, pp. 79–82.

4. Sauer, *Predigttäatigkeit*, pp. 67–73.

5. Hürlimann, *Die Aufklärung in Zürich*, pp. 105–106, 127; and Sauer, *Predigttäatigkeit*, pp. 64–67.

6. Some of the press reports on the affair, which we shall consider later, put the number of worshipers at 3,000, but most of the reports gave the more conservative figure of 1,200.

7. Unless otherwise indicated, the following account is based on two sets of manuscript sources: the testimony given by witnesses to the official investigators on 16 September 1776 (StAZ A 27 153, KN, "Examina wegen dem letzten h. Bätt Tag in der Kirche zu Großen Münster verfälscht wordenen Communion-Wein") and the report submitted by the administrator of the cathedral chapter [*Stiftverwalter*], Caspar Hess, to the mayor and the Secret Council on 14 September 1776 (ZBZ Ms G 168). Hess's report was written in the first-person plural on behalf of all the cathedral canons, and when it mentions Hess, it does so in the third person. But it is clear that Hess wrote it: his is the only signature to appear at the end, and he launched the investigation that led to the drafting of the report. From now on, therefore, I shall identify the document as "Hess's report."

8. The buildings of the former convent were destroyed in the mid-nineteenth century in order to make way for a new building, which today houses the theological seminary of the University of Zurich. Of the various parts of the former convent, only the cloister was spared destruction and remains intact today. My reconstruction of the eighteenth-century site is based on the descriptions in Salomon Voegelin, *Das alte Zürich*, vol. 1 of *Eine Wanderung durch Zürich im Jahr 1504* (Zurich, 1878), pp. 316–324; and Daniel Gutscher, *Das Grossmünster in Zürich*, pp. 20–22.

9. I infer that the sexton's servant must have entered through one of the doors in the cloister since these were the only ones that could be opened from the outside. She reported that on her way out, she locked the "church door"—that is, the door to the cathedral—but left open three other doors in the cloister. Presumably, the doors she left open were ones that led to other buildings in the convent complex rather than to the cathedral.

10. On the nature of the moisture discovered by the sexton, the sources are contradictory. In his testimony to the investigators on 16 September, the sexton spoke of "red spots," which he assumed came from wine spilled the previous evening; Hess's report, based on his investigation conducted on the day of the communion service itself, describes the moisture found by the sexton as "spots" of a "glue-like substance" identical to that smeared on the cup. Which of the two sources is the more trustworthy? My inclination is to follow the testimony given by the sexton to the investigators, who recorded the sexton's words, more or less verbatim, in the form of a transcript. Hess's report is a synthetic narrative that does not quote any of the witnesses directly. But it is of course possible that the sexton simply changed his mind about what he had seen in the interval from 12 September to 16 September.

11. For the precise chronology of events, I am relying on a published account: [Johann Caspar Lavater], "Wahre Geschichte der Nachtmahl-Vergiftung in

Zürich," *Teutscher Merkur* 1st quarter (1777), p. 265. According to this account, the congregation began assembling a quarter of an hour after the "second ringing of the bells." Since the bell ringer's assistant, Heinrich Pfister, gave testimony to the investigators that he rang the "first" bell at five o'clock, the second bell must have been rung at six, and worshipers must have begun arriving at 6:15.

12. During the Reformation, all benches and chairs had been removed from the cathedral, but pictures of the cathedral from the eighteenth century often depict chairs set up along the side of the cathedral, in the choir behind the pulpit, and in the gallery. Only the central axis of the nave (which today is filled with rows of pews) remained completely unencumbered.

13. [Lavater], "Wahre Geschichte," p. 269.

14. Gessner and his colleagues submitted two separate reports to Hess, and two copies of each of them has survived: "Herrn Chorherr Geßners Untersuchung oben gemeldeten verfälschten Weins" and "Eine gleiche Untersuchung von Herrn Doctor Schinz und Herrn Doctor Ziegler von Wintherthur." ZBZ Ms G 168. StAZ A 27 153, KN.

15. StAZ BII 1074, GRP, 15 September 1776, pp. 56–58.

16. Soon after Burckhard died, his daughter died too, and Dr. Diethelm Lavater did perform an autopsy on the daughter, discovering not the "slightest trace of poisoning as a cause of illness." StAZ BII 974, RM, 26 September 1776, p. 88. But the register of the Secret Council (StAZ BII 1074, GRP, 24 September 1776, p. 59) makes it quite clear that no autopsy had been performed on the father:

> Herr Doctor Diethelm Lavater reported today [to the magistrates in the Secret Council] that he hears that the general talk is that Herr captain Burkhard (deceased) died as a result of the poisoned wine. As [Burckhard's] former physician, he testifies to having found not the least trace [of poisoning as a cause of death] and is prepared to maintain that the illness was already present in the deceased before the sacred day of prayer. . . . Herr Doctor Lavater also said that he had wanted to perform an autopsy on the deceased Herr captain [but] that *the surviving family members [of the deceased] would not permit it to occur* [Herr Doctor Diethelm Lavater habe hochdenenselben [i.e., the magistrates in the Secret Council] heute angezeigt, er höre daß durchgängig die Rede seyn Herr Quartierhauptmann Burckhard (sel.) seyn wegen dieses verfälscht wordenen Weins gestorben. Er als sein gewesener Medicus bezeuge hiervon nicht die mindeste Spur entdeckt zu haben und getraue sich zu behaupten daß die Krankheit schon vor dem heiligen Bättag in dem nunmehro verstorbenen Herrn gelegen . . . Herr Doctor Lavater habe sich auch geäußert daß er eine Lection mit dem verstorbenen Herrn Hauptquartierhauptmann solch habe wollen vornehmen. *Seine hinterlassene aber solches nicht geschehen lassen.*] (my emphasis).

How, then, to explain the contradictory claim made by the pastor Johann Caspar Lavater, brother of the physician Diethelm Lavater, who wrote in his published account of the affair ("Wahre Geschichte," p. 272): "Without any doubt both corpses [i.e., that of the father and that of the daughter] were opened and examined by doctors" ["Beyde Leichname sind also ohne allen Zweifel von Aerzten geöfnet und untersucht worden"]? An innocent error is unlikely, unless Diethelm had concealed the truth from his own brother. The most likely explanation is that Johann Caspar misrepresented the truth in order to discredit rumors about the effects of the poisoning. Because he stood in a very close relation to the ruling councils, his account had a quasi-official character, and one of its goals may have been to calm the passions and the anger aroused by the crime. Whatever the explanation, however, the archival evidence directly refutes the claim made by Johann Caspar that autopsies were performed on both father and daughter.

17. Johann Caspar Lavater, *Zwo Predigten*, p. 22.

18. As a consequence of its political fragmentation, Germany has no national library so newspapers from the eighteenth century lie scattered in dozens of provincial libraries. Tracking them down would be a lengthy, if not impossible, task. To study the press coverage of the poisoning in Zurich, I have concentrated on the newspapers contained in the microfilm collection of the Institut für Presseforschung at the University of Bremen. The collection comprises only a fraction of all the newspapers published in 1776, but despite a slight bias in favor of northern Germany, it covers a wide geographic range, and where the collection revealed a glaring hole, I supplemented it by making a trip to another library. Thus, the Bremen collection lacks the *Leipziger Zeitungen*, an important newspaper in the eighteenth century, which I consulted in the University Library in Leipzig. The main difficulty with the Bremen collection is that it does not distinguish between different types of periodicals: newspapers and journals are thrown together pell-mell. For the autumn of 1776, moreover, a few of the newspapers are available only in fragmentary form. Of the newspapers in the Bremen collection for which a complete set exists, only one—*Die neue europäische Zeitung* [Hanau]—neglects the events in Zurich altogether. The following, then, is a list of newspapers in the Bremen collection, as well as the *Leipziger Zeitungen*, that published reports on the affair of the poisoned communion wine in Zurich. Each date in parentheses corresponds to a separate news report on some aspect of the affair. The newspapers have been arranged according to the number of reports:

1. *Erlanger Real-Zeitung* (8 October 1776; 22 November 1776; 20 December 1776; 24 December 1776),
2. *Kayserlich-privilegirte Hamburgische neue Zeitung* (2 October 1776; 8 October 1776; 13 December 1776),
3. *Staats und gelehrte Zeitung des Hamburgischen unpartheyischen Correspondenten* (2 October 1776; 4 October 1776; 13 December 1776),

4. *Bayreuther Zeitungen* (28 September 1776; 3 October 1776; 2 November 1776),
5. *Altonäischer Mercurius* (10 October 1776; 12 December 1776),
6. *Nachrichten zum Nutzen und Vergnügen* [Stuttgart] (8 October 1776; 18 October 1776).
7. *Privilegirte Hildesheimische Zeitung* (5 October 1776; 14 December 1776).
8. *Schlesische privilegirte Zeitung* (7 October 1776; 16 December 1776),
9. *Berlinische Nachrichten von Staats- und Gelehrten Sachen* (also known under the title *Vossische Zeitung*) (10 December 1776),
10. *Leipziger Zeitungen* (20 November 1776),
11. *Wienerisches Diarium von Staats- vermischt und gelehrten Neuigkeiten* (12 October 1776),
12. *Frankfurter Kayserl. Reich-Ober-Post Amtszeitung* (28 September 1776).

The most extensive narrative accounts of events in Zurich appeared not in the newspapers but in two journals: Schubart's *Teutsche Chronik* (30 September 1776), pp. 619–622; and Wieland's *Teutscher Merkur* (see chapter 1, n. 11).

19. *Nachrichten zum Nutzen und Vergnügen* (8 October 1776), pp. 318–319. Virtually the same report, word-for-word, appeared in the *Altonäischer Mercurius* (10 October 1776). The reader may have noticed that this report mentions "mercury sublimate" but not "arsenic." For the explanation of this, see the discussion of the chemical analyses in chapter 2.

20. On the HC, see the entry in Holger Böning, ed., *Deutsche Presse. Bibliographische Handbücher zur Geschichte der deutschsprachigen periodischen Presse von den Anfängen bis 1815* (Stuttgart, 1996), vol. 1.1, pp. 183–224. Precise figures on newspaper press runs are difficult to come by. According to the best estimates (*Deutsche Presse*, p. 193), the *HC* was being printed at a run of 13,000 copies in 1789, 25,000–27,000 in 1798, and 28,000–30,000 in 1800. Even if the run in 1776 was somewhat lower—say, 10,000—we may still assume a readership of at least 30,000 because coffee houses, reading cabinets, and reading societies permitted newspapers to circulate through many hands. For such a newspaper as the *HC*, the multiplier effect can scarcely have been less than three and it was probably much higher. On the impact of such institutions on the circulation of newspapers, see Martin Welke, "Gemeinsame Lektüre und frühe Formen von Gruppenbildungen im 17. und 18. Jahrhundert: Zeitungslesen in Deutschland," in *Lesegesellschaften und bürgerliche Emanzipation*, ed. Otto Dann (Munich, 1981), p. 30.

21. *Frankfurter Kayserl. Reich-Ober-Post-Amtszeitung* (28 September 1776); *Bayreuther Zeitungen* (28 September 1776); *Hamburgischer unpartheyische Correspondent* (4 October 1776); *Privilegirte Hildesheimische Zeitung* (5 October 1776); and *Schlesische privilegirte Zeitung* (7 October 1776). All of these reports were the same, apart from a few words:

> On the twelfth of this month (which presumably was a day of repentance and prayer) the holy communion is supposed to have been administered to nearly 3,000 people; but the wine contained in three vessels, which had already been placed upon the altar the evening before, was poisoned. This was discovered when a few people shuddered in disgust after having received the wine and the wine appeared murky and bluish, whereupon [the communion service] came to a halt. Several people died and nearly thirty are still ill. . . . May so dreadful an event remain unconfirmed. [Am 12ten dieses (welcher vermutlich ein Buß und Bettag war) sollte das heilige Abendmahl an beynahe 3000 Menschen ausgetheilt werden; aber der Wein, der abends vorher schon auf den Altar gestellt worden war, ward in 3 Kannen [in two of the texts: "Gefäßen"] vergiftet. Man fand dieses, als einige Personen, die solchen empfangen, sich darüber geschüttelt hatten und der Wein trüb und blaulicht aussah, worauf man einhielt. Etliche [in two of the texts: einige] Personen sind gestorben und bey 30 noch krank. . . . Möchte eine so schauervolle Begebenheit unbestätigt bleiben.]

With one exception, all of the foregoing were dated, "Zurich, 21 September 1776." But one wonders whether the report, in fact, originated in Zurich. It is hard to believe that a Zurich correspondent would have described the communion table as an "altar." Also, note the tentative tone and the concluding sentence, which argue against the authorship of a Zurich correspondent. One of the above cited articles, the text of which is identical to the others, carries the dateline: "Basel, 28 September 1776."

22. *Teutsche Chronik* (30 September 1776); *Nachrichten zum Nutzen und Vergnügen* (8 October 1776); and *Altonäischer Mercurius* (10 October 1776). The article in the *Teutsche Chronik* was somewhat longer and more detailed than those in the *Nachrichten* and the *Mercurius*, which were virtually identical; because it was published first, it was probably the model for the others. Whole paragraphs from the *Teutsche Chronik* appeared unaltered in the *Nachrichten* and the *Mercurius*, and so too did the conclusion: "Do not believe it if you are told that anyone died or became ill. Do not believe that [the goal was to] poison the entire congregation or that the [poisoning] was aimed at the magistrates." ["Glauben Sie es nicht, wenn man Ihnen sagt: daß jemand davon gestorben, oder elend geworden sey. Glauben Sie es nicht, daß die ganze Gemeinde hätte vergiftet werden sollen; nicht, daß es auf den Magistrat abgesehen gewesen."] In the *Nachrichten*, however, one finds a final sentence absent from the *Teutsche Chronik* and the *Mercurius*: "What is, is more, more than enough." ["Mehr, mehr als genug, ist das, was ist."] The *Wienerisches Diarium* (12 October 1776) also published a report denying that anyone had died, but the wording of this report is different from that of the previous ones. Among the early reports, I have found only one that reports the poison-

ing without raising the question whether anyone had died or had been taken ill: *Kayserliche-privilegirte Hamburgische neue Zeitung* (2 October 1776). Note that some of the newspapers enumerated above (see chapter 1, n. 18) did not publish their first reports on the affair until November or December. Several of these later reports focused on the search for the criminal rather than on the crime itself. Their unspoken assumption was that the reader would already be familiar with the details of the crime, which did not need to be repeated. *Vossische Zeitung* (10 December 1776); and *Leipziger Zeitungen* (4 December 1776).

23. *Kayerlich-privilegirte Hamburgische neue Zeitung* (28 September 1776).

24. *Erlanger Real-Zeitung* (22 November 1776); and *Bayreuther Zeitungen* (2 November 1776).

25. Gonthier-Louis Fink, "Die Schweiz im Spiegel deutscher Zeitschriften (1772–1789): Bild und Wirklichkeit," in *Helvetien und Deutschland. Kulturelle Beziehungen zwischen der Schweiz und Deutschland in der Zeit von 1770–1830*, ed. Hellmut Thomke, Martin Bircher, and Wolfgang Proß (Amsterdam, 1994), pp. 57–78; and Günter Oesterle, "Die Schweiz—Mythos und Kritik. Deutsche Reisebeschreibungen im letzten Drittel des 18. Jahrhunderts," in *Helvetien und Deutschland*, pp. 79–100. Gradually, during the last decades of the eighteenth century, the myth of Switzerland came under attack, giving way to a more critical image of the country, an image that refelected contemporary realities as well as important differences among the various cantons. This shift in attitudes was in part a reaction to events described in this book (see chapter 7, below). On the geography of press coverage in Germany—especially northern Germany—see Jürgen Wilke, "Auslandsberichterstattung und internationaler Nachrichtenfluß im Wandel," *Publizistik* 31 (1986), pp. 53–90; and *Nachrichtenauswahl und Medienrealität in vier Jahrhunderten* (Berlin, 1984). Studies devoted to the French-language newspapers of Germany (admittedly, not a very representative sample) show that, in general, Britain, together with its North American colonies, and France were the foreign countries most likely to produce newsworthy events during the 1770s and 1780s. Karin Angelike, Matthias Beermann, and René Noir, "Frankophone Zeitungen an der deutschen Westgrenze," in *Kulturtransfer im Epochenumbruch. Frankreich-Deutschland 1770 bis 1815*, ed. Hans-Jürgen Lüsebrink and Rolf Reichardt (Leipzig, 1997), pp. 166–167; and Matthias Beermann, *Zeitung zwischen Profit und Politik. Der Courrier du bas rhin (1767–1810). Eine Fallstudie zur politischen Tagespublizistik im Europa des späten 18. Jahrhunderts* (Leizpig, 1996), pp. 203–212. With the exception of Geneva, Switzerland appears to have attracted scant attention from the influential *Gazette de Leyde*, studied by Jeremy Popkin (*News and Politics in the Age of Revolution: Jean Luzac's Gazette de Leyde* [Ithaca, 1989], p. 92). Not surprisingly, the American Revolution was one of the leading foreign news stories in German newspapers in the late 1770s. On the reception of the American Revolution in Germany, see Horst Dippel, *Germany and the American Revolution*, trans. Bernard Uhlendorf (Chapel

Hill, 1977); and *La révolution américaine vue par les périodiques de langue allemande 1773–1783. Actes du colloque*, ed. Roland Krebs and Jean Moes (Metz, 1992).

26. StAZ BII 974, RM, 3 October 1776, pp. 94–98.

27. StAZ BII 974, RM, 9 October 1776, p. 107.

28. StAZ A 27 153, KN, letter from the magistrate in the ducal Würtemberg residence of Stuttgart, 10 October 1776.

29. Of the five newspapers that carried the initial reports of deaths (see chapter 1, n. 21), only one—the *Bayreuther Zeitungen* (2 November 1776)—published a subsequent report affirming that no one had, in fact, died. But even this report was not exactly a retraction; it was presented as a letter from Leipzig that claimed to confirm, rather than contradict, an earlier report published (presumably) in a Leipzig newspaper. That this letter from Leipzig contradicted the report published previously in the *Bayreuther Zeitungen* went unmentioned: "We can assure you on the basis of a very reliable source that the attempted poisoning of the wine intended for the communion service in Zurich is fully substantiated and that the details of the event conform entirely to what we have previously reported." ["Aus einer sehr zuverläßigen Quelle können wir versichern, daß die in Zürich versuchte Vergiftung des zu dem Abendmahle bestimmten Weines völlig gegründet ist, und daß die Umstände der Sache demjenigen, was wir davon gemeldet haben, vollkommen gemäß sind."]

30. *Teutsche Chronik* (30 September 1776); *Erlanger Real-Zeitung* (24 December 1776); and [Lavater], "Wahre Geschichte," pp. 264–279. Lavater wrote his article for the *Teutscher Merkur* in response to a direct request from Wieland, who asked for an "authentic account" of what he called the "chalice poisoning." See Christian Martin Wieland to Johann Caspar Lavater, Weimar, 3 January 1777, *Wielands Briefwechsel*, vol. 5, *Briefe der Weimarer Zeit*, ed. Hans Werner Seiffert (Berlin, 1983), p. 580.

31. StAZ BII 974, RM, p. 73. In Old Regime Zurich, where church and state were so closely interwoven, it was typical for government decrees to be read from the pulpits. The Small Council specified that the decree was to be read and sermons preached in the four main parish churches of the city—that is, the cathedral, the Fraumünster, the Predigerkirche, and St. Peter's—as well as in the church at the orphanage, where Johann Caspar Lavater was the deacon, and in the French church. One may assume that the Small Council did not wish to involve the extramural districts of the canton in an affair that it considered a matter for the city alone.

32. The famous *Zürcher Zeitung*, forerunner of today's *Neue Zürcher Zeitung*, was not founded until 1780. In 1776, there were three main newspapers in Zurich: the *Monatliche Nachrichten einicher* [*sic*] *Merkwürdigkeiten*, the *Wöchentliche Freytags-Zeitung*, and the *Montagszeitung*, none of which mentioned the affair of the poisoned communion wine. On press censorship in Old Regime Zurich, see Christoph Guggenbühl, "Skizze einer Geschichte der Zürcher Zensur im Ancien

Régime," in *Zensur und Pressefreiheit. Kommunikationskontrolle in Zürich an der Wende zum 19. Jahrhundert* (Zurich, 1998), pp. 35–88; and Thomas Bürger, "Aufklärung in Zürich. Die Verlagsbuchhandlung Orell, Gessner Füssli & Comp. in der zweiten Hälfte des 18. Jahrhunderts," *Archiv für Geschichte des Buchhandels* 48 (1997), pp. 161–175.

33. Guggenbühl, *Zensur und Pressefreiheit*, p. 59. The newspaper was entitled *Nova Turici collecta* (from 1778, *Züricherische Staatsanzeigen*). The ZBZ owns two copies of the newspaper for the autumn 1776: Msc. S 633 and Ms E 122. Both of the copies are fragmentary, but they complement one another and form a complete set if read in tandem. Scholars have long known about a few famous handwritten gazettes edited in eighteenth-century Paris—notably, that of Grimm—but manuscript news letters were probably more widespread than is commonly realized. See Mark Lehmstedt, "Handschriftliches Publizieren am Beginn des 19. Jahrhunderts: Kajetan Burgers handgeschriebene politische Zeitung aus München (1801–1804)," *Buchhandelsgeschichte. Aufsätze, Rezensionen und Berichte zur Geschichte des Buchwesens* 3 (1997), pp. 114–123.

34. ZBZ Msc. S 633, *Nova Turici collecta*, 4 October 1776.

35. StAZ A 27 153, KN, 16 September 1776, "Examina wegen dem letzten h. Bätt Tag in der Kirche zu Großen Münster verfälscht wordenen Communion-Wein."

36. StAZ A 27 153, KN, 16 September 1776, "Bericht . . . betreffend die vorgenommene Untersuchungen wegen dem am vergangenen h. Bättag verfälscht wordenen Communion-Wein."

37. StAZ BII 974, RM, 18 September 1776, pp. 71–74.

38. StAZ A 27 153, KN, 16 September 1776, "Examina wegen dem letzten h. Bätt Tag in der Kirche zu Großen Münster verfälscht wordenen Communion-Wein."

39. The exterior staircase that led directly from the Zwingli Platz to the gallery was dismantled sometime in the nineteenth century. The information about the state of the locks comes from the interrogation of Wirz conducted by the investigators on 16 September 1776. StAZ A 27 153, KN, "Examina wegen dem letzten h. Bätt Tag in der Kirche zu Großen Münster verfälscht wordenen Communion-Wein."

40. The initial suspicions of Wirz's guilt, the rumors of his flight, and the investigators' questioning of him were all discussed in the Secret Council session on 24 September 1776. StAZ BII 1074, GRP, p. 58. Later, during his interrogation, Wirz made reference to some sort of financial suit in which he had become entangled so he was almost certainly telling the truth when he spoke of his debts. See StAZ A 27 153, KN, 26 September 1776, "1. Examen mit Meister Hartmann Wirz Todtengräber von hier."

41. StAZ BII 1074, GRP, 24 September 1776, p. 60. The Council cited as the reason for arresting Wirz at this moment the testimony given by someone

named Fäsi, the son of a former gravedigger, to Johannes Scheuchzer, one of the two members of the Secret Council appointed to investigate the crime on 15 September. On the content of Fäsi's testimony, see chapter 3, below.

42. This detail emerges from the testimony of Wirz's wife. StAZ A 27 153, KN, 26 September 1776, "Verhör mit des Todtengräber Wirzen Ehefrau von hier."

43. ZBZ Msc. S 633, *Novi Tiguri collecta*, 4 October 1776. Sauer (*Predigttätigkeit*, pp. 427–432) provides a brief discussion of the various sermons delivered in response to the poisoning of the communion wine. The most important of them—those delivered by Johann Caspar Lavater—are discussed at length in chapter five, below.

44. ZBZ Ms E 122, *Nova Turici collecta*, 15 November 1776. This fantasy of the prisoner being flayed with hot-pincers and drawn and quartered by horses calls to mind the real tortures visited upon Damien after his failed attempt at regicide almost two decades earlier. For a description of Damien's execution, see Michel Foucault, *Discipline and Punish. The Birth of the Prison*, trans. Alan Sheridan (New York, 1979), pp. 3–6.

45. One needs to distinguish, of course, between judicial torture, which was still practiced in Zurich (the last known application of torture for the purpose of extracting a confession dates from 1777), and torture as part of the ritual of execution. The general tendency of the Zurich authorities in the eighteenth century was to pare down the elaborate ritual of execution and to "reduce" all capital sentences to one uniform mode of punishment: beheading by the executioner's sword. As recently as 1730, however, a young girl condemned of having poisoned her parents was burned alive at the stake. Erich Wettstein, *Die Geschichte der Todesstrafe im Kanton Zürich* (Winterthur, 1958), pp. 65–66, 144–145. For an overview of torture and punishment in German-speaking Europe during the early modern period, see Richard van Dülmen, *Theatre of Horror. Crime and Punishment in Early Modern Germany*, trans. Elisabeth Neu (Cambridge, 1990).

46. See chapter 3, note 1, below.

Chapter Two

Proof and Persuasion

1. William Jordan, *The French Monarchy and the Jews: From Philip Augustus to the Last Capetians* (Philadelphia, 1989), pp. 245–248, 191–194; Miri Rubin, *Gentile Tales. The Narrative Assault on Late Medievel Jews* (New Haven, 1999); and Hsia, *The Myth of Ritual Murder: Jews and Magic in Reformation Germany* (New Haven, 1988).

2. Arlette Farge and Jacques Revel, *The Vanishing Children of Paris: Rumor and Politics before the French Revolution*, trans. Claudia Miéville (Cambridge, Mass., 1991).

3. By treating all of these various episodes as "narratives," this approach is vulnerable to an obvious objection: while Jews did not sacrifice Christian children at Passover or conspire with lepers and Muslims to poison the wells of France, the blood banks in France in the mid-1980s were contaminated with the AIDS virus. Well, yes; but the "fact" of the contamination alone does not explain why the story of contaminated blood has proved so captivating, or why it is now being recast as a story of poisoning. On this point, a personal anecdote may prove illuminating. In conversations, I have told the story of the poisoned communion wine to several people—none of them professional historians—who maintained that they already knew it. They cannot have known it really, since, so far as I am aware, no one before me has taken the trouble to excavate it from the archives. But the illusion of familiarity speaks volumes.

4. For an anthropological approach to the problem of purity, pollution, and taboo, see Mary Douglas, *Purity and Danger: An Analysis of the Concepts of Pollution and Taboo* (London and New York, 1966).

5. Jeremy Popkin, *News and Politics in the Age of Revolution: Jean de Luzac's Gazette de Leyde* (Ithaca, 1989), pp. 2–3. According to Popkin, there were, by 1785, at least 151 newspapers published in Germany.

6. Holger Böning, "'Ist das Zeitungslesen auch dem Landmanne zu verstatten?' Überlegungen zum bäuerlichen Lesen in der deutschen Aufklärung," in *Hören Sagen Lesen Lernen. Bausteine zu einer Geschichte der Kommunikativen Kultur. Festschrift für Rudolf Schenda zum 65. Geburtstag*, ed. Ursula Brunold-Bigler and Hermann Bausinger (Bern, 1995), pp. 39–53.

7. Wilke, *Nachrichtenauswahl und Medienrealität*, pp. 124–169.

8. See chapter 1, note 25, above.

9. The layout of an eighteenth-century newspaper was very different from that of a modern newspaper. News stories were not laid out in parallel columns or grouped together under thematic headings; they simply followed one another in a linear sequence, separated only by datelines (e.g., Zurich, 12 September 1776; Philadelphia, 13 September 1776). Because the headline had not yet been invented, it was impossible to distinguish, typographically, between major news stories and minor ones.

10. For a summary of the debate on the dangers and the utility of the newspaper, see Werner Storz, *Die Anfänge der Zeitungskunde. Die deutsche Literatur des 17. und 18. Jahrhunderts über die gedruckten, periodischen Zeitungen* (Halle, 1931).

11. Kaspar Stieler, *Zeitungs Lust und Nutz* (1695; reprint, Bremen, 1969).

12. Wilke (*Nachrichtenauswahl und Medienrealität*, p. 162) has traced the evolution in the contents of a single German newspaper, the *HC*, at sixty year intervals from the seventeenth to the twentieth century. According to Wilke's findings, news stories devoted to crimes made up just under 10 percent of the news stories on nonpolitical subjects in the years 1736 and 1796; the vast majority of

the crimes reported were serious crimes (i.e., theft, murder, assassination). His conclusion is that crime figured *less* prominently in the "media reality" of the eighteenth century than is generally assumed on the basis of newspapers from the twentieth century. But even if it was less important than it later became, the crime story did belong to the "media reality" of the eighteenth century. It is important to note, moreover, that the *HC* had the reputation of being one of the most soberminded and judicious of all the German-language newspapers in the eighteenth century, so it probably accorded a smaller space to crime stories than did its less prestigious competitors. At the other end of the spectrum, however, the elite Francophone gazettes ignored crime entirely and concentrated exclusively on serious political news. Cf. Beermann, *Zeitung zwischen Profit und Politik*, pp. 189–190.

13. The thesis of a "reading revolution," now widely discussed in the scholarly literature, goes back to a single chapter in a book by the German historian Rolf Engelsing, *Der Bürger als Leser. Lesergeschichte in Deutschland 1500–1800* (Stuttgart, 1974), pp. 182–215.

14. I owe this point to Dr. Mark Lehmstedt.

15. On the "art of newspaper reading" in the late eighteenth century, see the discussion in Beermann, *Zeitung zwischen Profit und Politik*, pp. 226–236. In 1777, the Göttingen professor and journal editor August Ludwig Schlözer offered his students a course on the "art of newspaper reading." The issue of how to read newspapers was also taken up in the periodical press itself: "Über die Kunst, Zeitungen zu lesen," *Journal von und für Deutschland* 9, no. 7 (1792) pp. 620–622.

16. The priority given to eyewitness accounts goes back to the classic and oft-reprinted work by Stieler, which inaugurated the discussion on the appropriate use of newspapers. *Zeitungs Lust und Nutz*, p. 51.

17. Because newspapers were frequently read in a social setting, they also provided the subject matter for discussions. It is likely that the many press reports on the affair of the poisoned communion wine prompted talk about the affair in reading societies, reading cabinets, and coffee houses. On newspaper reading as a collective activity, see Erich Schön, *Der Verlust der Sinnlichkeit oder die Verwandlungen des Lesers. Mentalitätswandel um 1800* (Stuttgart, 1993), pp. 177–222.

18. The report claimed, erroneously, that the event had taken place on a Sunday and that the wine in the cups had been poisoned. *HC* (2 October 1776).

19. *HC* (4 October 1776). This report was identical to several other reports published in different newspapers at about the same time, and conformed to what I described earlier as the first version of events. See chapter 1, note 21, above.

20. *HC* (13 December 1776).

21. *Erlanger Real-Zeitung*, 92 (22 November 1776), pp. 743–44. This report implied that the denials had in fact been published in "some papers" [*einige Blätter*].

22. [Lavater], "Wahre Geschichte," pp. 270–271.

23. *Nachrichten zum Nutzen und Vergnügen* (8 October 1776); *Altonäischer Mercurius* (10 October 1776).

24. The newspapers that reported "several" deaths (see chapter 1, note 21, above) made no mention of the chemical analysis, but neither did they affirm unequivocally that the wine had been poisoned. Instead, they concluded by declaring: "May so dreadful an event remain unconfirmed." ["Möchte eine so schauervolle Begebenheit unbestätigt bleiben."] Those newspapers that denied the reports of deaths (see chapter 1, note 22, above) affirmed the fact of the poisoning and cited the results of the chemical analysis as evidence. The later and more detailed stories, which also affirmed the fact of the poisoning, went so far as to name Gessner explicitly. *Bayreuther Zeitungen* (2 November 1776); *Erlanger Real-Zeitung* (22 November 1776); and [Lavater], "Wahre Geschichte."

25. Urs Boschung: "Erkenntnis der Natur zur Ehre Gottes und zum Nutzen des werten Vaterlands: Der Naturforscher Johannes Gessner (1709–1790)," in *Alte Löcher—neue Blicke. Zürich im* 18. Jahrhundert, ed. Helmut Holzhey and Simone Zurbuchen (Zurich, 1997), pp. 299–318.

26. The following discussion is based on Charles Gillespie, *The Edge of Objectivity. An Essay in the History of Scientific Ideas* (Princeton, 1960), pp. 151–260; William H. Brock, *The Norton History of Chemistry* (New York, 1993), pp. 41–172; Thomas Hankins, *Science and the Enlightenment* (Cambridge, 1985). Thomas Browan, *The Transformation of German Academic Medicine, 1750–1820* (Cambridge, 1996)

27. In the printed and manuscript sources, Gessner and his colleagues are described by turns as *Physicus* and *Naturforscher* ([Lavater], "Wahre Geschichte," p. 271), as *Kunsterfahrene* (*Erlanger-Real-Zeitung* [24 December 1776], p. 821), and as *Aerzte* and *Naturforscher* (Lavater, *Zwo Predigten*, p. 18). I have found only one mention of a "chemist" [*chemici*], which occurs in Hess's original report submitted to the Secret Council on Saturday, 14 September (ZBZ Ms G 168), but it refers only to Dr. Ziegler from Winterthur, not to Gessner or to Schinz.

28. Two copies of the reports submitted by Gessner and by Schinz and Ziegler have survived: one in the ZBZ, the other in the StAZ. Only those in the ZBZ are labeled and signed; none of them is dated. But we know from Hess's report that the experiments were performed on Thursday, the twelfth, and Friday, the thirteenth. "Herrn Chorherr Geßners Untersuchung oben gemeldeten verfälschten Weins," and "Eine gleiche Untersuchung von Herrn Doctor Schinz und Herrn Doctor Ziegler von Wintherthur." ZBZ Ms G 168; StAZ A 27 153, KN.

29. Two copies of the report submitted by Hirzel have also survived: one in the ZBZ, the other in the StAZ. The copy in the ZBZ is labeled and signed but undated; that in the StAZ is dated but unlabeled and unsigned. The date of the latter is 17 September 1776; the title on the former is: "Eine gleiche Untersuchung von Herrn Doctor und Stadtarzt Hirzel." ZBZ Ms G 168; StAZ A 27 153, KN.

Chapter Three

"Not Wirz, Not the Gravedigger"

1. The biographical information on Wirz is drawn from the handwritten genealogical reference work compiled by Carl Keller-Escher: *Promptuarium genealogicum. d.h Genealogie züricherischer Bürgergeschlechter bis zum Anschluß an den Bürgeretat von 1824* (Zurich, n.d.). ZBZ Ms. Z II 1–6 a. Most of the information given by Keller-Escher coincides with that in other genealogical reference works, except as regards Wirz's date of birth, which the other works give as 1727 rather than 1729. If Wirz had been born in 1727, then he would have been forty-nine years old at the time of his arrest rather than forty-seven. Cf. Wilhelm Hofmeister, *Tabellen der Stadtbürgerschaft von Zürich erstellt um 1780–1800*. ZBZ Gen D 159; *Schweizerisches Geschlechterbuch* (Zurich: Genealogisches Institut, 1943), vol. 7, p. 680. The latter states incorrectly that Wirz was the sexton at the main cathedral.

2. Recall that when Wirz was first brought in for questioning, the investigators were surprised that he maintained his composure and answered them in a "soft" voice, which they considered unusual for him. See chapter 1, above. During Wirz's trial, as we shall see presently, witnesses bore out this image of him, presenting him as a man given to fits of rage, and subsequent events would confirm that he had a hot temper, despite his advanced years: even at forty-seven, he was quick to settle disputes with his fists.

3. For a vivid depiction of the role of violence in the working-class culture of Old Regime Europe, see the autobiography of the journeyman glazier Jacques-Louis Ménétra (the original manuscript published in French under the title, *Journal de ma vie. Jacques-Louis Ménétra. Compagnon vitrier au 18e siècle*, ed. Daniel Roche [Paris, 1982]) and the foreword by Robert Darnton to the English translation of the autobiography (*Journal of My Life by Jacques-Louis Ménétra*, trans. Arthur Goldhammer [New York, 1986], pp. vii–xvi). According to Richard van Dülmen (*Der ehrlose Mensch. Unehrlichkeit und soziale Ausgrenzung in der frühen Neuzeit* [Cologne, 1999], p. 14), the high level of daily violence reflected the ethos of a "society of orders." In such a society, honor was of such great importance that any challenge to it—a slight, an insulting remark, a lack of respect—called forth a swift and violent response. For an interpretation that considers the phenomenon of violence within the broader framework of the "civilizing process," see Norbert Elias, *The Development of Manners. Changes in the Code of Conduct and Feeling in Early Modern Times*, trans. Edmund Jephcott, vol. 1 of *The Civilizing Process* (New York, 1978), esp. pp. 191–217.

4. Generally speaking, the demographic situation of Zurich was brighter in the eighteenth century than it had been in the previous century. The plague had vanished, and there were no demographic catastrophes comparable to those of the

"black years" at the end of the seventeenth century. Nevertheless, a devastating famine struck Zurich—and indeed much of western and central Europe—in 1770–1771. See Wilhelm Abel, *Massenarmut und Hungerkrisen im vorindustriellen Deutschland*, 2d ed. (Göttingen, 1977), pp. 46–54; Rudolf Braun, *Le déclin de l'ancien régime en Suisse. Un tableau de l'histoire économique et sociale du 18e siècle*, trans. Michel Thévanez (Lausanne, 1988), pp. 13–44. As for executions, they were becoming less common; but even so, 145 convicted criminals were executed, mainly through beheading, during the eighteenth century in the city of Zurich alone. Wettstein, *Die Geschichte der Todesstrafe*, p. 62. On the general theme of the changing relation to death in Western civilization, see Philippe Ariès, *Western Attitudes towards Death from the Middle Ages to the Present*, trans. Patricia Ranum (Baltimore, 1974). To modern readers, it might appear that Wirz remarried with unseemly haste after the deaths of his various wives (he waited barely three months after the death of his third wife before marrying again) and that such haste betokened a coldness and indifference toward the value of human life, but it is unlikely that his behavior would have appeared in the same light to his contemporaries. The canonically prescribed period of mourning in Old Regime Zurich was three months, after which time a widower was at liberty to remarry. Johann Jacob Wirz, *Historische Darstellung der urkundlichen Verordnungen, welche die Geschichte des Kirchen- und Schulwesens in Zürich wie auch die moralische und einiger Massen die physische Wolfart unseres Volks betreffen: von der Reformation an bis auf die gegenwärtige Zeiten, zusammengetragen von Joh. Jacob Wirz* (Zurich, 1793–1794), vol. 2, p. 34.

5. Werner Danckert, *Unehrliche Leute. Die verfemten Berufe* (Bern and Munich, 1979), pp. 50–51.

6. *Bayreuther Zeitungen*, 120 (3 October 1776); *Wienerisches Diarium von Staats- vermischt und gelehrten Neuigkeiten*, 82 (12 October 1776).

7. Cited in Kathy Stuart, *Defiled Trades and Social Outcasts: Honor and Ritual Pollution in Early Modern Germany* (Cambridge, 1999), p. 241. Stuart concentrates on conflicts over honor and dishonor in Augsburg. For a broader treatment of the same subject, highlighting regional differences, see Dülmen, *Der ehrlose Mensch*. For speculation—some of it very speculative indeed—on the underlying causes of the dishonor that attached to grave-diggers, cf. Danckert, *Unehrliche Leute*, pp. 50–56.

8. After the massacre of the Jewish community in the mid-fourteenth century, some Jews did resettle in Zurich, but only for a very short time. In 1436, the Council expelled all Jews from Zurich, forbidding Jewish residence in the city "for all eternity." This decree of expulsion was never revoked under the Old Regime. See Bruno Fritzsche et al., *Geschichte des Kantons Zürich*, vol. 1, *Frühzeit bis Spätmittelalter* (Zurich, 1995), pp. 351–352. On Jews as scapegoats for collective misfortunes, see chapter 2, note 1, above.

9. Danckert, *Unehrliche Leute*, pp. 57–63. Dülmen (*Der ehrlose Mensch*, pp. 40–41) also mentions the association of the bell ringer [*Türmer-Nachtwächter*]

with the night, but he does not consider that this association alone was enough to account for the bell ringer's dishonor. The decisive factor in his view was that the bell ringer sometimes substituted for the gravedigger, burying the bodies of dishonorable people whom honorable artisans were unwilling to touch. Of course, all such explanations are merely speculative and cannot be proved. This is a point made forcefully by Stuart (*Defiled Trades and Social Outcasts*), who concentrates on the uses of dishonor rather than speculating on its origins.

10. On the importance of technology to what Weber called the "disenchantment of the world," see the essay by Ernst Bloch, "Technik und Geistererscheinungen," in *Literarische Aufsätze*, vol. 9 of *Gesamtausgabe* (Frankfurt, 1965), pp. 358–365.

11. On conflicts over honor in Zurich, see A. Lutz, "Handwerksehre und Handwerksgericht im alten Zürich," *Züricher Faschenbuch* 82 (1962), pp. 35–60. Lutz maintains that the executioner was the very "symbol" of dishonor in Old Regime Zurich, and that the same dishonor fell to all those who came in contact with the body of the condemned, including the gravedigger who had to bury the body. But the gravedigger who performed this dishonorable task must have been someone other than the master gravedigger—at least in the late eighteenth century, at which time the law did not discriminate against a master gravedigger such as Wirz. In all likelihood, Wirz and the other master gravediggers confined themselves to burying those who had died honorably.

12. According to Keller-Escher (*Promptuarium*), Wirz's father, Heinrich, was "Landschreiber" in Andelfingen, a rural district of the canton. The register of the Saffran guild, the largest of the twelve guilds in Zurich, indicates that Wirz was received into the guild in 1765, before which time he belonged to the Weggen guild. See StAZ W 6 Saffran 16, "Verzeichnis aller Herren Bügermeistern, Statthalteren, Zünftmeisteren, Rathsherren, Zwölferen von der loblichen Zunft zur Saffran." Documents from Wirz's trial frequently refer to him as "lieutenant" Hartmann Wirz. I infer that he must have occupied the rank of lieutenant in the urban militia since he was clearly not serving in any foreign regiment. Wirz's second wife, Anna Barbara Wirz, was a cousin to whom he was closely related. Before marrying her, therefore, he was obliged to petition the marriage court for clerical dispensation. See the entry for 6 March 1766 in the records of the *Ehegericht*. StAZ YY 1 257. Endogamy was common among those who exercised dishonorable trades, so it may tell us something about Wirz's standing in the urban community that he sought a marriage partner within prohibited degrees of affinity. Were his marriage options limited because other artisans were reluctant to have their daughters marry into the family of a gravedigger? One might have supposed as much, except that his fourth wife, Regula Michel, was the daughter of a master carpenter and the honor of carpenters was never in dispute.

13. The *Bayreuther Zeitungen* (3 October 1776) and the *Erlanger Real-Zeitung* (8 October 1776) described Wirz as a "gravedigger . . . from a good family"

["Todtengräber . . . von einer guten Familie"]. The *Privilegirte Hildesheimische Zeitung* (14 December 1776), the *Schlesische privilegirte Zeitung* (16 December 1776), and the *Vossische Zeitung* (10 December 1776) described him as the "honorable gravedigger Wirz" ["ehrlicher Todtengräber Wirz"].

14. On the development of the "inquisitorial" proceeding in German-speaking Europe during the late middle ages, see Eberhard Schmidt, *Einführung in die Geschichte der deutschen Strafrechtspflege*, third ed. (Göttingen, 1965), pp. 86–107.

15. Wettstein, *Geschichte der Todesstrafe*, pp. 102–108.

16. Following the example set by Carlo Ginzburg in his pioneering work, *The Cheese and the Worms*, historians of early modern Europe have mined judicial archives to recover the voices of artisans and peasants—members of a popular culture who stood in a subordinate relation to secular and ecclesiastical authorities. But the judicial archive does not preserve those voices unaltered. In Zurich, two principal transformations occurred when oral testimony was converted into a written record: it was translated into what was essentially High German and it was recast in the third person. In citing testimony from the trial, I have opted to reproduce the third-person form contained in the judicial transcripts, rather than converting it back into the first-person. The result—what literary scholars call "indirect discourse"—may occasionally sound somewhat wooden, and it certainly lacks the emotional intensity of "direct discourse," but it calls attention to the inevitable transformations that accompanied the shift from speech to writing and it forestalls the illusion of perfect and unmediated "presence." For a critique of Ginzburg along these lines, see Dominick LaCapra, "The Cheese and the Worms: The Cosmos of a Twentieth-Century Historian," in *History and Criticism* (Ithaca, 1985), p. 62.

17. StAZ A27 153, KN, 26 September 1776, "Examen mit Meister Hartmann Wirz Todten Gräber von hier"; "Verhör mit Heinrich Pfister von Richtenschweil 20 Jahre Alt"; "Verhör mit Todten Gräber Rordorf wegen des auf dem Rathhaus inhaftierten Todten Gräber Wirzen"; "Verhör mit Todten Gräber Rordorfen Knecht Johannes Roduner von St G [St. Gall?] 53 Jahr alt und ledigen Stands." The testimony most damaging to Wirz came from Roduner. When asked why three bell ringers were in the tower, Roduner replied: "Because Master Wirz left at 12 o'clock at night, though he should have remained in the tower" ["weilen Meister Wirz nach 12 Uhr in der Nacht, da er doch auf dem Thurm hätte bleiben sollen, weggangen"]. Had he been able to see whether Wirz was carrying anything? the magistrates then asked him. "No—he had not observed the slightest thing, he [Wirz] left without a lantern, just as he often came and went without a lantern" ["Nein—er habe nicht das Mindeste bemerket, er [Wirz] seyn ohne Licht weggegangen wie er oft ohne Licht gekommen, und ohne Licht weggangen seyn"].

18. To confirm the point, the magistrates asked Roduner to repeat his testimony in a second interrogation. StAZ A27 153, KN, 30 September 1776, " 2ter Verhör mit Johannes Roduner."

19. StAZ A27 153, KN, 26 September 1776, "Examen mit Meister Hartmann Wirz Todten Gräber von hier."

20. StAZ A27 153, KN, 30 September 1776, "2ter Examen mit dem auf dem Rathaus arrestierten Todten Gräber Wirz von hier."

21. StAZ A27 153, KN, 26 September 1776, "Verhör mit Frau Regula Michel [maiden name of Wirz's wife] des Todten Gräber Wirzen Ehefrau von hier"; "Verhör mit Heinrich Pfister von Richtenschweil 20 Jahre Alt." KN, 30 September 1776, "Verhör mit Heinrich Pfister des Todten Gräber Wirzen Knecht."

22. Fäsi gave his original testimony to the investigator Johannes Scheuchzer on the afternoon of 24 September, before Wirz was placed under arrest. Indeed, his testimony was one of the principal points cited by the Secret Council in support of its decision to imprison Wirz and to bring his case before the Small Council for trial. StAZ BII 1074, GRP, 24 September 1776, p. 59. Here, however, I have followed the more extensive testimony given by Fäsi one month later. See StAZ A27 153, KN, 21 October 1776, "Verhör mit Herrn Pedell Fäsi wegen dem auf dem Rathaus inhaftierten Todten Gräber Wirz." The precise words attributed by Fäsi to Wirz on 21 October were as follows: "Ich will dem Donnerspfaff dem Obrist Pfarrer [i.e, Ulrich] auch noch eins werden lassen, ich will ihm einen einschenken, daß man an mich denken muß." It is difficult, in translation, to capture the double meaning of *einschenken*. Usually, the word means simply "to pour"—for example, "Darf ich euch noch etwas Wein einschenken?" But here it also carries a second meaning, akin to that of the American colloquialism, "I'm going to lay into him."

23. StAZ A27 153, KN, 26 September 1776, "Verhör mit Todten Gräber Rordorfen Knecht Johannes Roduner von St G [St. Gall?] 53 Jahr alt und ledigen Stands."

24. StAZ A27 153, KN, 26 September 1776, "Examen mit Meister Hartmann Wirz Todten Gräber von hier."

25. The Small Council took the decision to arrange a confrontation in its session of 19 October 1776. StAZ BII 974, RM, p. 122.

26. StAZ A27 153, KN, 21 October 1776, "Verhör mit Herrn Pedell Fäsi wegen dem auf dem Rathaus inhaftierten Todten Gräber Wirz"; "Verhör mit Roduner." It is not clear what Fäsi meant by the danger to his personal "security." Presumably, he feared retribution either from Wirz himself in the event of an acquittal or from Wirz's allies. By giving such damning testimony against Wirz, however, he must have assumed that he was paving the way for a condemnation. My guess is that he feared reprisals from Wirz's allies—a fear, moreover, that was hardly groundless since Wirz did enjoy some support among the population, as subsequent events would show. The words attributed by Fäsi to Wirz in his original testimony of 24 September were slightly different from those he repeated on 21 October. According to that original testimony, Wirz had not used the expression "to pour into" ["einschenken"]—he had said that "he wanted to show a thing or two to that damn cleric [i.e., Ulrich]—and to do so in such a way as to make the

whole city talk about it" ["Er wolle es dem verdammten Pfaff schon einmal machen, und zwar so, daß die ganze Stadt von ihm reden werde."]. The magistrates seem to have noticed this and other small differences between Fäsi's two versions of the episode in the bell tower. Hence the questions they put to him about the reliability of his memory after so long a period of time. But a very large and perhaps crucial discrepancy seems to have escaped their attention. In his original testimony of 24 September, Fäsi claimed to have kept silent about the episode in the bell tower and to have mentioned it to no one before revealing it to the investigator Johannes Scheuchzer. This stood in stark contradiction to the claim made by him on 21 October that he had spoken about the episode to the wife of the Antistes as well as to his own mother, wife, and sister. For Fäsi's original testimony, see StAZ BII 1074, GRP, 24 September 1776, p. 59.

27. StAZ A27 153, KN, 21 October 1776, "Examen mit Todten Gräber Wirzen bevorstehende Verhören betreffend."

28. StAZ A27 153, KN, 21 October 1776, "Confrontation." It is unclear from the documents whether the witnesses appeared in front of Wirz individually or together.

29. StAZ BII 974, RM, 26 October 1776, p. 128.

30. StAZ A27 153, KN, 5 November 1776, "Verhör mit dem auf dem Rathaus inhaftierten Todten Gräber Hartmann Wirz von hier." The Antistes was not interrogated in the town hall like a normal witness, so there is no separate transcript of the testimony given by him. His statements regarding Wirz were recorded in the entry for the Small Council session of 2 November 1776. StAZ BII 974, RM, p. 132.

31. Like the statements made by the Antistes, those made by his wife were recorded in the entry for the Small Council session of 2 November 1776. StAZ BII 974, RM, p. 132. For the testimony of the three women in Fäsi's family, see StAZ A27 153, KN, 28 October 1776, "Verhör auf dem Rathaus mit Todten Gräber Fäsis sel. Witwe von hier"; "Verhör mit Jungfrau Fäsi"; "Verhör mit Frau Herrn Pedells Eheliebste."

32. In the second half of the eighteenth century, as the use of torture in Zurich declined, the recourse to alternative methods—aggravating the conditions of imprisonment, reducing food rations, etc.—became more and more common. It should be pointed out, however, that the threat of torture remained a powerful weapon of intimidation even if its actual use was declining, and that torture was never legally abolished in Old Regime Zurich even though no criminal suspects were tortured after 1777. The most infamous of the dungeons in Old Regime Zurich, the Wellenberg, was fitted out with a special torture chamber. Torture was also used against prisoners held in Oetenbach, a former convent that served after the Reformation as both an orphanage and a prison. It is unclear, however, whether torture was used against prisoners held in the town hall. On the importance of torture to the criminal justice system of Old Regime Zurich and its decline in the

late eighteenth century, see Wettstein, *Geschichte der Todesstrafe*, pp. 113–114, 145; Hans v. Grebel, *Die Aufhebung des Geständniszwanges in der Schweiz* (Zurich, 1900). For a more general discussion of torture and its centrality to the inquisitorial proceeding in German-speaking Europe, see Schmidt, *Einführung*, pp. 86–107; Dülmen, *Theatre of Horror*, pp. 5–23. The movement to abolish torture on the Continent coincided with the Enlightenment, but this coincidence does not mean that it resulted from the Enlightenment—that it was a response to the moral outrage provoked by such polemicists as Beccaria and Voltaire. Cf. John H. Langbein, *Torture and the Law of Proof. Europe and England in the Ancien Régime* (Chicago, 1976); Edward Peters, *Torture* (New York, 1985), pp. 74–102.

33. StAZ BII 974, RM, 28 September 1776, p. 90; 3 October 1776, p. 98.

34. StAZ BII 974, RM, 5 October, 1776, p. 105.

35. StAZ A27 153, KN, 11 October 1776, "Verhör auf dem Rathaus mit Caspar Bertschinger Stattwächter—wegen des auf dem Rathaus inhaftierten Todten Gräber Wirzen Knecht"; "Verhör mit Heinrich Pfister des Todten Gräber Wirzen Knecht."

36. StAZ BII 974, RM, 6 November 1776, p. 137.

37. StAZ A27 153, KN, 5 October 1776, "Aufgenohmenes Verhör mit Todten Gräber Wirz welches er selbst verlangt."

38. Wirz gave his speech to the magistrates more than two weeks before his confrontation with Fäsi. In theory, therefore, he should not yet have known about Fäsi's damaging testimony. But in fact he did. He had learned about it from his son just before his arrest, as the judges quickly discovered when they interrogated Wirz for the first time on 26 September. See StAZ BII 974, RM, 28 September 1776, p. 90:

> To their astonishment the gracious magistrates had to infer from these [the interrogations conducted with Wirz and other witnesses on 26 September] that already before his arrest, lieutenant Wirz had received word of the report made by Herr Pedell Fäsi to Herr guild master and Bergherr Scheuchzer concerning the threat uttered against the honorable Herr Antistes Ulrich [Aus denen meine gnädige Herren aber mit Verwunderung entnehmen müßten, daß Lieut. Wirz von der Anzeige, welche Herr Pedell Fäsi dem Herrn Zunftmeister und Bergherr Scheuchzer wegen einer über ihro hochwürden Herrn Antistes Ulrich ausgestoßenen Drohung gemacht hat, schon vor seiner Inhaftierung Wissenschaft erhalten habe.].

39. StAZ A27 153, KN, 8 October 1776, "Verhör mit Johannes Roduner Todten Gräber Rordorfen Knecht"; "Verhör mit Todten Gräber Rordorf."

40. StAZ BII 974, RM, 6 November 1776, p. 137. Following the instructions of the Small Council, the investigating magistrates then interrogated Wirz

on the subject of the note. StAZ A 27 153, KN, 15 November 1776, "Examen mit dem auf dem Rathaus inhaftierten Todtengräber Wirz von hier."

41. Lavater, *Zwo Predigten*, p. 29. Speaking of the poisoner, Lavater declared: "May the shape of your face betray you" ["Die Gestalt deines Angesichts verrathe dich."]. Then, later, Lavater added that he would be able to spot the poisoner by "his impudent, downcast gaze or the furtive manner in which he averted his eyes" ["seinem frechen niedergeschlagenen, oder schnell sich wegwendenden, Blicke"]. *Ibid.*, p. 65.

42. On the vogue for physiognomy and the popularity of Lavater's writings on the subject, see Ellis Shookmann, "Wissenschaft, Mode, Wunder: Über die Popularität von Lavaters Physiognomik," in *Das Antlitz Gottes im Antlitz des Menschen. Zugänge zu Johann Kaspar Lavater*, ed. Karl Pestalozzi and Horst Weigelt (Göttingen, 1994), pp. 243–252.

43. StAZ BII 974, RM, 28 September 1776, p. 90.

44. StAZ BII 974, RM, 3 October 1776, p. 95.

45. Even before Schnitli made his revelations, the judges were aware that Wirz had undertaken various journeys in the months before the General Day of Prayer and Repentance. But in the light of those revelations, the journeys suddenly took on added significance. Wirz was questioned briefly about them during his first interrogation; in his second interrogation, he was questioned about them at considerable length; and his fourth interrogation was devoted to them exclusively. StAZ A27 153, KN, 26 September 1776, "Examen mit Meister Hartmann Wirz Todten Gräber von hier"; 30 September 1776, "2ter Examen mit dem auf dem Rathaus arrestierten Todten Gräber Hartmann Wirz von hier"; 17 October 1776, "4ter Examen mit dem auf dem Rathaus inhaftierten Hartmann Wirz Todten Gräber von hier."

46. On the subject of Wirz's travels, the judges received letters from the mayor and council of the city of St. Gall (5 October 1776); citizen and Vogt Hans Rudolf Spintli of Grüningen (7 October); a doctor in Trogen (9 and 22 October 1776); the Schultheiß und council of the city of Winterthur (14 and 21 October 1776); and a magistrate in Herisau (1 November 1776). StAZ A27 153, KN. To confirm Wirz's account, the judges also interrogated an innkeeper from Winterthur. KN, 22 October 1776, "Verhör mit Herrn Sülzer Wildmann Wirth von Winterthur und seinem Sohn Johann Heinrich Sülzer wegen dem auf dem Rathaus inhaftierten Todten Gräber Wirz von hier."

47. Two copies of the libels are preserved in StAZ A27 153, KN.

48. StAZ A27 153, KN, 7 October [*sic*] 1776, "Verhör mit Heinrich Wilhelm Pauder von Stuttgart Peruquier Gesell. Wegen abgewiesener Passquill auf der Oberen Brügg." The transcript of Pauder's interrogation was dated incorrectly. The actual date of the interrogation was 7 November. See also the short note written by Statthalter Reinhard, the official to whom Pauder delivered the libel after he had made his discovery. KN, 13 October 1776.

49. StAZ BII 1074, GRP, 13 October 1776, pp. 60–61. At its meeting on 13 October, the Secret Council was under the impression that only three copies of the libel had been posted. Later, however, both it and the Small Council spoke of four copies rather than three.

50. StAZ BII 974, RM, 16 October 1776, pp. 118–119.

51. On the issue of the "French alliance" and the resulting conflict, see Rolf Graber, *Bürgerliche Öffentlichkeit*, pp. 125–149.

52. Bruno Fritzsche et al., *Geschichte des Kantons Zürich*, vol. 2, p. 21.

53. Cited by Graber, *Bürgerliche Öffentlichkeit*, p. 126.

54. Ibid., p. 133.

55. The younger sister of Wirz's wife said that she stayed with her sister for fourteen consecutive nights, leaving her only during the day. Wirz's wife said that her sister stayed with her night and day for eight days. StAZ A 27 153, KN, 12 November 1776, "3ter Verhör mit Schantzen Zimmermann Michels Tochter wegen dem inhaftierten Felix Frey v. Niederhasli"; 15 November 1776, "Verhör auf dem Rathaus mit der inhaftierten Todten Gräber Wirzen Frau gebohrene Michlin." On the strained relations between Michel and his youngest daughter, see KN, 6 October [*sic*] 1776, "1. Verhör mit Meister Michel Schantzen Zimmermann von hier"; 9 November 1776, "2ter Verhör mit Meister Michel dem Schantzen Zimmermann wegen dem inhaftierten Felix Frey von Niederhasli." Note that all the interrogations of witnesses connected to the affair of the libels occurred during the week from 5 November to 12 November. Some of the transcripts are misdated, giving the month as "October" rather than "November."

56. Frey described his living conditions and his various sources of income in his first interrogation. StAZ A 27 153, KN, 5 November 1776, "1. Examen mit dem in Oetenbach inhaftierten Felix Frey von Niederhasli." The wife of the caretaker at the hostel reported that Frey slept there from time to time. It is unclear where he found shelter when he did not sleep at the hostel. KN, 8 November 1776, "Verhör mit Gesellenwirthe Frau von Wiedikon." On Frey's relations to Michel and Michel's daughter, see KN, 6 October (sic) 1776, "1. Verhör mit Meister Michel Schantzen Zimmermann von hier"; "1. Verhör mit Schantzen Zimmermann Michels Tochter Anna Maria Michel 20–21 Jahr alt."

57. The case against Frey and Michel rested mainly on the testimony of two witnesses: that of one of Michel's neighbors, the wife of a pastor named Steinbrüchel, and that of a bailiff to the Council named Waser. The former claimed to have overheard Frey and Michel make self-incriminating comments; the latter claimed that Michel's youngest daughter, Anna Maria, had revealed Frey's guilt to him in a conversation, saying that "he [Frey] had done it for the pay though not in our house" ["er habe gemacht um den Lohn, aber nicht in unserem Haus"]. StAZ A 27 153, KN, 9 November 1776, "Verhör mit alt Pfarrern Steinbrüchels von Buebikon Frau . . . den Schantzen Zimmermann Michel, und den inhaftierten Felix Frey von Niederhasli betrefend"; "Verhör mit Herrn Hauptmann und Raths-

procurator Waser." For the account of Frey's attempt to sell his shaving knife in a tavern, see KN, 7 October [*sic*] 1776, "Verhör mit Herrn Steinbrüchel von hier, den in Oetenbach inhaftierten Felix Frey von Niederhasli betref"; 7 November 1776, "2ter Examen mit dem in Oetenbach inhaftierten Felix Frey von Niederhasli." References to Frey's drinking are scattered throughout the testimony given by Frey himself and by other witnesses. KN, 5 November 1776, "1. Examen mit dem in Oetenbach inhaftierten Felix Frey von Niederhasli"; 6 October [*sic*] 1776, "1. Verhör mit Meister Michel Schantzen Zimmermann von hier."

58. Frey was arrested and interrogated for the first time on 5 November. In its meeting on the following day (StAZ BII 1074, GRP, 6 November 1776, p. 62), the Secret Council directed the torturer "unter ernstlicher Züchtigung an der Stud ein Examen vorzunehmen und denselben [Frey] zur [*sic*] Eingeständnis bringen zu trachten." None of the most common methods of torture—the rack, thumbscrew, legscrew—appears to have been used against Frey.

59. On the prison in Oetenbach, see Maria Crespo, *Verwalten und Erziehung. Die Entwicklung des Züricher Waisenhauses 1637–1837* (Zurich, 2001), pp. 64–65.

60. Both Michel and Frey were interrogated three times individually and once together. StAZ A27 153, KN, 6 October (sic) 1776, "1. Verhör mit Meister Michel Schantzen Zimmermann von hier"; 9 November 1776, "2ter Verhör mit Meister Michel dem Schantzen Zimmermann wegen dem inhaftierten Felix Frey von Niederhasli"; 12 November 1776, "3ter Verhör mit Schantzen Zimmermann Michel." KN, 5 November 1776, "1. Examen mit dem in Oetenbach inhaftierten Felix Frey von Niederhasli"; 7 November 1776, "2ter Examen mit dem in Oetenbach inhaftierten Felix Frey von Niederhasli"; 12 November 1776, "3ter Verhör mit dem in Oetenbach inhaftierten Felix Frey v. Niederhasli." KN, 12 November 1776, "Confrontation mit Michel and Frey."

61. StAZ BII 1074, GRP, 7 November, p. 64.

62. The order for the imprisonment of Michel's daughter came on 8 November. StAZ BII 1074, GRP, 8 November 1776, p. 66. The instructions regarding Lavater's visit to her and the application of torture followed two days later. GRP, 10 November, p. 69. Whether Michel's daughter was, in fact, tortured, or merely threatened with torture, is unclear. The instructions indicated that she was to be interrogated "under threat of flogging at the stake" ["unter androhender Züchtigung an der Stud"].

63. StAZ A27 153, KN, 6 October (sic) 1776, "1. Verhör mit Schantzen Zimmermann Michels Tochter Anna Maria Michel 20–21 Jahr alt"; 9 November 1776, "2ter Verhör mit Anna Maria Michel Schanzen Zimmermann Michels Tochter von hier"; 12 November 1776, "3ter Verhör mit Schantzen Zimmermann Michels Tochter wegen dem inhaftierten Felix Frey v. Niederhasli."

64. The transcripts of Frey's interrogations do not make any allusion to torture or to the presence of the torturer at the interrogations, but the register of

the Secret Council meetings makes unambiguous allusion to both of them. In its meeting of 7 November (StAZ BII 1074, GRP, pp. 64–65), the Secret Council repeated the order given by it the previous day, directing the "torturer" ["Zuchtmeister"] "to interrogate the prisoner under harsh flogging at the stake" ["unter ernstlicher Züchtigung an der Stud wiederum ein Examen vorzunehmen"]. Then, on 8 November (GRP, p. 66), it noted that "Frey had maintained his innocence and stood by his earlier testimony under harsh flogging at the stake" ["unter ernstlicher Züchtigung an der Stud seine Ohnschuld behauptet und auf seinen bisherigen Aussagen beharrt habe"]. And, finally, on 10 November (GRP, p. 68), it mentioned that Frey had made repeated protestations of his innocence to the "torturer" ["Zuchtmeister"].

65. StAZ BII 1074, GRP, 12 November 1776, pp. 70–71.

66. StAZ BII 974, RM, 16 November 1776, pp. 146–148. The sentence of banishment against Frey seems "illogical" if one assumes that proof of guilt is an either/or proposition—either it is absolutely certain or it is not—and that only two verdicts are possible: condemnation or acquittal. Such reasoning had always lain at the foundation of the inquisitorial proceeding, but it was beginning to break down in the seventeenth and eighteenth centuries as the range of criminal sanctions widened. It is possible, therefore, that the judges considered the evidence against Frey too weak to justify a capital sentence but still strong enough to warrant a lesser penalty—that is, banishment. On the gradual shift away from the requirement of absolute certainty in criminal trials, see Langbein, *Torture and the Law of Proof*, esp. pp. 47–49.

67. The incident in the bell tower is recounted in the manuscript news sheet. ZBZ Ms E 122, *Nova Turici collecta*, 3 December 1776.

68. Wirz's name appears in a census of Zurich inhabitants carried out by the *Physicalische Gesellschaft* in 1780. According to the census, he was then living in a house on the upper side of the Predigergäßlein, and presided over a household that included "two hearths, four underage boys, his wife, one underage girl, one male servant, and one female servant." StAZ BIX 13, 1780, "Volkszählung." Keller-Escher (*Promptuarium*) gives Wirz's date of death as 18 November 1795, at which time he would have been sixty-six years old.

Chapter Four

The Enlightenment in German-Speaking Europe

1. For a concise discussion on the importance of theology to the *Aufklärung*, see Horst Möller, *Vernunft und Kritik. Deutsche Aufklärung im 17. und 18. Jahrhundert* (Frankfurt a/M, 1986), pp. 71–109.

2. Such is the view taken by Marx in *The German Ideology* (1845–1846). Two years earlier, however, he still shared the view that the critique of religion was of fundamental importance and the necessary condition of human emancipation. Note the opening lines of the introduction to "Contribution to the Critique of Hegel's Philosophy of Right" (1844): "For Germany, the criticism of religion has been largely completed; and the criticism of religion is the premise of all criticism." *The Marx-Engels Reader*, ed. Robert Tucker (New York, 1978), p. 53.

3. See, for example, Geoff Eley, "German Historians and the Problem of Bourgeois Revolution," in Geoff Eley and David Blackbourn, *The Peculiarities of German History: Bourgeois Society and Politics in Nineteenth-Century Germany* (Oxford, 1984), pp. 51–62; and Richard Evans, "Whatever Became of the *Sonderweg*?" in *Rereading German History 1800–1996: From Unification to Reunification* (London, 1997), pp. 12–22.

4. François Furet; "La 'librairie' du royaume de France au 18e siècle," in *Livre et société dans la France du XVIIIe siècle* (Paris, 1965), pp. 2–32. Furet studied the requests for book privileges submitted by French booksellers to the Direction of the Book Trade and the "tacit permissions" granted to publications that the censors were unwilling to approve. To trace the evolution of the French literary market, he selected sample years from the beginning, middle, and end of the century, but he did not select the same sample years for the analysis of his two sources (the "tacit permissions" were a mid-century innovation). As a result, it is not possible to say precisely what percentage of total domestic book production was devoted to theology and religion in any given year. The main criticism of Furet's study is that it excluded the vast quantity of French books produced abroad and smuggled into the kingdom. But the French books published abroad were unlikely to be religious or theological works, so this criticism does not affect Furet's conclusion about the secularization of the French literary market. Cf. Robert Darnton, "Reading, Writing, and Publishing," in *The Literary Underground of the Old Regime* (Cambridge, Mass., 1982), pp. 167–208.

5. Rudolf Jentzsch, *Der deutsch-lateinische Büchermarkt nach den Leipziger Ostermeß-katalogen von 1740, 1770 und 1800 in seiner Gliederung und Wandlung* (Leipzig, 1912), pp. 314–315. According to Jentzsch, theological works made up 38.54 percent of the titles entered in the Leipzig catalogue in 1740, 24.47 percent in 1770, and 13.55 percent in 1800. So the German literary market was also undergoing a process of secularization, but not nearly so soon, so quickly, or so thoroughly as was the case in France. The main criticism of the Leipzig catalogues as a source for reconstructing the German literary market is that they exclude much of the south German Catholic literary production. This criticism, however, does not affect the general conclusion about the strength of demand for religious and theological works in Germany, for it is virtually certain that the literary market of southern Germany was more, rather than less, religious than its north German counterpart.

6. On the theology of the Aufklärung, see Karl Barth, *Die Protestantische Theologie im 19. Jahrhundert. Ihre Vorgeschichte und Geschichte* (Zurich, 1947), pp. 1–152; Karl Aner, *Die Theologie der Lessingzeit* (Halle, 1929); Henry Allison, *Lessing and the Enlightenment. His Philosophy of Religion and Its Relation to Eighteenth-Century Thought* (Ann Arbor, 1966).

7. Gotthold Ephraim Lessing, *Die Erziehung des Menschengeschlects*, vol. 13 of *Sämtliche Schriften*, ed. K. Lachmann (Stuttgart, 1893), pp. 414–436.

8. Jacobi's claim about Lessing's adherence to the doctrines of Spinoza prompted Mendelssohn to take up his pen in defense of Lessing, who had since died. This led to what has come to be called the "Pantheism controversy." See Frederick Beiser, *The Fate of Reason: German Philosophy from Kant to Fichte* (Cambridge, Mass., 1987), pp. 44–108.

9. Rudolf Vierhaus, "'Sie und nicht Wir.' Deutsche Urteile über den Ausbruch der französischen Revolution," in *Deutschland im 18 Jahrhundert. Politische Verfassung, soziales Gefüge, geistige Bewegungen* (Göttingen, 1987), pp. 202–215.

10. On the increasingly reflexive character of the Aufklärung in the period following the essay competition of the Berlin Academy, see Schneiders, *Die wahre Aufklärung*. The essays published in the *Berlinische Monatschrift* have been collected in a single volume: Norbert Hinske, ed., *Was ist Aufklärung? Beiträge aus der Berlinischen Monatschrift* (Darmstadt, 1981). A sample of some of the most important contributions to the debate on the nature of Enlightenment is now available in English: James Schmidt, ed., *What is Enlightenment? Eighteenth-Century Answers and Twentieth-Century Questions* (Berkeley, 1996), pp. 49–231. On the relation of Kant's essay "What is Enlightenment?" to its historical context, see Schmidt, "What Enlightenment Was: How Moses Mendelssohn and Immanuel Kant Answered the *Berlinische Monatschrift*," *The Journal of the History of Philosophy* 30, no. 1 (January 1992), pp. 77–101.

11. Steven Lestition, "Kant and the End of the Enlightenment in Prussia," *The Journal of Modern History* 65, no. 1 (March 1993), pp. 57–112.

12. Robert Darnton, "George Washington's False Teeth," *The New York Review of Books* 44, no. 5 (27 March 1997), pp. 34–38. For an example of the diffusionist model of analysis, see especially Robert Darnton, *The Business of Enlightenment: A Publishing History of the Encyclopédie 1775–1800* (Cambridge, Mass., 1979).

13. Friedrich Nicolai to Johann Georg Zimmermann, Berlin, 13 August 1765: "The so widely scattered world of scholarship in Germany has need of a point of unity, and I intended the German Library [to fill that need]" ["Die in Deutschland so sehr zerstreute Gelehrsamkeit hat einen Vereinigungspunkt nötig, und hiezu habe ich die Deutsche Bibliothek ersehen."]. Cited in Pamela Selwyn, *Philosophy in the Comptoir: The Berlin Bookseller-Publisher Friedrich Nicolai 1733–1811* (Ph.D. diss., Princeton University, 1992), p. 162. On the *ADB*, see also Ute Schneider, *Friedrich Nicolais Allgemeine deutsche Bibliothek als Integrationsmedium der Gelehrtenrepublik* (Wiesbaden, 1995).

14. Horst Möller, *Aufklärung in Preussen. Der Verleger, Publizist und Geschichtsschreiber Friedrich Nicolai* (Berlin, 1974), p. 206.

15. On the geographic dispersion of Nicolai's collaborators, see Selwyn, *Philosophy in the Comptoir*, p. 185.

16. Adolph Freiherr von Knigge, *Über Schriftsteller und Schriftstellerei* (Hanover, 1793), p. 9. Cited in Hans-Erich Bödeker, "Aufklärung als Kommunikationsprozeß," *Aufklärung. Interdisziplinäre Halbjahresschrift zur Erforschung des 18. Jahrhunderts und seiner Wirkungsgeschichte* 2, no. 2 (1987), p. 98: "Schriftstellerei ist also öffentliche Mitteilung der Gedanken; gedruckte Unterhaltung; laute Rede, an Jeden im Publikum gerichtet, der sie hören will; Gespräch mit der Leserwelt." Of course, the eighteenth century in Germany was also a great age of sociability and spoken conversation, marked by the growing number of clubs, societies, lodges, academies, coffee houses, etc. Cf. Otto Dann ed., *Lesegesellschaften und bürgerliche Emanzipation. Ein europäischer Vergleich* (Munich, 1981); Richard von Dülmen, *Die Gesellschaft der Aufklärer*; and Ulrich im Hof, *Das gesellige Jahrhundert.* But however numerous they may have been, the sites of sociability were dispersed. On letter-writing as a means of overcoming this geographic dispersion, see Hans-Erich Bödeker, "Lessings Briefwechsel," in *Über den Prozeß der Aufklärung in Deutschland im 18. Jahrhundert. Personenen, Institutionen und Medien* (Göttingen, 1987), pp. 113–138.

17. Immanuel Kant, "Beantwortung der Frage: Was ist Aufklärung?" in *Schriften zur Anthropologie, Geschichtsphilosophie, Politik und Pädagogik*, vol. 11 of *Werkausgabe*, ed. Wilhelm Weischedel (Frankfurt, 1977), p. 55.

18. For Kant, as Onora O'neill has argued, reason is not susceptible of a transcendental vindication. The principles of reason emerge through the process of communication, and the only vindication of which they are susceptible is immanent: what grounds their authority is their "publicizability"—that is, that they can stand the test of free and open examination. See Onora O'Neill, "The Public Use of Reason," in *Constructions of Reason* (Cambridge, 1989), pp. 28–50.

19. For an overview of censorship in late eighteenth-century Germany, see the discussion in Reinhard Wittmann, *Geschichte des deutschen Buchhandels* (Munich, 1991), pp. 138–142.

20. Writing to Nicolai, Lessing spoke disdainfully of what he called "Berlin liberty":

> Your Berlin liberty consists merely . . . in the liberty to market as much foolishness against religion as one wishes. Just let one person in Berlin stand up who wished to raise his voice in favor of the rights of subjects and against oppression and despotism . . . and you will soon learn which land remains down to the present day the most enslaved land in

> Europe. [Ihre Berlinische Freiheit reduziert sich . . . auf die Freiheit, gegen die Religion so viel Sottisen zu Markte zu bringen, als man will . . . Lassen Sie einen in Berlin auftreten, der für die Rechte der Untertanen, der gegen Aussaugung und Despotismus seine Stimme erheben wollte . . . und Sie werden bald die Erfahrung haben, welches Land bis auf den heutigen Tag das sklavischste Land in Europa ist.]

Lessing to Nicolai, 25 August 1769, in Lessing, *Sämtliche Schriften*, ed. Karl Lachmann and Franz Muncker (Stuttgart, 1904), vol. 17, p. 298. Lessing died a few years before Frederick II. If he had lived long enough to experience the reaction that set in after Frederick's death in 1786, perhaps he would have revised his hostile opinion of the roi philosophe. On Prussian censorship both before and after Frederick's death, see the discussion in Selwyn, *Philosophy in the Comptoir*, pp. 52–110.

21. Kant, "Was ist Aufklärung?" in *Werkausgabe*, vol. 11, p. 59.

22. Jürgen Wilke, *Literarische Zeitschriften des 18. Jahrhunderts (1688–1789)*, 2 vols. (Stuttgart, 1978).

23. Wittmann, *Geschichte des deutschen Buchhandels*, pp. 111–142.

24. In 1769, Lavater translated, under the title "Philosophical Examination of the Proofs for Christianity" ["Philosophische Untersuchung der Beweise für das Christentum"], excerpts from a work by the Genevan naturalist and philosopher Charles Bonnet, *Palingenesis or Ideas on the past and future state of living beings* [Palingénésie ou idées sur l'état passé et l'état futur des êtres vivans]. To his German translation Lavater then attached a dedication to Moses Mendelssohn, imploring him to examine Bonnet's arguments, and, if he were unable to refute them, "to do what wisdom, love of truth, and honesty require, to do what Socrates would have done if he had read this [Bonnet's] work and had found it to be irrefutable." Mendelssohn and all of his contemporaries interpreted this dedication as an attempt at conversion, and so, too, until recently, have all the scholars working on Mendelssohn and Lavater. For an alternative interpretation of Lavater's intentions, see the recently published article by Gisela Luginbühl-Weber, "'. . . zu thun, . . . was Sokrates getan hätte': Lavater, Mendelssohn und Bonnet über die Unsterblichkeit," in *Das Antlitz Gottes im Antlitz des Menschen*, pp. 114–148. According to Weber, Lavater's intention was not to convert Mendelssohn but rather to engage him in debate on a philosophical question: whether immortality pertains to the soul alone or to the whole person—a "mixed being" in whom soul and body are inextricably joined. In his *Phädon* (1767), Mendelssohn had argued for the first of these two positions; Lavater, following Bonnet, was committed to the second. Whatever Lavater's true intention, however, Nicolai certainly believed that Lavater was attempting to convert Mendelssohn. On Nicolai's reaction, see Martin Sommerfeld, *Friedrich Nicolai und der Sturm und Drang. Ein Beitrag zur Geschichte der deutschen Aufklärung* (Halle, 1921), p. 221.

25. Lavater's enmity toward Nicolai reached its zenith in the mid-1780s. For a discussion of this period in the relations between Lavater and Nicolai, see O. Guinaudeau, *Etudes sur J.-G. Lavater* (Paris, 1924), pp. 460–476; and Jürgen Sang, *Der Gebrauch öffentlicher Meinung. Voraussetzungen des Lavater-Blanckenburg-Nicolai Streites 1786* (Hildesheim, 1985).

Chapter Five

"And God Fell Silent": The Enlightenment on Trial (I)

1. For general studies devoted to Lavater's life and work, see O. Guinadeau, *Etudes sur J. ·G. Lavater* (Paris, 1924); Paul Wernle, *Der schweizerische Protestantismus im XVIII. Jahrhundert*, vol. 3, pp. 221–284; and Horst Weigelt, *J.K. Lavater. Leben, Werk und Wirkung* (Göttingen, 1991).

2. The Carolinum was the forerunner of the Zurich university. In the eighteenth century, Basel was the only Swiss city to have its own university.

3. Wernle, *Der schweizerische Protestantismus*, vol 2, pp. 412–436.

4. Johann Caspar Lavater, *Aussichten in die Ewigkeit, in Briefen an Herrn Joh. Georg Zimmermann, königl, Großbrittanischen Leibarzt in Hannover*, 3 vols. (Zurich, 1768–1773).

5. On the theme of transparency in the life and work of Rousseau, see Jean Starobinski, *Jean-Jacques Rousseau. Transparency and Obstruction*, trans. Arthur Goldhammer (Chicago, 1988). According to Lavater, no radical break existed between this world and the next. All of humanity was engaged in a movement toward ever-higher degrees of perfection, and this movement bridged the gap between life on earth and life in heaven. Eventually, moreover, all human beings would arrive at the same destination—a perfect reconciliation with God—though the elect would get there sooner, and hence enjoy the felicity of their blessed state for a longer period of time, than those who fell foul of God in this world.

6. On the relations between Lavater and Goethe, see Heinrich Funck, ed., *Goethe und Lavater. Briefe und Tagebücher*, vol. 16 of *Schriften der Goethegesellschaft*, ed. Erich Schmidt and Bernhard Suphan (Weimar, 1901); Johann Wolfgang Goethe, *Dichtung und Wahrheit* (Frankfurt, 1975), vol. 3, pp. 673–680; and Guinaudeau, *Etudes*, pp. 220–228.

7. Five Zurich pastors other than Lavater preached sermons on the poisoning of the communion wine: Kaspar Geßner, Rudolf Freytag, Johannes Tobler, Johann Rudolph Ulrich, and J. J. Escher. Of these, the last two had their sermons published. The sermons of the first three have survived in manuscript in the ZBZ Ms G 168. All of these sermons were delivered on Sunday, 29 September. Sauer, *Predigttätigkeit*, pp. 427–432.

8. Sauer provides a bibliography of Lavater's sermons, which lists the editions of Lavater's two sermons on the poisoned communion wine. Sauer, *Predigttätigkeit*, p. 465, 470, 472, 473, 476. Besides all of the various German and Swiss editions, there was also a Dutch translation published in Amsterdam.

9. BPUN, Johann Conrad Deinet to the Société Typographique de Neuchâtel, Frankfurt, 2 March 1777 [in French].

10. Johann Caspar Lavater to Philipp Erasmus Reich, Zurich, 5 February 1777, *Die Korrespondenz von Philipp Erasmus Reich*, ed. Mark Lehmstedt (forthcoming). My thanks to Dr. Lehmstedt for drawing my attention to this and other letters related to the publication of Lavater's sermons. On Reich, see Mark Lehmstedt, *Philipp Erasmus Reich 1717–1787. Verleger der Aufklärung und Reformer des deutschen Buchhandels* (Leipzig, 1988). Reich invested large sums of money in his luxurious edition of Lavater's *Physiognomik*, which turned out to be a commercial failure. Mark Lehmstedt, "Schweizer Literatur im Verlag der Weidmannischen Buchhandlung Leipzig," in *Helvetien und Deutschland*, pp. 115–129.

11. Johann Georg Zimmermann to Philipp Erasmus Reich, Hanover, 20 February 1777, *Die Korrespondenz von Philipp Erasmus Reich*.

12. On the preparation of the Leipzig edition, see Johann Caspar Lavater to Philipp Erasmus Reich, Baden, 21 February 1777; Lavater to Reich, Zurich, 15 March 1777; Lavater to Reich, Baden, 23 March 1777; and Lavater to Reich, 26 March 1777. All of the letters are in *Die Korrespondenz von Philipp Erasmus Reich*. Wieland sent Reich a copy of the "True History" from Weimar.

13. On the delays, which Reich attributed to Lavater's "negligence," see the letter from Zimmermann to Reich, Hanover, 30 March 1777, *Die Korrespondenz von Philipp Erasmus Reich*.

Johann Caspar Lavater, *Zwo Predigten bey Anlaß der Vergiftung des Nachtmahlweins. Nebst einigen historischen und poetischen Beylagen. Einzige ächte Ausgabe unter vielen äußerst elenden und fehlervollen von Chur, Schafhausen und Frankfurt* (Leipzig, 1777) 84 pages in-octavo. On 1 May 1777, Zimmermann wrote to Reich, acknowledging the receipt of a letter that Reich had sent to him during the fair. In this letter, Reich had announced the shipment of eight copies of Lavater's sermons. *Die Korrespondenz von Philipp Erasmus Reich*.

14. See chapter 2, note 25, above.

15. The vitalism of chemistry held a particular appeal for the pre-Romantics and the Romantics—from Diderot to Goethe—who rejected the mechanistic and atomistic world view derived from the physics of Galileo and Newton. Gillespie, *On the Edge of Objectivity*, pp. 184–201.

16. Lavater, *Zwo Predigten*, p. 21.

17. In fact, an anonymous pamphlet published in 1776 entitled *Bluttheologie* accused Lavater of being a crypto-Catholic and endorsing the Catholic doctrine of transubstantiation. It is likely that the author of this pamphlet was Lavater's

Zurich colleague, the theologian Johann Jakob Steinbrüchel. In 1786, shortly after arriving in Berlin, Mirabeau renewed the accusation of crypto-Catholicism, even claiming that Lavater was an agent of the Jesuits. In making such an inflammatory accusation, Mirabeau was deploying the same kind of rhetorical hyperbole as Lavater, who denounced all of his adversaries indiscriminately as "Spinozists" and "atheists." So Mirabeau's accusation should not be taken literally. Even if Lavater never converted to Catholicism, however, his theology may have had certain affinities with it. On the accusations of crypto-Catholicism made against Lavater by Steinbrüchel, Mirabeau and others, see Guinaudeau, pp. 372–373, 463–476. On the Zwinglian interpretation of communion, see W. P. Stephens, *Zwingli: An Introduction to His Thought* (Oxford, 1992), pp. 76–84.

18. Ibid, pp. 19–20:

> Who can account for it? Comprehend it? Explain it?—Out of revenge? . . . Indeed! Revenge against a whole congregation or half a congregation on account of one or two or ten people who the monster believed had offended him, toward whom his evil heart was angry—in order to be certain of slaying them, he gave a poisonous drink to a whole congregation or half a congregation, a congregation full of innocent, good, pious people who yearned for fellowship with Christ! Who can account for it?—comprehend it?—explain it? For reasons of greed? Avarice? To obtain a legacy? That too. . . . Who can shed light?. . . Oh, forgetfulness of God! Oh, impiety! The secrets of your wickedness are inscrutable like the secrets of God's mercy." ["Wer kanns ergründen? Wer kanns begreifen? Wer erklären?—Aus Rache?. . . Wie! Rache gegen eine ganze oder halbe Gemeine um eines, um zweener, um zehen willen, von denen der Unmensch sich beleidigt glaubte, gegen die sein böses Herz ergrimmt war—um diese gewiß zu treffen, einer Gemeine oder halben Gemeine, voll unschuldiger, guter Gottliebender, nach Christi Gemeinschaft sich sehender Menschen—einen Gifttrank bereiten! Wer kanns ergründen?—begreifen?—erklären?—Und aus Gewinnsucht? Geldsucht? Erbsucht? Auch das wieder. . . Wer kann Licht geben?. . . O Gottesvergessenheit! O Irreligion! die Geheimnisse deiner Greuel sind unergründlich, wie die Geheimnisse der Erbarmung Gottes."]

19. Lavater did devote one section of his first sermon to depicting the fate of the criminal (pp. 22–40). Some of the language he used in this section was ambiguous enough that it could be interpreted as referring to the torments of hell. But even here his main concern was not to conjure up a picture of hellfire and damnation; it was to move the criminal to confess his guilt by dangling before him the prospect of his torments on earth. Wherever he might try to hide, Lavater warned, the criminal will be unable to flee from God, to whom everything is always visible. Eventually, therefore, "the angel of the Lord will bring [him] back to the

place where [he] committed his monstrous deed, and into the city which will avenge itself upon [him] for his wickedness" (p. 26). And until that day, he will be subject to all manner of torments, haunted by the memory of a deed that will accompany him through all his waking and sleeping hours. It would be better, Lavater concluded, for the criminal to save his soul by confessing to his guilt than to endure this hell on earth. But what if the criminal did not confess his guilt, and the angel of the Lord failed to deliver him into the hands of the Zurich magistrates? Lavater did not say.

20. On one occasion, Lavater expressed his gratitude to God, whose "watchful providence" had frustrated the designs of the poisoner (p. 19). But no sooner did he mention the failure of the crime than he returned to his preferred theme: the wickedness of the attempted poisoning. By contrast, the failure of the crime figured prominently in the sermon of Antistes Ulrich, who interpreted the failure as a sign of God's benevolence and mercy toward the city of Zurich. Cf. the discussion of Ulrich's sermon in Sauer, *Predigttätigkeit*, p. 428.

21. The second sermon develops points adumbrated at the very end of the first sermon, so there is not, in fact, a sharp break between the two sermons. In what follows, I shall be referring to the second sermon and the last section of the first. Lavater, *Zwo Predigten*, pp. 40–66.

22. The praise of the "just" and "equitable" magistrates—some of it rather unctuous and ingratiating—runs on for two pages (pp. 57–59).

23. The cancer metaphor occurs twice (pp. 47, 63). Metaphors of disease and healing were common in Lavater's writings. Thus he frequently compared Christ to a physician and Christ's teachings to medicine. See Guinaudeau, *Etudes sur J. G. Lavater*, p. 270.

24. "Synodalrede gegen Deismus und kirchlichen Rationalismus (4 May 1779)" in Ernst Staehelin, ed., *Johann Caspar Lavaters ausgewählte Werke* (Zurich, 1943), vol. 3, pp. 1–27. After evoking the poisoning of the communion wine as evidence of creeping unbelief, Lavater focused his criticisms on two works: *Von dem Zwecke Jesu und seiner Jünger* (1777), which was the final installment of the Reimarus fragments edited by Lessing, and *System der reinen Philosophie, oder Glückseligkeitslehre des Christentums* (1778) by Gotthilf Steinbart. In the same year as the affair of the poisoned communion wine, Lavater also composed an extensive polemic against Johann Semler, a professor of theology at Halle and one of the leading Neologians, whom he blamed for having contributed to the decline of Christianity. On Lavater's attack against Semler and his speech before the Zurich synod, see Rudolf Dellsperger, "Lavaters Auseinandersetzung mit dem Deismus. Anmerkungen zu seiner Synodalrede von 1779," in *Das Antlitz Gottes*, pp. 92–101; Hürlimann, *Aufklärung in Zürich*, pp. 206–07; Weigelt, *Lavater*, pp. 38–39.

25. Lavater, *Zwo Predigten*, pp. 41–42. In all likelihood, Lavater's comment about the light-hearted jesting of his fellow citizens was mere rhetoric, the main purpose of which was to drive home his point that Zurich was rife with irreligion

and impiety. But what if he was telling the truth? Perhaps the secular and clerical elites did, in fact, treat the poisoning far more seriously than most of their fellow citizens, who were having a good laugh about the whole affair while drinking toasts to the poisoned communion wine at their local taverns. "Here's to the poisoned chalice," the revelers might have said as they raised their cups in the air. "Zum Wohl!" It is an interesting possibility if nothing else.

26. Lavater's vindication of Christianity in his sermons on the affair of the poisoned communion wine anticipated the position he would take two decades later in response to the French Revolution. The Revolution, he argued, was an example of how far man could fall in the absence of Christian faith: "Where irreligion prevails, so also do lawlessness, immorality, misery, and destruction. . . . All evil comes from irreligion, all salvation from religion." ["Wo Irreligion herrscht, muß Gesetzlosigkeit, Sittenlosigkeit, Jammer und Zerrüttung herrschen. Alles Uebel kommt mit der Irreligion! Alles Heil mit der Religion."] *Christliches Sonntagsblatt*, 1 (1792), p. 184. Cited in Weigelt, *Johann Kaspar Lavater*, p. 108.

27. So many points were swirling around in the maelstrom of Lavater's sermons that it was quite possible to agree with some of his points and disagree with others. In particular, Lavater's point about the contagious character of crime (what we would nowadays call the "copycat phenomenon") is likely to have met with widespread approval, coinciding as it did with the so-called "Werther fever"—a reported epidemic of suicides that gave rise to widespread panic and that contemporaries blamed on the baneful influence of Goethe's *Werther*. In its review of Lavater's sermons, the *Göttingische gelehrte Anzeigen*, an eminently sober-minded and judicious journal, took pains to praise Lavater's observations on the step-by-step process of moral decay and the contagious character of crime, even as it condemned his high-flown and intemperate rhetoric. See *Göttingische gelehrte Anzeigen* 35 (3 May 1777), pp. 421–22.

28. On Nicolai, see Selwyn, *Philosophy in the Comptoir*; Möller, *Aufklärung in Preussen*; Schneider, *Friedrich Nicolais Allgemeine deutsche Bibliothek*.

29. Klaus Berghahn, "Maßlose Kritik. Friedrich Nicolai als Kritiker und Opfer der Weimarer Klassiker," *Zeitschrift für Germanistik* 8 (February 1987), pp. 50–60; Walter Strauss, *Friedrich Nicolai und die kritische Philosophie. Ein Beitrag zur Geschichte der Aufklärung* (Stuttgart, 1927); and Möller, *Aufklärung in Preussen*, pp. 120–149.

30. Friedrich Nicolai, *Das Leben und die Meinungen des Herrn Magisters Sebaldus Nothanker*, 3 vols. (Berlin, 1773–76). On the diffusion of Nicolai's novel, see Richard Schwinger, *Friedrich Nicolais Roman 'Sebaldus Nothanker'. Ein Beitrag zur Geschichte der Aufklärung* (Weimar, 1897), p. 154. Nicolai's novel was also widely disseminated outside of Germany in the form of a French translation. Jeffrey Freedman, "Traduction et édition à l'époque des lumières," *Dix-huitème siècle* 25 (1993), pp. 79–100.

31. Immanuel Kant, preface to the 1st ed. *Kritik der reinen Vernunft*, vol. 3 of *Werkausgabe*, p. 13.

32. During the 1770s, Nicolai used his influence as journal editor, bookseller, and author to launch polemics against the Sturm und Drang, or what he called the "party of strength and miracles" [*Kraft- und Wunderpartei*], whose celebration of a lawless and individualistic freedom he denounced for undermining the ethic of social responsibility. Such leading Stürmer und Dränger as Goethe and Herder were far from sharing Lavater's vision of Christianity; but to Nicolai, they were birds of a feather, all of them given to the same flights of fancy and the same unbridled "enthusiasm" [*Schwärmerei*]. His campaign against Lavater thus belonged to a larger battle against the Sturm und Drang and the challenge posed by it to his conception of the Aufklärung. On this battle generally, see Martin Sommerfeld, *Friedrich Nicolai und der Sturm und Drang.*

33. Nicolai was not opposed to physiognomy as such. He objected to Lavater's "charlatanism," which gave physiognomy a bad name. On Nicolai's critique of Lavater's writings on physiognomy, see Sommerfeld, *Friedrich Nicolai und der Sturm und Drang*, pp. 226–236. See also Nicolai's letter of 4 October 1776 to Johann Georg Zimmermann in Hanover, where he discusses his first review of Lavater's *Physiognomische Fragmente*. LUB Kestner II A IV 1281.

34. [Georg Christoph Lichtenberg], *Timorus, das ist Verthedigung zweyer Israeliten, die durch die Kräftigkeit der laveterischen Beweisgründe und der Göttingischen Mettwurst bewogen den wahren Glauben angenommen haben* (Berlin, 1773). Lichtenberg described Nicolai as the "midwife" to the birth of his satirical work. Selwyn, *Philosophy in the Comptoir*, p. 242.

35. [Johann August Eberhard], *Betrachtungen über Wunderglauben, Schwärmerei, Toleranz, Spott- und Predigtwesen* (Berlin, 1777).

36. Johann Georg Zimmermann to Friedrich Nicolai, Hanover, 8 June 1776, SPKB NN, no. 33, folio 70. The metaphor of Nicolai and Lavater as generals in an ideological war was, of course, much overdrawn; to judge from the light tone of his letter, Zimmermann meant it more in jest than in earnest. In 1776, the battle line between Berlin and Zurich—*Nicolaiten* and *Lavaterianer*—was still fluid. As a friend and correspondent of both Nicolai and Lavater, Zimmermann stood somewhere between the two antagonists, and so too did others of his contemporaries—for instance, Johann Spalding, Isaak Iselin, Johann Basedow—who felt under no compulsion to join one camp or the other. The military image fits the period of the late 1780s far better than it does that of the mid-1770s. It was then that the battle line hardened and then, too, that Zimmermann broke unequivocally with Nicolai, echoing Lavater's tirades against the rank immorality fostered by the "deism" and "atheism" of the Berlin Aufklärung. On Zimmermann's relations to Nicolai and Lavater, see August Ohage, "Zimmermanns Anteil an Lavaters *Physiognomischen Fragmenten*" and Sigrid Habersaat, "Zimmermann und die Berliner Aufklärung: Friedrich Nicolai," both in *Johann Georg Zimmermann. König-*

lich großbritanischer Leibarzt (1728–1795), ed. Hans-Peter Schramm, Wolfenbütteler Forschungen, vol. 82 (Wiesbaden, 1998), pp. 109–122, 179–184.

37. By the 1770s, it was becoming less and less common for Nicolai to write reviews, so it is a measure of the importance attached by him to the review of Lavater's sermons that he took on the responsibility for it himself, rather than farming it out to one of his collaborators. See Selwyn, *Philosophy in the Comptoir*, p.168.

38. In principle, the review also covered the sermon of the Antistes Johann Rudolf Ulrich, but it barely mentioned it after the first page. "Nachtrag zur Gottesgelahrtheit," *Anhang zu dem fünf und zwanzigsten bis sechs und dreyßigsten Bande der allgemeinen deutschen Bibliothek. Erste Abtheilung*, pp. 637–664 (henceforth: Nicolai, "Review of Lavater"). According to Selwyn (*Philosophy in the Comptoir*, p. 163), it was quite typical for reviews in the *ADB* to go well beyond a mere discussion of the book or books under consideration.

39. As editor of the *ADB*, Nicolai admonished his collaborators to exercise "impartiality" toward the books assigned to them for reviewing. See Selwyn, *Philosophy in the Comptoir*, p. 165.

40. Möller, *Aufklärung in Preussen*, pp. 56–57.

41. Friedrich Nicolai, *Geschichte eines dicken Mannes. Worin drey Heurathen und drey Körbe nebst viel Liebe*, 2 vols. (Berlin-Stettin, 1794); *Leben und Meinungen Sempronius Gundibert's eines deutschen Philosophen. Nebst zwei Urkunden der neuesten deutschen Philosophie* (Berlin-Stettin, 1798).

42. For Kant's response to Nicolai, see Immanuel Kant, *Über die Buchmacherei. Zwei Briefe an Herrn Friedrich Nicolai*, in *Kants gesammelte Schriften*, ed. Royal Prussian Academy of Sciences (Berlin, 1912–23), vol. 8.

43. Nowadays, prejudice usually means prejudice "against" rather than prejudice "for." In the Aufklärung, however, the opposite was the case: *Vorurteil* ("fore"-judgment) was also a *Fürurteil* (judgment "for"). The general tendency of the Aufklärung was to evaluate prejudice negatively—to invest it with a pejorative connotation absent from the original juridical sense of prejudice as *praejudicium*—and to assign to it a positive content. Werner Schneiders, *Aufklärung und Vorurteilskritik. Studien zur Geschichte der Vorurteilstheorie* (Stuttgart, 1983), pp. 45–46.

44. Nicolai, "Review of Lavater," p. 659.

45. Friedrich Nicolai, *Einige Zweifel über die Geschichte der Vergiftung des Nachtmahlweins welche zu Zürich geschehen sein soll* (Berlin and Stettin, 1778).

46. Johann Eberhard to Friedrich Nicolai, Halle, 6 February 1779, SPKB NN, no. 51, folio 193. Nicolai was deeply devoted to Eberhard, and several decades later, he would honor him in a eulogy (*Gedächtnißschrift auf Johann August Eberhard* [Berlin-Stettin, 1810]), which singled out for special praise Eberhard's polemical defense of Socrates: *Neue Apologie des Sokrates—Oder Untersuchung der Lehre von der Seligkeit der Heiden* (1772). In this work, Eberhard had explicitly rejected the necessity of Christianity to salvation and denounced the monstrous injustice

of condemning all the pagans of antiquity to eternal punishment in hell. Lavater's sermons, which made Christianity the indispensable foundation of all morality, must therefore have been especially offensive to him. On Nicolai's eulogy of Eberhard, see Möller, *Aufklärung in Preussen*, pp. 178–183.

47. On Runge's response to Nicolai's pamphlet (which I have been unable to track down), see Guinaudeau, *Etudes sur J.-G. Lavater*, p. 682, n. 65. Runge made his claim in the 29 March 1780 issue of a periodical entitled *Neue Beilage.*

48. Isaak Iselin to Friedrich Nicolai, Basel, 29 October 1779, *Profile der Aufklärung. Friedrich Nicolai-Isaak Iselin*, ed. Holger Jacob Friesen (Bern, 1997), pp. 514–515. Nicolai reported the attempts of the Zurich authorities to block the circulation of his pamphlet in his response to Iselin. See Friedrich Nicolai to Isaak Iselin, Berlin, 30 November 1779, *Profile der Aufklärung*, p. 518.

49. Lavater to Eberhard Gaupp, Zurich, 29 January 1779, ZBZ FA Lav Ms 560, no. 194.

50. Anna Barbara von Muralt, "Anekdoten aus Lavaters Leben," ZBZ FA Lav Ms 15.7. The manuscript of Muralt's journal in the ZBZ is a copy; the original document is in private hands. The event in question took place on 28 January 1779. It was the annual "Charlemagne dinner" [*Carli Mahl*], which honored the emperor Charlemagne as a Christian saint on the anniversary of his death. It is unlikely that Muralt herself would have been present at the dinner. Presumably, she learned of what had transpired there from Lavater. Whether Usteri's smile was, in fact, "malicious" and his tone "coarse" is impossible to say. The important thing is that Lavater experienced them as such.

51. Johann Georg Zimmermann to Friedrich Nicolai, Hanover, 21 March 1779, SPKB NN, no. 35, folio 75. On Zimmermann's relations to Lavater and Nicolai, see note 36, above.

52. Johann Gottfried Herder to Johann Caspar Lavater, Weimar, July 1779, *Johann Gottfried Herder Briefe*, ed. Wilhelm Dobbek and Günter Arnold (Weimar, 1986), vol. 4, p. 98. On Herder's relations to Nicolai, see Martin Sommerfeld, *Friedrich Nicolai und der Sturm und Drang*, pp. 158–210.

53. The review appeared in the book review supplement entitled "Von gelehrten Sachen," *HC* (16 January 1779).

Chapter Six

Radical Evil: The Enlightenment on Trial (II)

1. All of these documents are among Lavater's papers (ZBZ FA Lav 48i).

2. An undated copy of Lavater's letter to Spalding has survived among Lavater's papers (ZBZ FA Lav Ms 49i). It was common for Lavater to have copies

made of his letters, and there is no reason to think that these copies differed in any important ways from the originals. In what follows, therefore, I shall be citing the copy of Lavater's letter to Spalding rather than the original, which I have been unable to locate. I am also assuming that the letter was, in fact, sent, for it seems unlikely that Lavater would have gone to the trouble of having a copy made of so long a letter if he had not sent it. On the other hand, none of the surviving letters written by Spalding to Lavater in subsequent years make reference to the letter in which Lavater responded to Nicolai.

3. On Spalding, see Joseph Schollmeier, *Johann Joachim Spalding. Ein Beitrag zur Theologie der Aufklärung* (Gütersloh, 1967).

4. Lavater to Spalding, ZBZ FA Lav Ms 49i: "Everyone should, of course, wish that the entire affair were merely an invention or [the result] of misunderstanding. The deed, if it occurred, as the news said, is such a disgrace to my fatherland and to humanity that it should immediately, had that been possible, have been erased [and declared] not to have taken place." ["Jeder Mensch sollte freylich wünschen, daß alles an der Geschichte Erdichtung oder Mißverstand seyn mögte. Die That, wenn sie, wie die Nachricht sagte, geschehen ist, ist so sehr Schande meines Vaterlandes und der Menschheit, daß sie, wenn es möglich gewesen wäre, sogleich als Nichtgeschehen hätte vertilgt werden sollen."]

5. Lavater begins by directing his condemnation against Zurich citizens who endorse Nicolai's position, rather than against Nicolai himself, a foreigner to whom he concedes the right to express doubt. But this is a concession in appearance only, for Lavater then goes on to insinuate that the review was not the work of Nicolai at all but that of the poisoner or poisoners:

> What concerns me in this whole affair is the *suppression of truth*, prepared and deviously orchestrated from afar. . . . Thus every friend of truth and justice must feel pain in his soul, but not because *foreigners* express doubt about the affair—that is reasonable and can occur out of the most honorable intentions. [No, he must feel pain] that citizens of our city, witnesses of everything that occurred at the time, apply themselves, under the pretense of love for humanity, to destroying a *fact*, the *certainty* and *demonstrability* of which are almost without parallel. This, I confess, made Nicolai's work appear in my eyes to be highly important—for it hands an intolerable victory both to the infamous author or authors of the most evil deed and to those who have been led, presumably through the treacherous subtlety of the latter, *to doubt the fact* and if this [i.e., Nicolai's] work does not come from the criminals themselves, then it is hard to conceive how thoughts and words heard so often here [in Zurich] found their way to Berlin [and how these came to be] supported by the addition of an *hypothesis* which no soul *here* would

> have dared openly to express but which nevertheless must deceive anyone unfamiliar with the affair. [Aber was mir bey dieser ganzen Sache Mühe macht, ist die von langer Hand her vorbereitete und künstlich eingefädelte *Unterdrückung der Wahrheit* . . . so muß es jeden Freund der Wahrheit und des Rechts in der Seele schmerzen nicht—daß *Fremde* Zweifel gegen die Geschichte äußern—das ist vernünftig and kann aus den schönsten Absichten geschehen—aber daß Bürger unserer Stadt, Zeugen von allem dem, was um jene Zeit vorgegangen, unter dem Schein von Menschenliebe, alles anwenden ein *Faktum* zu vernichtigen das an *Gewißheit* und *Erweislichkeit* kaum seines gleichen hat. Dies, ich gestehe es, machte die nicolaische Schrift in meinen Augen höchst wichtig—weil sie dem oder den verruchten Urhebern der boshaftesten That, und allen denen die vermutlich durch die geheime Feinheit derselben auf die *Bezweifelung des Faktums* geleitet worden sind, einen unerträglichen Triumph in die Hände spielt und, wenn diese Schrift nicht von diesen Urhebern selbst herrrührt, so ist kaum so begreifen, wie Gedanken und Worte, die hier so oft gehört worden, nach Berlin gekommen und mit einem Zusatz von *Hypothese*, die *hier* auszusprechen keine Seele gewagt hätte und die dennoch jedem der Sache unkundigen täuschen muß, unterstützt worden."]

Lavater to Spalding, ZBZ FALav. Ms 49i. Note that the manuscript of Lavater's letter to Spalding is full of underlined words and dashes, as if Lavater were trying to recreate the emotional intensity of an oral performance.

6. Lavater to Spalding, ZBZ FA Lav. Ms 49i: "All cold and warm hearts that have no other interest than that of truth and *that are familiar with the affair* suffer [in horror] and seethe [with rage] at the enormous audacity [which seeks to] 'doubt away' the most proven fact." ["Alle kalte und warme Herzen die kein Interesse als das Interesse der Wahrheit haben *und der Sache kundig sind*, schmachten und glühen unter der enormen Effronterie, das erwiesenste Faktum, wegzuzweifeln."]

7. [Johann Caspar Lavater], *Predigten über die Existenz des Teufels und seine Wirkungen, nach Anleitung der Versuchungsgeschichte Jesu. Von einem schweizerischen Gottesgelehrten* (Frankfurt and Leipzig, 1778).

8. Sauer provides an overview of all of Lavater's sermons on the devil and the temptation of Christ, of which only six were published in the 1778 edition. See Sauer, *Predigttätigkeit*, pp. 179–183.

9. Lavater, *Predigten über die Existenz des Teufels und seine Wirkungen*, pp. 8–11. Lavater was fond of such general phrases as the "genius of our century" or the "spirit of the age," which he used almost invariably in a pejorative sense. See Gerhard Ebeling, "Genie des Herzens unter dem genius saeculi—Johann Caspar

Lavater als Theologe," in *Das Antlitz Gottes*, p. 27. In his sermons on the devil, however, the "spirit of our philosophy" and other such phrases are likely to have had a precise referent: the contemporary controversy over the existence of the devil [*Teufelsstreit*], initiated by Johan Semler, a theology professor at the University of Halle. On the *Teufelsstreit*, see Karl Aner, *Die Theologie der Lessingzeit*, pp. 234–252. Lavater's sermons on the devil also coincided with the Gassner affair, a controversy centering on a Catholic priest named Gassner who had performed a series of much-publicized exorcisms. Lavater took an active interest in Gassner and defended him against accusations of charlatanism. On Lavater's relations to Gassner, see O. Guinaudeau, *Etudes sur J.-G. Lavater*, pp. 374–387.

10. Lavater, *Predigten über die Existenz des Teufels und seine Wirkungen*, p. 99:

> If you have ever in your life seen how a godless man sneers maliciously at the fall of a pious man, then you have seen something of the *Schadenfreude* that Satan experiences [when he contemplates] the destruction to which, sooner or later, sin leads.—How abominable are the cunning and the treachery of the seducer toward the seduced!—Oh, the cunning of Satan!—Oh, the *Schadenfreude* of Satan! [Hast du einmal in deinem Leben das boshafte Hohnlachen eines Gottlosen über den Fall eines Frommen gesehen,—so hast du etwas von Schadenfreude Satans über das Verderben, worin früh oder späth die Sünde stürzt, gesehen.—Wie abscheulich die List und die Bosheit des Verführers gegen den Verführten ist!—O List des Satans!—O Schadenfreude Satans!]

11. On the problem of rendering *Schadenfreude* in English, see John Portmann, *When Bad Things Happen to Other People* (New York, 2000), pp. 3–6.

12. Lavater, *Predigten über die Existenz des Teufels und seine Wirkungen*, pp. 86–87:

> According to Scripture, this enemy of man, this devil, takes pleasure in evil and misfortune, just as God and Christ take pleasure in the good, in the freedom and happiness of men. Just as Christ does everything to prevent evil and to foster the good, so also does Satan, through his angels, do all that he can in order to prevent the good and to spread and bring forth evil. . . . Evil lies in his heart just as the good lies in that of our Lord. [Dieser Menschenfeind, dieser Teufel hat nach der Schrift Freude am Bösen und Unglück, wie Gott und Christus Freude hat am Guten, an der Freiheit und Glückseligkeit der Menschen. Wie Christus alles thut, das Böse zu verhindern, und das Gute zu beförd-ern; so thut der Satan durch seine Engel alles, was er kann, das Gute zu verhindern, und das Böse auszubreiten, und empor zu bringen. . . Das Böse liegt ihm am Herzen, so wie unserm Herrn das Gute.]

13. Max Horkheimer and Theodor Adorno, "Juliette oder Aufklärung und Moral," in *Dialektik der Aufklärung. Philosophische Fragmente* (Frankfurt, 1969), pp. 74–107; and Jacques Lacan, "Kant avec Sade," in *Ecrits* (Paris, 1966), pp. 763–90. To be sure, Sadian characters appear to derive little actual pleasure from violating the moral law, and Kant explicitly rejects pleasure as a legitimate motive for obeying the moral law. In this sense, Kantian and Sadian ethics differ from Lavater's presentation of divine love and diabolic *Schadenfreude*, which links both good and evil to the emotion of pleasure [*Freude*]. What unites them is that Kant, Sade, and Lavater all postulate a kind of radical autonomy in which a perfectly free will becomes the determining ground of all action and neither prior influences nor ulterior goals enter into consideration.

14. *Preidgten über die Existenz des Teufels und seine Wirkungen*, p. 15:

> To wish to explain away the miraculous in Scripture means to explain away Scripture, to deny God's revelation. But whoever does not wish to deny Scripture and God's revelation should not be surprised at this or that unusual or miraculous occurrence which conflicts with daily experience. . . . Is it still possible for the impartial reader of Scripture to retain the slightest doubt that Scripture partly presupposes and partly affirms the existence of a Satan, a malign and powerful prince, a fallen angel, a tempter of men? [Das Wunderbare in der Schrift wegerklären wollen, heißt die Schrift wegerklären, heißt die Offenbarungen Gottes leugnen. Wer aber die Schrift und die Offenbarungen Gottes nicht leugnen will, dem sollte dieß oder jenes Ungewöhnliche, Wunderbare, das mit der täglichen Erfahrung streitet, nicht mehr unerwartet seyn. . . . Kann wohl dem uneingenommenen Schriftleser noch der mindeste Zweifel übrig bleiben, daß die Schrift das Daseyn eines Satans, eines Boshaften, mächtigen Fürsten, eines gefallenen Engels, eines Verführers der Menschen theils voraussetze, theils behaupte?]

15. On Deinet's relations to Lavater, see Jeffrey Freedman, "Zwischen Frankreich und Deutschland. Buchhändler als Kulturvermittler," in *Kulturtransfer im Epochenumbruch. Frankreich-Deutschland 1770–1815*, ed. Hans-Jürgen Lüsebrink and Rolf Reichardt (Leipzig, 1997), vol. 1, pp. 453–460. Deinet provides an example of just how difficult it is to establish a clear boundary between the Aufklärung and its adversaries. He was a passionate admirer of Lavater, but he also thought highly of Nicolai's novel *Sebaldus Nothanker*.

16. *Frankfurter gelehrte Anzeigen*, 20–21 (9–12 March 1779).

17. After the completion of this book, I became aware of a contemporary version of Faust by the playwright Friedrich ["Maler"] Müller in which the poisoning of the communion wine figures as an example of diabolic evil: *Fausts Leben dramatisirt von Mahler Müller. Erster Theil.* (Mannheim, 1778), pp. 23–24. In the first scene of Müller's play, the devils complain about the lack of great villains

among contemporary humanity, whereupon Lucifer cites the poisoner of the communion wine as a counterexample, describing him as a truly diabolic figure who stands apart from his "insipid century." In Lucifer's speech, the poisoner appears as a kind of romantic hero, the great man who liberates himself from the chains of philistine convention, like the Renegade of Avignon in Diderot's *Nepheu de Rameau*, whose crime points beyond moral categories to an aesthetic conception of the diabolic. Such a conception could hardly be further removed from Lavater's account of diabolic *Schadenfreude*, but if nothing else, Müller's *Faust* shows that Lavater was not alone in associating the poisoning of the communion wine with the devil. My thanks to Dr. Eckhard Faul of the University of the Saarland for bringing Müller's play to my attention.

18. On this theme generally, see Gerhard Sauder, "Aufklärung des Vorurteils—Vorurteile der Aufklärung," *Deutsche Vierteljahresschrift für Literaturwissenschaft und Geistesgeschichte* 57, no. 2 (1983), pp. 259–277; Werner Schneiders, *Aufklärung und Vorurteilskritik: Studien zur Geschichte der Vorurteilstheorie* (Stuttgart, 1983).

19. Nicolai, "Review of Lavater," p. 657.

20. Hegel, preface to *Enzyklopädie der philosophischen Wissenschaften*, 2d ed. (1827), ed. Nicolin and Pöggeler (Hamburg, 1969), p. 5. Cited in Christoph Schulte, *Radikal Böse. Die Karriere des Bösen von Kant bis Nietzsche* (Munich, 1988), p. 154.

21. For Kant's anthropological conception of radical evil, see *Die Religion innerhalb der Grenzen der bloßen Vernunft* (1793), especially the first chapter, "Von der Einwohnung des bösen Prinzips neben dem guten: Oder über das radikale Böse in der menschlichen Natur," vol. 8 of *Werkausgabe*, pp. 665–705. On the theodicy problem, see *Über das Mißlingen aller philosophischen Versuche in der Theodizee* (1791), vol. 11 of *Werkausgabe*, pp. 103–124. Kant's notion of radical evil has been the object of considerable controversy. One school of thought, already expressed by some of Kant's contemporaries, holds that such a notion amounted to an act of apostasy against the Enlightenment and that it resurrected the old Christian doctrine of original sin in a new guise. Another school argues that Kant's notion of radical evil remained fundamentally different from the doctrine of original sin because for Kant, man sins against himself (he violates a law of his own making rather than a divine commandment) and thus incurs the obligation to redeem himself—correct his bad disposition [*Gesinnung*]—through his own efforts without recourse to divine grace. For a modified version of the first school of thought, see Gordon Michalson, *Fallen Freedom: Kant on Radical Evil and Moral Regeneration* (Cambridge, 1990); for the position that emphasizes Kant's break with Christianity, see Christoph Schulte, *Radikal Böse*, pp. 13–154.

22. The strength of the Leibnizian tradition is, of course, another peculiarity of the Aufklärung. Leibniz composed his *Theodicy* in response to the article

"manichéens," which Pierre Bayle wrote in his *Dictionnaire philosophique*, and he set the terms in which the Aufklärung discussed the theodicy problem until Kant recast them. But Leibniz had nothing like the same influence in France as he did in Germany. In *Candide*, Voltaire took up the defense of Bayle against Leibniz. In so doing, he arrived at conclusions that anticipated Kant's by more than thirty years. That physical suffering and moral evil have nothing to do with one another, as witness the Lisbon earthquake; that moral evil has the same ontological status as moral good and that it is not simply a *privatio boni*—all of this, I would argue, was already present in *Candide*. For a recent discussion of *Candide* and its relation to Leibniz's *Theodicy*, see Daniel Gordon, introduction to *Candide*, trans., ed. Daniel Gordon (Boston and New York, 1999), pp. 18–24.

23. For Leibniz (as also for Hegel), the doctrine of sufficient reason amounted to a metaphysical statement: it said that whatever exists has its ground in some underlying rational necessity, in the plan or order of the entire cosmos. Such a doctrine occupied a central place in Leibniz's theodicy (as it did in Hegel's), but Nicolai was taking the doctrine in a much more limited sense: not as a metaphysical statement but as a statement about contingent events. The claim made by Nicolai was simply that any event "A" must be the result of some other event or set of conditions "B," but not that "A" and "B" are necessary elements in the best of all possible worlds or logical deductions of the Idea.

24. See chapter 4, note 8, above.

25. Immanuel Kant, *Kritik der reinen Vernunft*, vol 4 of *Werkausgabe*, pp. 426–433.

26. The partial rehabilitation of prejudice in the Aufklärung went back to the work of the popular philosopher Georg Friedrich Meier (*Beyträge zu der Lehre von den Vorurtheilen des menschlichen Geschlechts* [Halle, 1766]), who distinguished between the form of a prejudice and its content. From a formal standpoint, Meier argued, prejudice was always an error (it was, as Christian Wolff had said, "an overhasty," because insufficiently grounded, judgment), but a judgment may be wrong from the standpoint of its form and true in regard to its content. So it was misguided to attempt to eliminate all prejudices, many of which were not only unavoidable; they were the form in which a large segment of humanity came to an apprehension of truth. Here, as elsewhere, the Aufklärung was a good deal less radical and more circumspect than its French counterpart. In his *Essai sur les préjugés* (1770), D'Holbach denounced prejudices unconditionally, arguing that they were ipso facto harmful and that they were incompatible with virtue and happiness. Such uncompromising radicalism was foreign to the spirit of the "popular philosophers" in Germany (e.g., Thomas Abbt, Friedrich Karl Freiherr von Moser), most of whom followed Meier in his partial rehabilitation of prejudice. On Meier and the influence of his theory of prejudice, see Werner Schneiders, *Aufklärung und Vorturteilskritik*, pp. 203–262.

27. That neither Nicolai nor Lavater ever distinguished between the form of a prejudice and its content is hardly surprising. Such a distinction emerged out of theoretical reflection on the problem of prejudice, and Nicolai and Lavater were practicing the critique of prejudice, not developing a theory. The theory of prejudice developed by the Aufklärung reached its culmination in the thought of Kant, who took over the formalist conception of prejudice and raised it to a meta-theoretical plane. According to Kant, prejudice was not any particular instance of a precipitate or overhasty judgment, it was a general rule: the rule of judging without reflection. It therefore stood opposed not to true statements [*Sätze*] but to true principles [*Grundsätze*]. Kant was quite willing to accept that a provisional judgment, as opposed to prejudice, was a necessary step on the way to a definitive judgment. But a provisional judgment could easily harden into a prejudice in the mind of a sloppy thinker, and Kant would almost certainly have argued that this had occurred in Nicolai's critique of Lavater. On the Kantian theory of prejudice, see Schneiders, *Aufklärung und Vorurteilskritik*, pp. 263–323. In view of the theory of prejudice developed by the Aufklärung, it is impossible to accept the unqualified verdict of Gadamer, who argues that the "prejudice against prejudice" was the blind spot of the Enlightenment. Cf. Hans Georg Gadamer, *Truth and Method*, 2d ed., rev., trans. Joel Weinsheimer and Donald G. Marshall (New York, 1994), p. 270.

28. Here I am taking issue with Isaiah Berlin ("The Counter-Enlightenment," in *Against the Current. Essays in the History of Ideas* [Oxford, 1981], pp. 1–25), who presents the "counter-Enlightenment" as an implacable foe of the Enlightenment—as an antagonist, rather than a partner in dialogue. Of course, some opponents of the Enlightenment were implacable foes. Such a description fits the French anti-philosophes studied by Darrin McMahon ("The Counter-Enlightenment and the Low-Life of Literature in Pre-Revolutionary France," *Past & Present*, no. 159 [May 1998], pp. 77–112), who were more interested in discrediting the philosophes than engaging with them. But it does not fit the mainly German figures mentioned by Berlin—Hamann, Herder, Jacobi, Möser, Lavater—whose thought evolved out of an ongoing dialogue with such Aufklärer as Kant, Iselin, Lessing, and Mendelssohn. The peculiar feature of the German situation was precisely that critics of the Enlightenment contributed to what Jürgen Habermas has described as the "enlightening of Enlightenment." See Habermas, "The New Intimacy between Culture and Politics: Theses on Enlightenment in Germany," in *The New Conservatism. Cultural Criticism and the Historians' Debate*, ed., trans. Shierry Weber Nicholson (Cambridge, Mass., 1989), p. 201. For a similar argument applied to Rousseau and his relation to the philosophes, see Mark Hulling, *The Autocritique of Enlightenment: Rousseau and the Philosophes* (Cambridge, 1994). My thanks to Professor James Schmidt for helping me to clarify my thinking on this important point.

CHAPTER SEVEN

The Sword of Justice

1. Johann Wolfgang von Goethe, *Briefe aus der Schweiz* (1779), cited in Holger Böning, *Der Traum von Freiheit und Gleichheit. Helvetische Revolution und Republik (1798–1803). Die Schweiz auf dem Weg zur bürgerlichen Demokratie* (Zurich, 1998), p. 1. On the myth of Swiss liberty and its gradual erosion during the last decades of the eighteenth century, see the bibliographic references in chapter 1, note 25, above.

2. The discussion of the career and trial of Johann Heinrich Waser presented in this chapter is based largely on the work of Rolf Graber: "Der Waser Handel. Analyse eines soziopolitischen Konflikts in der alten Eidgenossenschaft," *Schweizerische Zeitschrift für Geschichte* 30 (1980), pp. 321–356; "Geschichte eines Justizmordes im alten Zürich," *Tagesanzeiger Magazin* 21 (24 May 1780), pp. 16–25; and *Bürgerliche Öffentlichkeit und spätabsolutistischer Staat. Sozietätenbewegung und Konfliktkonjunktur in Zürich 1746–1780* (Zurich, 1993), pp. 149–166. For an older treatment of the affair, which is less sympathetic to the victim than that offered by Graber, cf. Hans Martin Stückelberger, *Johann Heinrich Waser von Zürich* (Zurich, 1932).

3. On the meaning of "patriotism" in the eighteenth century, see Rudolf Vierhaus, "'Patriotismus'—Begriff und Realität einer moralisch-politischen Haltung," in *Deutschland im 18. Jahrhundert. Politische Verfassung, soziales Gefüge, geistige Bewegungen* (Göttingen, 1987), pp. 96–109. The second half of the eighteenth century saw the founding of a great many "patriotic" societies devoted to implementing the ideals of patriotism. For a survey of those societies, see the articles in Rudolf Vierhaus, ed., *Deutsche patriotische und gemeinnützige Gesellschaften* (Munich, 1980).

4. See chapter 3, note 4, above.

5. [Johann Heinrich Waser], "Bevölkerung des löbl. Cantons Zürich, in verschiedenen Zeitaltern," *Briefwechsel meist historischen und politischen Inhalts* 32 (1780), pp. 102–106.

6. [Johann Heinrich Waser], "Schweizer-Blut und Franz-Geld, politisch gegen einander abgewogen von einem alten Schweizer," *Briefwechsel meist historischen und politischen Inhalts* 32 (1780), p. 67. Zwingli himself had denounced the trade in mercenaries, so Waser's position had a venerable pedigree within the Zurich Church.

7. Two of Waser's studies managed to pass the censors and were, in fact, published in Zurich: one study devoted to the population of the Swiss cantons (*Abhandlung über die Grösse der ganzen Lobl. Eidgenossenschaft und des Cantons Zürich insonderheit* [1775]) and another on prices and wages in Zurich (*Betrach-*

tungen über die Zürcherischen Wohnhäuser vornehmlich in Absicht auf die Brandcassen und Bürger-Protocoll, samt einigen andern dahin einschlagenden öconomisch-politischen Bemerkungen [1778]). But the permission for the publication of the first of these two studies was withdrawn two days after the work left the press. Unable to pass the censors, most of Waser's writings remained in manuscript, some of them in fragmentary form. For a list of these manuscripts, see the bibliography in Graber, *Bürgerliche Öffentlichkeit*, pp. 216–217.

8. [Johann Heinrich Waser], "Ursprung und Beschaffenheit des Kriegs-Fonds in Zürich," *Briefwechsel meist historischen und politischen Inhalts* 31 (1780), pp. 57–66; "Schweizer-Blut und Franz-Geld, politisch gegen einander abgewogen von einem alten Schweizer" and "Bevölkerung der lobl. Cantons Zürich, in verschiedenen Zeitaltern," *Briefwechsel* 32 (1780), pp. 67–81, 102–106; and "Disputen in Zürich, über das Staats-Recht dieses Cantons, bei Gelegenheit der französischen Allianz," *Briefwechsel* 33 (1780), pp. 151–196.

9. On the politicization of the Aufklärung and the ideal of publicity, see especially Hans-Erich Bödeker, "Prozesse und Strukturen politischer Bewußtseinsbildung der deutschen Aufklärung," in *Aufklärung als Politisierung—Politisierung der Aufklärung* (Hamburg, 1987), pp. 10–31; and Rudolf Vierhaus, "Politisches Bewußtsein in Deutschland vor 1789," in *Deutschland im 18. Jahrhundert*, pp. 183–201. See also Jürgen Habermas, *Strukturwandel der Öffentlichkeit. Untersuchungen zu einer Kategorie der bürgerlichen Gesellschaft* (Darmstadt and Neuwied, 1962), esp. pp. 92–94.

10. On Necker, see Jean Egret, *Necker, ministre de Louis XVI* (Paris, 1975), pp. 169–179. On the significance of the *Compte rendu* for the development of the concept of "public opinion," see Keith Baker, "Public Opinion as Political Invention," in *Inventing the French Revolution* (Cambridge, 1990), esp. pp. 190–197.

11. StAZ A 20: Pfarrer Waser, "2ter Verhör" (13 April 1780).

12. Johann Heinrich Füßli to Louis Simond, Zurich, 11 June 1823. Letter in French reprinted in: Louis Simond, appendix to *Voyage en Suisse, fait dans les années 1817, 1818, 1818*, vol. 2, 2d ed., rev. and corr. (Paris, 1824). Cited in Peter Walser-Wilhelm, "'. . . bis die Gerechtigkeit die Muse der Historie ihr zum Beystand aufgerufen.' Zum Waser-Handel 1780: Bonstetten, Johannes von Müller und Lavater," in *Das Antlitz Gottes*, p. 335. Either the passage of time had dimmed Füßli's memory, and he genuinely believed that bread, rather than wine, was supposed to have been poisoned, or he may have been expressing his contempt for the whole affair by confusing an important detail.

13. Lavater to Goethe, Zurich, 8 April 1780, *Goethe und Lavater*, pp. 108–109.

14. Lavater to Goethe, Zurich, 12, 13 May 1780, *Goethe und Lavater*, p. 113.

15. The following account is based on a copy of the manuscript in the ZBZ FA Lav Ms. 50, "*Wasers letzte Stunden* am 27. Mai 1780 Morgens zwischen 10 und 12 uhr von Johann Caspar Lavater zusammengeschrieben." Clergymen were ex-

pected to visit condemned men before their executions, so Lavater could have justified his visit to Waser as the fulfillment of a pastoral duty.

16. *Wasers letzte Stunden*, pp. 42–46.

17. It is unclear what Lavater meant by the "five fingerprints on the tablecloth of the communion table." No other document mentions anything of the sort.

18. The official text of the judgment is reprinted as an appendix in Stückelberger, *Waser*, pp. 114–115: "Urteilsspruch des unglücklichen Heinrich Wasers gewesenen Pfarrers beim Kreuz" (27 May 1780).

19. Graber, *Bürgerliche Öffentlichkeit*, p. 159; and Stückelberger, *Waser*, p. 105.

20. On Lavater's campaign to justify the condemnation of Waser, see O. Guinaudeau, *Etudes sur Lavater*, pp. 395–398; Peter Walser-Wilhelm, "Zum Waser-Handel 1780," pp. 317–336.

21. Graber, "Geschichte eines Justizmordes," p. 25. In the end, friends persuaded Schlözer not to carry through with his plans. But he expressed his outrage in a series of critical "commentaries" published in a 1781 issue of the *Göttinger Magazin*, as well as in letters to Lavater. In one such letter, dated 15 November 1780, Schlözer declared: "[U]njust murders are the characteristic of oligarchic forms of government. Even despots respect the public; only Council members do not." Cited in Stückelberger, pp. 135–36. For an overview of the reactions to Waser's execution, see the discussion in Stückelberger, pp. 116–140.

22. Friedrich Nicolai to Isaak Iselin, Berlin, 5 October 1780, *Profile der Aufklärung*, pp. 531–532.

Chapter Eight

The Search for Truth

1. On iconoclasm in Zurich during the Reformation, see Lee Palmer Wandel, *Voracious Idols and Violent Hands. Iconoclasm in Reformation Zurich, Strasbourg, and Basel* (Cambridge, 1994), pp. 53–101. On iconoclasm in the Reformation generally, see Carlos M. N. Eire, *War against the Idols. The Reformation of Worship from Erasmus to Calvin* (Cambridge, 1986). On the behavior of Protestant and Catholic crowds during the Wars of Religion in France, cf. Natalie Davis, "The Rites of Violence," in *Society and Culture in Early Modern France* (Stanford, 1975), pp. 152–188.

2. On the intellectual challenge posed by the atrocities and the carnage of the twentieth century, see, for example, Jonathan Glover, *Humanity: A Moral History of the Twentieth Century* (New Haven, 2000); and Alain Finkielkraut, *In*

the Name of Humanity: Reflections on the Twentieth Century, trans. Judith Friedlander (New York, 2000).

3. Here, of course, I am betraying my own bias in favor of the Enlightenment. For an alternative view presented by a religious historian who considers that the concept of the devil remains as plausible today as at any time in the past, see Jeffrey Burton Russell, *The Prince of Darkness: Radical Evil and the Power of Good in History* (Ithaca, 1988).

4. Philosophers whom we might label "postmodern" may very well speak about something called "radical evil." The important point, however, is not whether they speak about it, but how they do so. Consider, for example, the introduction to a recently published collection of essays, *Radical Evil* (ed. Joan Copjec [London, 1996], pp. vii–xxviii). The author, Joan Copjec, attempts to connect Kant's notion of radical evil to the phenomenon of modern evil by drawing on the insights of such contemporary French thinkers as Lacan, Deleuze, Jean-Luc Nancy, and Philippe Lacoue-Labarthe. Because the Kantian imperative to act from duty contradicts man's nature as a sensuous being, she argues, the experience of guilt is inevitable. So the Kantian subject is, in fact, a self-divided subject, the site of internal contradictions analogous to those described by Freud with the concepts of the ego and the superego. What gives fascism its appeal is that it holds out the (false) promise of overcoming those contradictions: it is the collective phantasy of omnipotence by which modern man seeks in vain to recover his self-alienated freedom. Now, this may very well be a plausible reading of Kant, and it may even shed light on the psychological appeal of fascism, but it has precious little to do with radical evil—or, in any case, with radical evil conceived as a freely chosen act of the will. On Copjec's reading, guilt is pervasive, a constitutive aspect of the modern experience. So it is not possible to say of anyone in particular that he or she is, *fundamentally*, wicked.

5. It may well be that modern man is, in fact, ensnared in a web of constraints so all-encompassing as to negate his freedom, and that the social sciences are merely registering this fact, not constructing it. But even if this were so, it would not alter the basic point that it has become increasingly difficult to conceive of anything like radical evil, which presupposes some ultimate determining ground of action. On the more general difficulty of conceiving of radical evil in the contemporary world, see Schulte, *Radikal Böse*, pp. 323–352. One place, of course, where some version of the morally responsible subject has survived—and indeed must survive—is in courts of law. But even here radical evil is not at issue—it is rather a question of degrees of guilt and freedom. If nevertheless legal scholars speak of "radical evil," they have in mind something quite different from the concept of an evil will as the ultimate determining ground of action. Thus the noted legal scholar Carlos Santiago Nino, a major proponent of international human rights tribunals, alludes to "the kind of collective behavior that *leads* [my emphasis] to radical evil." Nino cites Kant; but he clearly does not have Kant in mind,

for it would make no sense to speak of anything *leading* to radical evil in the Kantian sense of the term. Presumably, Nino is using "radical" as an intensifier: what he means by "radical evil" is a very, very dreadful crime. Carlos Santiago Nino, *Radical Evil on Trial* (New Haven, 1996), p. ix.

6. On the many dodges and evasions performed by historians in order to skirt the issue of Hitler's radical culpability in the Holocaust, see the important book by Ron Rosenbaum, *Explaining Hitler* (New York, 1999). In the final chapter of his book, Rosenbaum presents the portrait of a "laughing Hitler," an arch-criminal who gleefully contemplated the monstrosity of his crime. Such a portrait calls to mind Lavater's notion of diabolic *Schadenfreude*.

7. In this connection, it is interesting to note that Hess's original report submitted to the Secret Council on Saturday, 14 September 1776, described jimson weed, one of the plants discovered by Gessner, as the sort of thing used by rogues or rascals to sicken and daze their victims: "welches Spitzbuben zum erbrechen und betäuben brauchen." This was before it had become common to describe the poisoner as "godless," "monstrous," "diabolic," "villainous," "inhuman," etc. If my reading of the evidence is accurate, then Hess's original intuition was on the mark: Wirz was a "Spitzbube"—a rogue or rascal, nothing more and nothing less. ZBZ Ms G 168.

8. Friedrich Nicolai, *Über meine gelehrte Bildung, über meine Kenntnis der kritischen Philosophie und meine Schriften dieselbe betreffend, und über die Herren Kant, J.B. Erhard, und Fichte* (Berlin and Stettin, 1799), 41–43.

Bibliography

OR THE RECONSTRUCTION OF EVENTS IN ZURICH, I have relied almost exclusively on manuscript sources, all of which are housed either in the Zurich State Archives or in the Zurich Central Library. To follow the reception of the affair in the wider world of German-speaking Europe, however, I had to travel farther afield, making research trips to the Institute for the Study of the Press at the University of Bremen and to the State Library in Berlin. The Institute in Bremen owns an extensive microfilm collection of eighteenth-century German newspapers, which allowed me to study the press coverage of the crime; the State Library in Berlin houses the papers of Friedrich Nicolai.

Manuscript Sources

Staatsarchiv des Kantons Zürich (StAZ)

A27 153: *Kundschaften und Nachgänge.* All documents relevant to criminal investigations in Zurich, including the transcripts of interrogations conducted by judges with witnesses and prisoners.

BII 974: *Ratsmanuale.* Bound register of decisions, judgments, and proclamations made by the Small or Daily Council.

BII 1074: *Geheimen Rats Protocoll.* Bound register of decisions, judgments, and proclamations made by the Secret Council.

A20: Pfarrer Waser 1744–1794. All documents relevant to the criminal investigation of Johann Heinrich Waser.

YY I 257: *Ehegericht.* Records of the marriage tribunal, including judgments on requests for clerical dispensations.

W 6 Saffran 16: *Verzeichnis aller Herren Bügermeistern, Statthalteren, Zünftmeisteren, Rathsherren, Zwölferen von der loblichen Zunft zur Saffran.* Register of all members of the Saffran guild.

StAZ BIX 13, 1780: *Volkszählung.* Census of Zurich residents conducted by the *Physikalische Gesellschaft.*

Zentralbibliothek Zürich (ZBZ)

Msc. S 633; Ms E 122. Copies of the handwritten newspaper, *Nova Turici collecta.*

FA Lav. Ms 49i. Copy of letter written by Johann Caspar Lavater to Johann Joachim Spalding, undated.

FA Lav Nos 48.1. Dossier compiled by Johann Caspar Lavater in 1778 containing assorted documents related to the case of the poisoned communion wine.

FA Lav Ms. 50: "*Wasers letzte Stunden* am 27 Mai 1780 Morgens zwischen 10 und 12 uhr von Johann Caspar Lavater zusammengescrieben." Conversations between Johann Caspar Lavater and Johann Heinrich Waser in the Wellenberg dungeon.

FA Lav Ms 560. Letters of Lavater.

FA Lav Ms 15.7: "Anekdoten aus Lavaters Leben." Manuscript copy of a journal kept by Lavater's cousin, Anna Barbara von Muralt.

Ms G 168. Report submitted by the cathedral canon Caspar Hess to the Secret Council on 14 September 1776; reports of chemical analyses performed on the tainted wine.

Ms. Z II 1–6 a. Keller-Escher, Carl. *Promptuarium genealogicum. d.h Genealogie züricherischer Bürgergeschlechter bis zum Anschluß an den Bürgeretat von 1824.* Zurich, 19— [precise year not indicated]. Genealogical reference work devoted to the citizens of Old Regime Zurich.

Gen D 159. Hofmeister, Wilhelm. *Tabellen der Stadtbürgerschaft von Zürich erstellt um 1780–1800.* Genealogical reference work devoted to the citizens of Old Regime Zurich.

Staatsbibliothek Preußischer Kulturbesitz Nachlaß Nicolai (SPKB NN).

Letters of Johann Georg Zimmermann to Friedrich Nicolai, 8 June 1777 and 21 March 1779.

Letter of Johann August Eberhard to Friedrich Nicolai, 6 February 1779.

Leipziger Universitätsbibliothek (LUB)

Kester II AIV 1281. Letter of Friedrich Nicolai to Johann Georg Zimmermann, 4 October 1776.

Bibliothèque Publique et Universitaire de Neuchâtel

Letter of Johann Conrad Deinet to the Société Typographique de Neuchâtel, 2 March 1777.

Printed Sources

Journals and Newspapers

Allgemeine deutsche Bibliothek, "Nachtrag zur Gottesgelahrtheit." In *Anhang zu dem fünf und zwanzigsten bis sechs und dreyßigsten Bande der allgemeinen deutschen Bibliothek. Erste Abtheilung* (1778), pp. 637–664. [Nicolai's review of Lavater's sermons]

Altonäischer Mercurius (10 October 1776; 12 December 1776).

Bayreuther Zeitungen (28 September 1776; 3 October 1776; 2 November 1776).

Berlinische Nachrichten von Staats- und Gelehrten Sachen (10 December 1776).

Briefwechsel meist historischen und politischen Inhalts 31, 32, 33 (1780).

Erlanger Real-Zeitung (8 October 1776; 22 November 1776; 20 December 1776; 24 December 1776).

Frankfurter gelehrte Anzeigen 20–21 (9 and 12 March 1779).

Frankfurter Kayserl. Reich-Ober-Post Amtszeitung (28 September 1776).

Göttingische gelehrte Anzeigen 35 (3 May 1777).

Kayserlich-privilegirte Hamburgische neue Zeitung (2 October 1776; 8 October 1776; 13 December 1776).

Journal von und für Deutschland 9, no. 7 (1792).

Leipziger Zeitungen (20 November 1776).

Nachrichten zum Nutzen und Vergnügen (8 October 1776; 18 October 1776).

Privilegirte Hildesheimische Zeitung (5 October 1776; 14 December 1776).

Schlesische privilegirte Zeitung (7 October 1776; 16 December 1776).

Staats und gelehrte Zeitung des Hamburgischen unpartheyischen Correspondenten (2 October 1776; 4 October 1776; 13 December 1776; 16 January 1779).

Teutsche Chronik (30 September 1776).

Teutscher Merkur first quarter (1777).

Wienerisches Diarium von Staats- vermischt und gelehrten Neuigkeiten (12 October 1776).

Published Correspondence

Goethe, Johann Wolfgang, and Johann Caspar Lavater. *Goethe und Lavater. Briefe und Tagebücher*. Vol. 16 of *Schriften der Goethegesellschaft*. Edited by Erich Schmidt and Bernhard Suphan. Weimar, 1901.

Herder, Johann Gottfried. *Johann Gottfried Herder Briefe*. Edited by Wilhelm Dobbek and Günter Arnold. Vol. 4. Weimar, 1986.

Lessing, Gotthold Ephraim. *Sämtliche Schriften*. Edited by Karl Lachmann and Franz Muncker. Vol. 17. Stuttgart, 1904.

Nicolai, Friedrich, and Isaak Iselin. *Profile der Aufklärung. Friedrich Nicolai-Isaak Iselin*. Edited by Holger Jacob Friesen. Bern, 1997.

Reich, Philipp Erasmus. *Die Korrespondenz von Philipp Erasmus Reich*. Edited by Mark Lehmstedt. Forthcoming.

Wieland, Christoph Martin. *Wielands Briefwechsel*. Vol. 5, *Briefe der Weimarer Zeit*. Edited by Hans Werner Seiffert. Berlin, 1983.

Documentary Collections

Blühm, Elger, and Rolf Engelsing, editors. *Die Zeitung. Deutsche Urteile und Dokumente von den Anfängen bis zur Gegenwart*. Bremen, 1967.

Hinske, Norbert, editor. *Was ist Aufklärung? Beiträge aus der Berlinischen Monatschrift*. Darmstadt, 1981.

Schmidt, James, editor. *What is Enlightenment? Eighteenth-Century Answers and Twentieth-Century Questions*. Berkeley, 1996.

Wirz, Johann Jacob. *Historische Darstellung der urkundlichen Verordnungen, welche die Geschichte des Kirchen- und Schulwesens in Zürich wie auch die moralische und einiger Massen die physische Wolfart unseres Volks betreffen: von der Reformation an bis auf die gegenwärtige Zeiten, zusammengetragen von Joh. Jacob Wirz*. 2 vols. Zurich, 1793–1794.

Published Works

Goethe, Johann Wolfgang. *Dichtung und Wahrheit*. 3 vols. Frankfurt, 1975.

Kant, Immanuel. *Kritik der reinen Vernunft*. Vols. 3 and 4 of *Werkausgabe*. Edited by Wilhelm Weischedel. Frankfurt, 1977.

———. *Die Religion innerhalb der Grenzen der bloßen Vernunft*. Vol. 8 of *Werkausgabe*.

———. *Über das Mißlingen aller philosophischen Versuche in der Theodizee* and "Beantwortung der Frage: Was ist Aufklärung?" Vol. 11 of *Werkausgabe*.

Lavater, Johann Caspar. *Zwo Predigten bey Anlaß der Vergiftung des Nachtmahlweins. Nebst einigen historischen und poetischen Beylagen. Einzige ächte Ausgabe unter vielen äußerst elenden und fehlervollen von Chur, Schafhausen und Frankfurt*. Leipzig, 1777.

———. *Aussichten in die Ewigkeit, in Briefen an Herrn Joh. Georg Zimmermann, königl, Großbrittanischen Leibarzt in Hannover*. 3 vols. Zurich, 1768–1773.

———. *Predigten über die Existenz des Teufels und seine Wirkungen*. Frankfurt and Leipzig, 1778.

———. "Synodalrede gegen Deismus und kirchlichen Rationalismus (4 May 1779)." Vol. 3 of *Johann Caspar Lavaters ausgewählte Werke*. Edited by Ernst Staehelin. Zurich, 1943.

[Lavater, Johann Caspar]. "Wahre Geschichte der Nachtmahl-Vergiftung in Zürich." *Teutscher Merkur* first quarter (1777).

Lessing, Gotthold Ephraim. *Eine Duplik* and *Die Erziehung des Menschengeschlects.* Vol. 13 of *Sämtliche Schriften.* Edited by Karl Lachmann. Stuttgart, 1893.

[Lichtenberg, Georg Christoph]. *Timorus, das ist Verthedigung zweyer Israeliten, die durch die Kräftigkeit der laveterischen Beweisgründe und der Göttingischen Mettwurst bewogen den wahren Glauben angenommen haben.* Berlin, 1773.

Müller, Friedrich ("Mahler"). *Fausts Leben dramatisirt von Mahler Müller. Erster Theil.* Mannheim, 1778.

Nicolai, Friedrich. *Leben und Meinungen des Herrn Magisters Sebaldus Nothanker.* 3 vols. Berlin, 1773–1776.

———. *Einige Zweifel über die Geschichte der Vergiftung des Nachtmahlweins welche zu Zürich geschehen sein soll.* Berlin and Stettin, 1778.

———. *Geschichte eines dicken Mannes. Worin drey Heurathen und drey Körbe nebst viel Liebe.* 2 vols. Berlin and Stettin, 1794.

———. *Leben und Meinungen Sempronius Gundibert's eines deutschen Philosophen. Nebst zwei Urkunden der neuesten deutschen Philosophie.* Berlin and Stettin, 1798.

———. *Über meine gelehrte Bildung, über meine Kenntnis der kritischen Philosophie und meine Schriften dieselbe betreffend, und über die Herren Kant, J.B. Erhard, und Fichte.* Berlin and Stettin, 1799.

Stieler, Kaspar. *Zeitungs Lust und Nutz.* Edited by Gert Hagelweide. Bremen, 1969.

[Waser, Johann Heinrich]. "Ursprung und Beschaffenheit des Kriegs-Fonds in Zürich"; "Schweizer-Blut und Franz-Geld, politisch gegen einander abgewogen von einem alten Schweizer"; "Bevölkerung der lobl. Cantons Zürich, in verschiedenen Zeitaltern." *Briefwechsel meist historischen und politischen Inhalts* 31, 32 (1780).

Secondary Literature

Abel, Wilhelm. *Massenarmut und Hungerkrisen im vorindustriellen Deutschland.* Göttingen, 1977.

Allison, Henry. *Lessing and the Enlightenment. His Philosophy of Religion and Its Relation to Eighteenth-Century Thought.* Ann Arbor, 1966.

Aner, Karl. *Die Theologie der Lessingzeit.* Halle, 1929.

Angelike, Karin, Matthias Beermann, and René Noir. "Frankophone Zeitungen an der deutschen Westgrenze." In *Kulturtransfer im Epochenumbruch. Frankreich-Deutschland 1770 bis 1815*, edited by Hans-Jürgen Lüsebrink and Rolf Reichardt. Vol 1. Leipzig, 1997.

Ariès, Philippe. *Western Attitudes towards Death from the Middle Ages to the Present*, translated by Patricia Ranum. Baltimore, 1974.

Baker, Keith. *Inventing the French Revolution.*Cambridge, 1990.

Barth, Karl. *Die Protestantische Theologie im 19. Jahrhundert. Ihre Vorgeschichte und Geschichte.* Zurich, 1947.

Beermann, Matthias. *Zeitung zwischen Profit und Politik. Der Courrier du bas rhin (1767–1810). Eine Fallstudie zur politischen Tagespublizistik im Europa des späten 18. Jahrhunderts.* Leizpig, 1996.

Beiser, Frederick. *The Fate of Reason: German Philosophy from Kant to Fichte.* Cambridge, Mass., 1987.

Berghahn, Klaus. "Maßlose Kritik. Friedrich Nicolai als Kritiker und Opfer der Weimarer Klassiker." *Zeitschrift für Germanistik* 8 (February 1987), pp. 50–60.

Berlin, Isaiah. "The Counter-Enlightenment." In *Against the Current.* Oxford, 1981.

Bloch, Ernst. "Technik und Geistererscheinungen." In *Literarische Aufsätze.* Vol 9 of *Gesamtausgabe.* Frankfurt, 1965.

Bödeker, Hans-Erich. "Aufklärung als Kommunikationsprozeß." *Aufklärung. Interdisziplinäre Halbjahresschrift zur Erforschung des 18. Jahrhunderts und seiner Wirkungsgeschichte* 2, no. 2 (1987), pp. 89–111.

———. "Lessings Briefwechsel." In *Über den Prozeß der Aufklärung in Deutschland im 18. Jahrhundert. Personenen, Institutionen und Medien.* Göttingen, 1987.

———."Prozesse und Strukturen politischer Bewußtseinsbildung der deutschen Aufklärung." In *Aufklärung als Politisierung—Politisierung der Aufklärung.* Hamburg, 1987.

Böning, Holger. "'Ist das Zeitungslesen auch dem Landmanne zu verstatten?' Überlegungen zum bäuerlichen Lesen in der deutschen Aufklärung." In *Hören Sagen Lesen Lernen. Bausteine zu einer Geschichte der Kommunikativen Kultur. Festschrift für Rudolf Schenda zum 65. Geburtstag*, edited by Ursula Brunold-Bigler and Hermann Bausinger. Bern, 1995.

———. *Der Traum von Freiheit und Gleichheit. Helvetische Revolution und Republik (1798–1803). Die Schweiz auf dem Weg zur bürgerlichen Demokratie.* Zurich, 1998.

———, ed. *Deutsche Presse. Bibliographische Handbücher zur Geschichte der deutschsprachigen periodischen Presse von den Anfängen bis 1815.* Stuttgart, 1996.

Boschung, Urs. "Erkenntnis der Natur zur Ehre Gottes und zum Nutzen des werten Vaterlands: Der Naturforscher Johannes Gessner (1709–1790)." In *Alte Löcher—neue Blicke. Zürich im 18. Jahrhundert*, edited by Helmut Holzhey and Simone Zurbuchen. Zurich, 1997.

Braun, Rudolf. *Le déclin de l'ancien régime en Suisse. Un tableau de l'histoire économique et sociale du 18e siècle*, translated by Michel Thévanez. Lausanne, 1988.

Broman, Thomas. *The Transformation of German Academic Medicine, 1750–1820*. Cambridge, 1996.

Brock, William H. *The Norton History of Chemistry*. New York, 1993.

Bürger, Thomas. "Aufklärung in Zürich. Die Verlagsbuchhandlung Orell, Gessner Füssli & Comp. in der zweiten Hälfte des 18. Jahrhunderts." *Archiv für Geschichte des Buchhandels* 48 (1997).

Copjec, Jean, ed. *Radical Evil*. London, 1996.

Crespo, Maria. *Verwalten und Erziehung. Die Entwicklung des Züricher Waisenhauses 1637–1837*. Zurich, 2001.

Danckert, Werner. *Unehrliche Leute. Die Verfemten Berufe*. Bern and Munich, 1979.

Dändliker, Karl. *Geschichte der Stadt und des Kantons Zürich*. Vol. 3, *Von 1712 bis zur Gegenwart*. Zurich, 1912.

Dann, Otto, ed. *Lesegesellschaften und bürgerliche Emanzipation. Ein europäischer Vergleich*. Munich, 1981.

Darnton, Robert. "Reading, Writing, and Publishing." In *The Literary Underground of the Old Regime*. Cambridge, Mass., 1982.

———. "George Washington's False Teeth." *The New York Review of Books* 44, no. 5 (27 March 1997), pp. 34–38.

———. *The Business of Enlightenment: A Publishing History of the Encyclopédie 1775–1800*. Cambridge, Mass., 1979.

———. Foreword to *Journal of My Life by Jacques-Louis Ménétra*, edited by Daniel Roche. Translated by Arthur Goldhammer. New York, 1986.

Davis, Natalie Zemon. *The Return of Martin Guerre*. Cambridge, Mass., 1983.

———. "The Rites of Violence." In *Society and Culture in Early Modern France*. Stanford, 1975.

Dippel, Horst. *Germany and the American Revolution*, translated by Bernard Uhlendorf. Chapel Hill, N.C., 1977.

Douglas, Mary. *Purity and Danger: An Analysis of the Concepts of Pollution and Taboo*. London and New York, 1966.

Dülmen, Richard van. *Die Gesellschaft der Aufklärer. Zur bürgerlichen Emanzipation und aufklärerischen Kultur in Deutschland*. Frankfurt, 1996.

———. *Theatre of Horror: Crime and Punishment in Early Modern Germany*, translated by Elisabeth Neu. Cambridge, 1990.

———. *Der ehrlose Mensch. Unehrlichkeit und soziale Ausgrenzung in der frühen Neuzeit*. Cologne, 1999.

Ebeling, Gerhard. "Genie des Herzens unter dem genius saeculi—Johann Caspar Lavater als Theologe." In *Das Antlitz Gottes im Antlitz des Menschen. Zugänge zu Johann Kaspar Lavater*, edited by Karl Pestalozzi and Horst Weigelt. Göttingen, 1994.

Egret, Jean. *Necker, ministre de Louis XVI*. Paris, 1975.

Ehrensperger, Alfred. *Die Theorie des Gottesdienstes in der späten deutschen Aufklärung (1770–1815)*. Zurich, 1971.

Eire, Carlos M. N. *War against the Idols. The Reformation of Worship from Erasmus to Calvin*. Cambridge, U.K., 1986.

Eley, Geoff. "German Historians and the Problem of Bourgeois Revolution." In *The Peculiarities of German History: Bourgeois Society and Politics in Nineteenth-Century Germany*, by Geoff Eley and David Blackbourn. Oxford, 1984.

Elias, Norbert. *The Development of Manners: Changes in the Code of Conduct and Feeling in Early Modern Times*. Vol. 1 of *The Civilizing Process*, translated by Edmund Jephcott. New York, 1978.

Engelsing, Rolf. *Der Bürger als Leser. Lesergeschichte in Deutschland 1500–1800*. Stuttgart, 1974.

Evans, Richard. "Whatever Became of the *Sonderweg*?" In *Rereading German History 1800–1996: From Unification to Reunification*. London, 1997.

Farge, Arlette and Jacques Revel. *The Vanishing Children of Paris. Rumor and Politics before the French Revolution*, translated by Claudia Miéville. Cambridge, Mass., 1991.

Fink, Gonthier-Louis. "Die Schweiz im Spiegel deutscher Zeitschriften (1772–1789): Bild und Wirklichkeit." In *Helvetien und Deutschland. Kulturelle Beziehungen zwischen der Schweiz und Deutschland in der Zeit von 1770–1830*, edited by Hellmut Thomke, Martin Bircher, and Wolfgang Proß. Amsterdam, 1994.

Finkielkraut, Alain. *In the Name of Humanity: Reflections on the Twentieth Century*, translated by Judith Friedlander. New York, 2000.

Foucault, Michel. *Discipline and Punish. The Birth of the Prison*, translated by Alan Sheridan. New York, 1979.

Freedman, Jeffrey. "Traduction et édition à l'époque des lumières." *Dix-huitème siècle* 25 (1993), pp. 79–100.

———. "Zwischen Frankreich und Deutschland. Buchhändler als Kulturvermittler." *Kulturtransfer im Epochenumbruch. Frankreich-Deutschland 1770–1815*, edited by Hans-Jürgen Lüsebrink and Rolf Reichardt. Vol. 1. Leipzig, 1997.

Fritzsche, Bruno, et al. *Geschichte des Kantons Zürich*. Vol. 1, *Frühzeit bis Spätmittelalter.* Vol 2., *Frühe Neuzeit—16. bis 18. Jahrhundert*. Zurich, 1995–1996.

Furet, François. "La 'librairie' du royaume de France au 18e siècle." In *Livre et société dans la France du XVIIIe siècle*. Paris, 1965.

Gadamer, Hans Georg. *Truth and Method*, 2d ed., translated by Joel Weinsheimer and Donald G. Marshall. New York, 1994.

Gillespie, Charles. *The Edge of Objectivity. An Essay in the History of Scientific Ideas.* Princeton, 1960.

Ginzburg, Carlo. *The Cheese and the Worms. The Cosmos of a Sixteenth-Century Miller*, translated by John and Anne Tedeschi. New York, 1982.

———. "Clues: Roots of an Evidential Paradigm." In *Clues, Myths and the Historical Method*, translated by John and Anne Tedeschi. Baltimore, 1989.

———. *The Judge and the Historian*, translated by Anthony Shugaar. London, 1999.

Glover, Jonathan. *Humanity: A Moral History of the Twentieth Century.* New Haven, 2000.

Gordon, Daniel. Introduction to *Candide*, by Voltaire, translated and edited by Daniel Gordon. Boston-New York, 1999.

Graber, Rolf. "Der Waser-Handel. Analyse eines soziopolitischen Konflikts in der Alten Eidgenossenschaft." *Schweizerische Zeitschrift für Geschichte* 30 (1980), pp. 321–356.

———. *Bürgerliche Öffentlichkeit und spätabsolutistischer Staat. Sozietätenbewegung und Konfliktkonjuktur in Zürich 1746–1780*. Zurich, 1993.

———. "Geschichte eines Justizmordes im alten Zürich." *Tagesanzeiger Magazin* 21 (24 May 1780), pp. 16–25.

Grebel, Hans von. *Die Aufhebung des Geständniszwanges in der Schweiz.* Zurich, 1900.

Guggenbühl, Christoph. *Zensur und Pressefreiheit. Kommunikationskontrolle in Zürich an der Wende zum 19. Jahrhundert.* Zurich, 1998.

Guinaudeau, O. *Etudes sur J.-G. Lavater.* Paris, 1924.

Gutscher, Daniel. *Das Grossmünster in Zürich. Eine Baugeschichtliche Monographie.* Bern, 1983.

Habermas, Jürgen. *Strukturwandel der Öffentlichkeit. Untersuchungen zu einer Kategorie der bürgerlichen Gesellschaft.* Darmstadt and Neuwied, 1962.

———. "The New Intimacy between Culture and Politics: Theses on Enlightenment in Germany." In *The New Conservatism. Cultural Criticism and the Historians' Debate*, edited and translated by Shierry Weber Nicholson. Cambridge, Mass., 1989.

Hankins, Thomas. *Science and the Enlightenment.* Cambridge, 1985.

Hinske, Norbert. Introduction to *Was ist Aufklärung? Beiträge aus der Berlinischen Monatschrift.* Darmstadt, 1981.

Horkheimer, Max and Theodor Adorno. *Dialektik der Aufklärung. Philosophische Fragmente.* Frankfurt, 1969.

Hsia, Po-Chia R. *Social Discipline in the Reformation: Central Europe 1550–1750.* London and New York, 1989.

———. *The Myth of Ritual Murder: Jews and Magic in Reformation Germany.* New Haven, 1988.

Hulling, Mark. *The Autocritique of Enlightenment: Rousseau and the Philosophes.* Cambridge, 1994.

Hürlimann, Martin. *Die Aufklärung in Zürich. Die Entwicklung des Züricher Protestantismus im 18. Jahrhundert.* Leipzig, 1924.

Im Hof, Ulrich. *Das gesellige Jahrhundert. Gesellschaft und Gesellschaften im Zeitalter der Aufklärung.* Munich, 1982.

Jentzsch, Rudolf. *Der deutsch-lateinische Büchermarkt nach den Leipziger Ostermeß-katalogen von 1740, 1770 und 1800 in seiner Gliederung und Wandlung.* Leipzig, 1912.

Jordan, William. *The French Monarchy and the Jews: From Philip Augustus to the Last Capetians.* Philadelphia, 1989.

Krebs, Roland and Jean Moes, ed. *La révolution américaine vue par les périodiques de langue allemande 1773–1783. Actes du colloque.* Metz, 1992.

Langbein, John H. *Torture and the Law of Proof: Europe and England in the Ancien Régime.* Chicago, 1977.

Lehmstedt, Mark. "Schweizer Literatur im Verlag der Weidmanischen Buchhandlung Leipzig." In *Helvetien und Deutschland. Kulturelle Beziehungen zwischen der Schweiz und Deutschland in der Zeit von 1770–1830*, edited by Hellmut Thomke, Martin Bircher, and Wolfgang Proß. Amsterdam, 1994.

———. "Handschriftliches Publizieren am Beginn des 19. Jahrhunderts: Kajetan Burgers handgeschriebene politische Zeitung aus München (1801–1804)." *Buchhandelsgeschichte. Aufsätze, Rezensionen und Berichte zur Geschichte des Buchwesens* 3 (1997), pp. 114–123.

———. *Philip Erasmus Reich 1717–1787. Verleger der Aufklärung und Reformer des deutschen Buchhandels.* Leipzig, 1988.

Lestition, Steve. "Kant and the End of the Enlightenment in Prussia." *The Journal of Modern History* 65, no. 1 (March 1993), pp. 57–112.

Luginbühl-Weber, Gisela. "'Zu thun was Socrates getan hätte': Lavater, Mendelssohn und Bonnet über die Unsterblichkeit." In *Das Antlitz Gottes im Antlitz des Menschen. Zugänge zu Johann Kaspar Lavater*, edited by Karl Pestalozzi and Horst Weigelt. Göttingen, 1994.

Lutz, A. "Handwerksehre und Handwerksgericht im alten Zürich." *Züricher Faschenbuch* 82 (1962), pp. 35–60.

McMahon, Darrin. "The Counter-Enlightenment and the Low-Life of Literature in Pre-Revolutionary France." *Past & Present*, no. 159 (May, 1998), pp. 77–112.

Michalson, Gordon. *Fallen Freedom: Kant on Radical Evil and Moral Regeneration.* Cambridge, 1990.

Möller, Horst. *Vernunft und Kritik. Deutsche Aufklärung im 17. und 18. Jahrhundert.* Frankfurt, 1986.

———. *Aufklärung in Preussen. Der Verleger, Publizist und Geschichtsschreiber Friedrich Nicolai.* Berlin, 1974.

Nino, Carlos Santiago. *Radical Evil on Trial.* New Haven, 1996.

Oesterle, Günter. "Die Schweiz—Mythos und Kritik. Deutsche Reisebeschreibungen im letzten Drittel des 18. Jahrhunderts." In *Helvetien und Deutschland. Kulturelle Beziehungen zwischen der Schweiz und Deutschland in der*

Zeit von 1770–1830, edited by Hellmut Thomke, Martin Bircher, and Wolfgang Proß. Amsterdam, 1994.

O'neill, Onora. "The Public Use of Reason." In *Constructions of Reason*. Cambridge, 1989.

Pestalozzi, Karl and Horst Weigelt, ed. *Das Antlitz Gottes im Antlitz des Menschen. Zugänge zu Johann Kaspar Lavater*. Göttingen, 1994.

Peters, Edward. *Torture*. New York, 1985.

Popkin, Jeremy. *News and Politics in the Age of Revolution: Jean Luzac's Gazette de Leyde*. Ithaca, 1989.

Portmann, John. *When Bad Things Happen to Other People*. New York, 2000.

Rosenbaum, Ron. *Explaining Hitler*. New York, 1999.

Rubin, Miri. *Gentile Tales: The Narrative Assault on Late Medieval Jews*. New Haven, 1999.

Russell, Jeffrey Burton. *The Prince of Darkness: Radical Evil and the Power of Good in History*. Ithaca, 1988.

Sabean, David Warren. *Power in the Blood. Popular Culture and Village Discourse in Early Modern Germany*. Cambridge, 1984.

Sang, Jürgen. *Der Gebrauch öffentlicher Meinung. Voraussetzungen des Lavater-Blanckenburg-Nicolai Streites 1786*. Hildesheim, 1985.

Sauder, Gerhard. "Aufklärung des Vorurteils—Vorurteile der Aufklärung." *Deutsche Vierteljahresschrift für Literaturwissenschaft und Geistesgeschichte* 57, no. 2 (1983), pp. 259–277.

Sauer, Klaus Martin. *Die Predigttätigkeit Johann Kaspar Lavaters (1741–1801). Darstellung und Quellengrundlage*. Zurich, 1988.

Schmidt, Eberhard. *Einführung in die Geschichte der deutschen Strafrechtspflege*. 3d. Göttingen, 1965.

Schmidt, James. Introduction to *What is Enlightenment? Eighteenth-Century Answers and Twentieth-Century Questions*. Berkeley, 1996.

———. "What Enlightenment was: How Moses Mendelssohn and Immanuel Kant Answered the *Berlinische Monatschrift*." *Journal of the History of Philosophy* 30, no. 1 (January, 1992), pp. 77–101.

Schneider, Ute. *Friedrich Nicolais Allgemeine deutsche Bibliothek als Integrationsmedium der Gelehrtenrepublik*. Wiesbaden, 1995.

Schneiders, Werner. *Aufklärung und Vorurteilskritik: Studien zur Geschichte der Vorurteilstheorie*. Stuttgart, 1983.

———. *Die Wahre Aufklärung. Zum Selbstverständnis der deutschen Aufklärung*. Freiburg and Munich, 1974.

Schollmeier, Joseph. *Johann Joachim Spalding. Ein Beitrag zur Theologie der Aufklärung*. Gütersloh, 1967.

Schön, Erich. *Der Verlust der Sinnlichkeit oder die Verwandlungen des Lesers. Mentalitätswandel um 1800*. Stuttgart, 1987.

Schram, Hans-Peter, ed. *Johann Georg Zimmermann. Königlich großbritanischer Leibarzt (1728–1795)*. Wolfenbütteler Forschungen, Vol. 82. Wiesbaden, 1998.

Schulte, Christoph. *Radikal Böse. Die Karriere des Bösen von Kant bis Nietzsche*. 2d ed. Munich, 1991.

Schwinger, Richard. *Friedrich Nicolais Roman 'Sebaldus Nothanker'. Ein Beitrag zur Geschichte der Aufklärung*. Weimar, 1897.

Selwyn, Pamela. *Philosophy in the Comptoir: The Berlin Bookseller-Publisher Friedrich Nicolai 1733–1811*. Ph.D. diss., Princeton University, 1992.

———. *Everyday Life in the German Book Trade. Friedrich Nicolai as Bookseller and Publisher in the Age of Enlightenment 1750–1810*. University Park, 2000.

Shookmann, Ellis. "Wissenschaft, Mode, Wunder: Über die Popularität von Lavaters Physiognomik." In *Das Antlitz Gottes im Antlitz des Menschen. Zugänge zu Johann Kaspar Lavater*, edited by Karl Pestalozzi and Horst Weigelt. Göttingen, 1994.

Sommerfeld, Martin. *Friedrich Nicolai und der Sturm und Drang. Ein Beitrag zur Geschichte der deutschen Aufklärung*. Halle, 1921.

Starobinski, Jean. *Jean-Jacques Rousseau. Transparency and Obstruction*, translated by Arthur Goldhammer. Chicago, 1988.

Stephens, W. P. *Zwingli: An Introduction to His Thought*. Oxford, 1992.

Storz, Werner. *Die Anfänge der Zeitungskunde. Die deutsche Literatur des 17. und 18. Jahrhunderts über die gedruckten, periodischen Zeitungen*. Halle, 1931.

Strauss, Walter. *Friedrich Nicolai und die kritische Philosophie. Ein Beitrag zur Geschichte der Aufklärung*. Stuttgart, 1927.

Stuart, Kathy. *Defiled Trades and Social Outcasts: Honor and Ritual Pollution in Early Modern Germany*. Cambridge, 1999.

Stückelberger, Hans Martin. *Johann Heinrich Waser von Zürich*. Zurich, 1932.

Vierhaus, Rudolf. *Deutschland im 18 Jahrhundert. Politische Verfassung, soziales Gefüge, geistige Bewegungen*. Göttingen, 1987.

Vierhaus, Rudolf, ed. *Deutsche patriotische und gemeinnützige Gesellschaften*. Munich, 1980.

Voegelin, Salomon. *Das alte Zürich*. Vol. 1 of *Eine Wanderung durch Zürich im Jahr 1504*. Zurich, 1878.

Walser-Wilhelm, Peter. " 'Bis die Gerechtigkeit die Muse der Historie ihr zum Beystand aufgerufen.' Zum Waser-Handel 1780: Bonstetten, Johannes von Müller und Lavater." In *Das Antlitz Gottes im Antlitz des Menschen. Zugänge zu Johann Kaspar Lavater*, edited by Karl Pestalozzi and Horst Weigelt. Göttingen, 1994.

Wandel, Lee Palmer. *Voracious Idols and Violent Hands. Iconoclasm in Reformation Zurich, Strasbourg, and Basel*. Cambridge, 1994.

Weigelt, Horst. *J. K. Lavater. Leben, Werk und Wirkung*. Göttingen, 1991.

Welke, Martin. "Gemeinsame Lektüre und frühe Formen von Gruppenbildungen im 17. und 18. Jahrhundert: Zeitungslesen in Deutschland." In *Lesegesellschaften und bürgerliche Emanzipation*, edited by Otto Dann. Munich, 1981.

Wernle, Paul. *Der schweizerische Protestantismus im 18. Jahrhundert.* 3 volumes. Tübingen, 1924.

Wettstein, Erich. *Die Geschichte der Todesstrafe im Kanton Zürich.* Winterthur, 1958.

Wilke, Jürgen. "Auslandsberichterstattung und internationaler Nachrichtenfluß im Wandel." *Publizistik* 31 (1986), pp. 53–90.

———. *Nachrichtenauswahl und Medienrealität in vier Jahrhunderten. Eine Modellstudie zur Verbindung von historischer und empirischer Publizistikwissenschaft.* Berlin, 1984.

———. *Literarische Zeitschriften des 18. Jahrhunderts (1688–1789).* 2 volumes. Stuttgart, 1978.

Wittmann, Reinhard. *Geschichte des deutschen Buchhandels.* Munich, 1991.

Index

Page references followed by *i* indicate illustrations.